Praise for
UNCONTAINABLE

"UNCONTAINABLE is a love story. Kip and Sharon's love for each other and their precious family, their business journey of joy, and, most of all, their pure and uncontainable love for their employees and their families is clear and happy proof that the future of business is building loving cultures."

—Roy Spence, co-founder and chairman, GSD&M, founder and CEO, Purpose Institute, and bestselling author of *It's Not What You Sell, It's What You Stand For* and *The 10 Essential Hugs of Life*

"UNCONTAINABLE is an inspired journey that is fueled by Kip Tindell's passionate, purposeful leadership and the unique culture that he has created. The Container Store is more than a store; it is truly 'the promise of a better, happier life' and an example of how to achieve sustainable success and impact through soul vs. sell."

—Mindy Grossman, CEO, HSNi, Inc.

"If you've ever wondered why you love The Container Store, then you need to read UNCONTAINABLE. Throughout the book, Kip Tindell lays out his personal pathway toward creating a beloved, best-in-class business in which every stakeholder ends up in a better place: the embodiment of Conscious Capitalism."

—Danny Meyer, bestselling author of *Setting the Table: The Transforming Power of Hospitality in Business* and CEO, Union Square Hospitality Group

UNCONTAINABLE

How Passion, Commitment,
and Conscious Capitalism
Built a Business
Where Everyone Thrives

KIP TINDELL

Chairman & CEO of The Container Store

with Paul Keegan and Casey Shilling

GRAND CENTRAL
PUBLISHING

NEW YORK   BOSTON

Copyright © 2014 by Rufus Tindell LLC
All rights reserved. In accordance with the U.S. Copyright Act of 1976, the scanning, uploading, and electronic sharing of any part of this book without the permission of the publisher constitutes unlawful piracy and theft of the author's intellectual property. If you would like to use material from the book (other than for review purposes), prior written permission must be obtained by contacting the publisher at permissions@hbgusa.com. Thank you for your support of the author's rights.

Foundation Principles™ is a registered trademark of The Container Store.
1 Great Person = 3 Good People℠; Fill the Other Guy's Basket to the Brim. Making Money Then Becomes an Easy Proposition.℠; Man in the Desert Selling℠; Communication IS Leadership℠; The Best Selection, Service & Price℠; Intuition Does Not Come to an Unprepared Mind. You Need to Train Before It Happens.℠; and Air of Excitement℠ are all service marks of The Container Store.

Conscious Capitalism® is a registered trademark of Conscious Capitalism, Inc.

Grand Central Publishing
Hachette Book Group
1290 Avenue of the Americas
New York, NY 10104

www.HachetteBookGroup.com

Printed in the United States of America

RRD-C

First Edition: October 2014
10 9 8 7 6 5 4 3 2 1

Grand Central Publishing is a division of Hachette Book Group, Inc.
The Grand Central Publishing name and logo is a trademark of Hachette Book Group, Inc.

The publisher is not responsible for websites (or their content) that are not owned by the publisher.

Library of Congress Cataloging-in-Publication Data

Tindell, Kip.
    Uncontainable : how passion, commitment, and conscious capitalism built a business where everyone thrives / Kip Tindell, with Paul Keegan. — First edition.
        pages cm
    Includes index.
    Summary: " 'You're going to sell what? Empty Boxes?' Back in 1978, Kip Tindell (Chairman & CEO of The Container Store) and his partners had the vision that people were eager to find solutions to save both space and time—and they were definitely onto something. A new category of the retailing industry was born—storage and organization. Today, with stores nationwide and with more than 5,000 loyal employees, the company couldn't be stronger. Over the years, The Container Store has been lauded for its commitment to its employees and focus on its original concept and inventory mix as the formula for its success. But for Tindell, the goal never has been growth for growth's sake. Rather, it is to adhere to the company's values-based business philosophies, which center on an employee-first culture, superior customer service and strict merchandising. The Container Store has been named on *Fortune* magazine's 100 Best Companies To Work For list for 15 consecutive years. Even better, The Container Store has millions of loyal customers. In *Uncontainable*, Tindell reveals his approach for building a business where everyone associated with it thrives through embodying the tenets of Conscious Capitalism. Tindell's seven Foundation Principles are the roadmap that drives everyone at The Container Store to achieve the goals of the company. *Uncontainable* shows how other businesses can adapt this approach toward what Tindell calls the most profitable, sustainable, and fun way of doing business. Tindell is that rare CEO who fully embraces the 'Golden Rule' of business— where all stakeholders—employees, customers, vendors, shareholder, the community—are successful through a harmonic balance of win-wins."—Provided by publisher.
    ISBN 978-1-4555-2685-7 (hardback)—ISBN 978-1-4789-8260-9 (audiobook)— ISBN 978-1-4789-8261-6 (audio download) 1. Tindell, Kip. 2. Container Store. 3. Specialty stores—United States—History. I. Title.
    HF5465.U6C657 2014
    381'.45668497092—dc23
    [B]
                                                                                    2014011902

Contents

Acknowledgments

It's with my deepest gratitude and love that I dedicate this book to all of the 1=3, wonderful employees of The Container Store—past, present, and future. It's because of your boundless devotion, hard work, love of life, passion for our brand, and spirit of innovation that The Container Store continues to make people's lives better—creating value for all of our stakeholders. And a very special thank you to our incredible management team, whom I believe with my whole heart and soul is the best in retail. Thank you for helping to build our business and to guide us into, and through, the future. You know it was hard for me not to write a book about each of you...

Melissa Reiff, first a dear friend, then an extraordinary colleague! You and Ron mean so very much to me. I'm continuously astounded by your compassionate commitment to communication and excellence. Thank you for your continued partnership and your incredible leadership that touches each and every one of our thousands of employees every single day. Jodi Taylor—the day we found you was like a dream come true. You're simply the best at what you do and I'm so fortunate to have you in my foxhole. Sweet, yet resolute. So smart and funny. Tom Birmingham, whose 360-degree understanding of the company's operations allows him to see how IT can support the interdependence of our stakeholders in order to help our company fulfill our higher purpose. Karla Buie, my wonderful assistant—thank you for your patience, positivity, and never-fading radiant smile in all you do to support me both professionally and personally.

Amy Carovillano, who after years in store management stepped into a role she never dreamed would allow her to be responsible for developing the happiest distribution center team on the planet. Melissa Collins, who masterfully ensures our creative look and feel touches the hearts and minds of every customer. Peggy Doughty, who has served as the utmost model for integrity all while using her *über* visual merchandising talent to bring beauty and order to our customers' shopping experiences. Eva Gordon, who has beautifully blended art and science into the hiring, leadership, and development of our store teams. Natalie Levy, your contributions to our company are innumerable. Thank you for always stepping up without hesitation in order to serve the greater good. Joan Manson, the only person who could have introduced loss prevention to our company in such a sophisticated and excellent way that continues to enhance our culture, not harm it. Jeff Miller, a newbie to our company, but whose vision and commitment have already made an immeasurable impact on our accounting practices—and more. Brooke Minteer, thank you for your incredible tenacity for problem solving and love for creatively crafting our glorious vendor relationships, by far one of my most favorite aspects of our business. Val Richardson, beloved by the retail real estate community for her brilliant, gracious, and sweet, but firm, way of negotiating the best deals around. Audrey Robertson, your playful spirit has endeared you to us all while your soulful connection to what we stand for has strengthened the bond among all our stakeholders. John Thrailkill, who so genuinely believes that earning profits in a conscious way does nothing but create more value for all, and he does exactly that so unfailingly. Joe Wilkinson, who embraces excellence and fun in all of the awesomely, unending things he achieves for our company. Matt Vonderahe, who has leveraged his passions for finance, marketing, and purpose into a position that's raising the bar for our financial communications. Lucy Witte, a true brand guardian who will forever in her own delightful way keep us on the straight and narrow!

Casey Shilling, my dear friend and colleague without whom this book would never have been written. Our work together over the past eighteen years has allowed you to know what I want to say, well, better than I do. There's nothing you can't do, there's nothing you won't take on, and no matter the challenge or hand dealt, there's not a doubt you'll play it beautifully with grace, perseverance, a contagious smile, and Air of Excitement like no other!

And to my other collaborator on this book, Paul Keegan, whom I met when he was covering The Container Store's designation on *Fortune* magazine's 100 Best Companies to Work For list in 2010. Paul, you immediately understood our culture and I adore how you quickly developed such an appreciation for Conscious Capitalism. I've so valued your work on this journey with us—not only for your wonderful writing ability but for your keen musical talent as a brilliant jazz trumpeter with your band, the Blue Soul Jazz Quintet, in Manhattan. Thank you for helping to bring our story to life.

And to Sharon Tindell, my wife, the greatest person I've ever met, and undoubtedly the most brilliant chief merchant in all of retail. There hasn't been anything more fulfilling than building this business with you for the past thirty-six years—it's been like building a family farm. It's *thrilling* and has given me so much pride and joy to be able to watch you achieve so much and be admired by all. Garrett and I have received so much of the credit for The Container Store, but it's you who has the most to do with the company's success. You've inspired and moved me to be better, work harder, care even more, and do whatever it takes to be able to feel like I've competently partnered with you. Thank you for jointly undertaking the passion and commitment and sacrifices and devotion to build this special company together. Not a day has gone by that I have ever wished for another path.

With all of you and for all of you, I'll give it my heart and my soul to ensure the future is bright, opportunities are endless, and everyone—and I mean everyone—associated with our business can and will thrive! Here's to making more magic happen together!

Kip

Kip Tindell will donate a portion of his revenues from the book to The Container Store's Employee First Fund—a fund that provides grants to employees of The Container Store experiencing unforeseen emergencies like a major medical situation, a catastrophic event, or other grave challenges that they are not financially prepared to deal with.

UNCONTAINABLE

Selling Empty Boxes?

One of my greatest pleasures in life is fly-fishing. There's a dance to it, a rhythm. The trick is to cast your fly so it lands on the water just like an insect, and then you need to manage that fly in the water so it drifts naturally as if it's not attached. It's truly an art you could spend several lifetimes perfecting.

My favorite spot is in western Colorado, near our place, where my wife, Sharon, and I spend a few weeks each summer. The beauty is breathtaking. You become one with the stream and the wind, and the feeling of quiet and peace is mystical.

In the summer of 2008, I needed that feeling more than ever. The company we had started thirty years earlier, The Container Store, was in crisis. The economic earthquake we now call the Great Recession was rattling markets around the world, and our sales were suddenly falling for the first time in our history. This was not an experience we were accustomed to. We had seen nothing but phenomenal growth, year after year, ever since my friend and business partner Garrett Boone and architect John Mullen and I opened our first store with a $35,000 investment. (Initial cash capital was provided by Garrett, his father, and John, who were founding directors, officers, and shareholders of the company. I kicked in the last $5,000 of the investment several months after we opened.)

My dad's Texas oilman buddies (and distinctly non–targeted customers) thought we were crazy: "What? You boys are going to sell empty boxes?" But we knew we were onto something special, creating an entirely new retail category of storage and organization products to help busy folks save precious space and, ultimately, time. Even back in the late '70s, when the pace of life was incomprehensibly slower, we fortunately somehow knew you had to be reasonably organized to accomplish half of what you wanted to in life. But as the recession began to take hold in 2008, we realized we were in serious trouble. Though The Container Store, during the downturn, was still doing vastly better than most retailers, our overall store sales were down, into the negative single digits, and falling fast. I've always said that the difference between the highest-flying, most successful retailer and bankruptcy is not much more than 10 percent in sales. Conversely, if you have an incremental 10 percent, successful retail sales and earnings will likely triple or more. If the recession worsened, we could lose the business.

And it was not only The Container Store I was worried about. It was a frightening time for everyone, and there seemed a very real chance that the retailers I most loved and admired for quality, service, style, selection, and innovation—companies like Whole Foods, Crate & Barrel, and Neiman Marcus—would no longer exist. The only stores left standing would thrive on price and price alone. Not value. Not excellence. Just price, and nothing more. A bad-enough cup of coffee is not even worth ten cents. For someone who believes in the magic of retail, this was a world I couldn't even imagine. But this world was clearly on the horizon.

For most of that year, the challenges of the Great Recession kept me home in Dallas, where our company is headquartered. But in July, Sharon and I finally managed to spring loose for a few weeks in Colorado. That's usually where our best ideas come to us, a place where we can allow our minds to wander freely. My wife is always amazingly calm and showed little outward panic. But I could tell she was worried, too. Sharon is our chief merchandising officer and, without question, the most remarkable, impressive person I have ever met (and was lucky enough to marry).

We were dating, in our midtwenties, when we opened that first store. Sharon was a behind-the-scenes player back then, and today is probably the single most indispensable person in the entire company. Garrett (who is now retired and chairman emeritus) and I have always agreed that if it weren't for Sharon, we might still have just that one cute and darling first store in Dallas. Sharon and I don't have children, but our stores (and our employees) have always been our babies. We feel as fierce about protecting our company—and our 6,000 exceptional, loyal employees—as any parent whose family faces grave and immediate danger.

———◇———

It was an overcast morning when I packed up my fishing gear, kissed Sharon good-bye, and headed for my favorite trout stream on my friend Henry's ranch. We had a conference call scheduled that afternoon with our president and chief operating officer, Melissa Reiff, to make some tough decisions. Next to Sharon, Melissa is my closest confidante, a great friend and business associate for more than thirty years. It would be impossible to exaggerate how essential she has been to the company's success since she came aboard in 1995.

Sharon and Melissa, in fact, are part of an interesting

pattern I have noticed over the years: My most trusted advisers are women. In fact, fourteen of the top nineteen executive positions at The Container Store are held by women. And, along those lines, almost 70 percent of our employee base is female. I hate making generalizations—though it's hard to talk about this without making what sounds like one. I'm very blessed with lots of male friends and colleagues whom I love, and I'm proud to have their friendship. But in my experience, women make much better executives than men. They communicate better and listen better, which I consider the two most crucial leadership qualities. Women also tend to be very good at collaboration and teamwork, which are extremely important at The Container Store. I would never dream of making a major decision without first having deep discussions with Sharon and Melissa, along with other executives, managers at our stores, and employees.

In any event, on that gray morning in July of 2008, as the economy crumbled, I was faced with one of the most wrenching decisions of my life: To save the company, did we have to lay off employees?

Payroll is usually one of the biggest expenses for any company, of course. And for most companies, terminating employees through systematic layoffs is the quickest and easiest way to offset a drop in corporate revenue. No wonder millions and millions of jobs vanished from the American economy in 2008 and 2009, creating an unemployment crisis. But The Container Store has always been different. We have built our brand on the joyful conviction that our employees are our top priority, our most treasured asset. We offer pay, benefits, training, and creative freedom that most retailers wouldn't even dream of providing—and much more. But we also provide something more intangible and harder to quantify. We truly love our employees and are committed to caring for their whole being—not just as workers. They're all extraordinary folks—that's the only kind we hire—and we fully support their efforts to become the best people they can possibly be, both on the job and at home.

I can't tell you how many times an employee has come up to me and said "Working here has helped me become a much better person" or "Having this job has really helped my marriage." I get choked up at company events when a wife stands up, with tears in her eyes, and says, "The Container Store has made my husband a better father to our children. Thank you so much!" Good Lord! Where do you hear stuff like that in business? And how do you get used to hearing it?

But here's the twist: Treating your employees with affection and respect is not only the right thing to do, it also happens to be the fastest road to success. In fact, it's much more successful than any other business methodology. We know this approach defies conventional business wisdom, most famously expressed by economist Milton Friedman. The only reason a corporation exists, Friedman said, is to maximize the return of the shareholder. Well, with all due respect to Friedman, we've found that if you really and truly take better care of the employees than anybody else (instead of just myopically focusing on the shareholder), your employees will truly take better care of your customers.

In short, if those two groups of people—your employees and your customers—are ecstatic, then wonderfully and ironically, your shareholders are going to be ecstatic as well. It's about creating a business where everyone associated with it thrives—everyone! This is not just theory, or wishful thinking. The numbers we've posted for the last three decades prove the point. Our EBITDA (earnings before interest, taxes, depreciation, and amortization) margins are consistently in double digits, and our CAGR (compound annual growth rate) since inception is over 21 percent. That growth rate is even more remarkable when you consider that we haven't made a lot of acquisitions to boost revenue. We bounced back from the Great Recession with record sales each year since 2010, despite a still sluggish economy. We're now among the retail industry leaders in terms of new-store growth. We've vanquished hundreds of copycat rivals over the years—in the '80s there were hundreds of "direct" competitors: Susie's Containers, Store This…Store That. Back then, everyone from mom-and-pop stores to many of the biggest retailers was trying to sell some form of storage and organization.

Today we say that everyone and no one is our competition—because, from the grocery store to the big retailers like Target, Bed Bath & Beyond, and Walmart, everyone dabbles in storage and organization, and some devote several aisles to it. But nobody singularly focuses on storage and organization the way we do. Not only did we create our retail category, but we've helped it become one of the fastest-growing sectors of the housewares industry. As the pace of modern life accelerates and people realize that being organized is not a luxury anymore, but a necessity, making our customers more productive, more relaxed, and happier becomes vitally important. Truly, our purpose—and we say this with all humility—is to improve the quality of life through the joyful, calming, and time-saving gifts that come with being organized.

At The Container Store, we never lose sight of the fact that our success stems directly from our enthusiastic and highly motivated employees. Our turnover rate is less than 10 percent in a retail industry that averages about 100 percent, and we get thousands and thousands of job inquiries but only hire about 3 percent of all applicants. We've been named one of *Fortune* magazine's 100 Best Companies to Work For for fifteen years straight. We didn't throw our hat into the ring until the third year *Fortune* published that list—and by golly, we not only got on the list, we got number one! We were number one the following year, too, then number two for the next two years.

Fortune even sent a reporter down from New York to go

undercover as an employee to see if we were the real thing. Our unique workplace culture has been praised in countless books, academic papers, television programs, and other media coverage. Goodness, you never quite get used to the incredible feeling of hiring people who tell you they studied your company in their MBA courses at some of the most highly regarded business schools in America.

Yes, I know I'm bragging big-time here, but understand I'm bragging on behalf of the thousands of Container Store employees who have built and maintained our success. They're the ones I salute.

Anyone walking through our doors can't help but be affected by the passion, energy, creativity, and, yes, love that our employees demonstrate every day on the job. You may be noticing my frequent use of the word "love." That makes some businesspeople uneasy, but we're not shy about using the word (after a business meeting with us, you might even get a hug). Of course, there are some CEOs who believe you have to create a climate of fear to get results. There have been those notorious "rank and yank" corporate policies that actually required managers to rank their employees, then fire the bottom 10 percent each year—yes, they were required to fire people. Imagine!

Yes, of course we've had to part ways with some employees for justifiable cause or lack of productivity—that's to be expected in any business. But those brutal "rank and yank" management tactics and the like are what give business a bad reputation. Guys went to World War II and came back with a militaristic "aye-aye, sir" idea of management. Well, that may work for waging war, but it's a wretched way to run a business. We believe instead in the vision of Herb Kelleher, the legendary cofounder of Southwest Airlines, who said, "A company is stronger if it is bound by love rather than by fear." I think I heard him say that more than forty years ago, and I was completely taken by it.

Many companies function the way Herb suggests, of course, especially smaller ones started by passionate entrepreneurs. But many big companies do, too—more than you might think. I'm proud to be part of a movement called Conscious Capitalism that was started a few years ago by John Mackey, cofounder of Whole Foods Market, who was, amazingly enough, my college roommate back at the University of Texas at Austin. One of the fundamental principles of Conscious Capitalism®, as embodied by companies such as Whole Foods, Google, Starbucks, Zappos, Southwest Airlines, and many others, is that businesses should have a higher purpose than merely making money.

Don't get me wrong. We're all dyed-in-the-wool capitalists. But we also believe that companies should be managed for the simultaneous benefit of all stakeholders—including employees, vendors, customers, the environment, and our communities— and should have a positive net impact on the world. And guess what? The success of The Container Store and these remarkable companies reveals a surprising irony: Not making profit your number one priority actually makes you a lot more profitable.

At The Container Store, we've been practicing Conscious Capitalism for thirty-six years, since long before there was a name for it. Our unique corporate culture comes from what we call our Foundation Principles™, which had their humble origins in a battered manila folder I began keeping as a student at Jesuit College Preparatory School of Dallas. Whenever I found a quote, an idea, or an article that really blew me away, I would drop it into what I called my Philosophy Epistle File. I know that sounds awfully Catholic, and it makes me grin now. But it was a treasured file that started with life philosophies and then began to reflect what I thought were some of the wisest business philosophies.

Back then, I began to passionately believe—as I still do today—that you should have the same code of conduct in life and business. There shouldn't be a looser code for one or the other. I continued this habit of collecting ideas and business strategies during my college days at the University of Texas at Austin and referred to that Philosophy Epistle File often as we launched and grew the business. I drew on it heavily during a store meeting in Houston in 1989, at a pivotal time in our company's development, which I'll get to later in the book. I'll discuss these seven principles in great depth, but for now, it's enough to say that many of them go back to the Golden Rule we all learned as kids: "Do unto others as you would have them do unto you." Simple...right? Do you know anyone who disagrees with the Golden Rule?

But back to July 2008, in Colorado. I parked my ATV near the river and sat for a while, lost in thought. With sales falling sharply, layoffs would certainly be the easy way out. I knew they would also be emotionally devastating, a betrayal of everything we believed in, everything that made our company great. You can't go around saying you're an employee-first culture and then start laying people off.

Thousands of our cherished employees, most with families to support, were counting on us. On the other hand, if we didn't take drastic steps and the recession worsened, there might not even be a company for long. With the stock market plunging, economists feared another depression. Why not sacrifice a few jobs now to preserve the jobs of many?

As I arrived at my fishing spot, I thought about my favorite movie, *It's a Wonderful Life*. It may sound sentimental, but Jimmy Stewart's passion about how important the Bailey Building and Loan Association is to the people of Bedford Falls never fails to bring tears to my eyes. One of my firmest convictions is that our wake—those waves and ripples of consequences that follow our every action—is much bigger than we can ever imagine. Everything you do and everything you don't do affects the people around you and your business, far, far more than you realize.

Even the most self-centered, egotistical person you know wildly underestimates the power of his wake.

Each and every one of our employees is mindful of the power of their wake in all they do—how they support and develop their colleagues, how they work with a customer or a vendor, and how they contribute to the community. I love reading the comments from our customers about the impact our employees have on their lives—not just their storage problems, mind you...their lives! When you get an entire organization that's mindful of its wake, some pretty incredible things can happen. Now, I know real life is not a Frank Capra movie with Clarence coming down from Heaven and bells ringing when an angel gets his wings and all. But I've always believed there's a lot of magic in real life.

I waded into the water, the powerful current pulling hard at my legs, and cast my fly toward a clump of rocks. One thing I love about fly-fishing is that it's nearly impossible to think about anything else while you're doing it. Your conscious mind must be still, allowing your instincts to take over. Developing that intuition requires years of practice, of course, and goodness knows I've spent endless hours in streams like this, dating back to my boyhood in Louisiana. I'm a daydreamer by nature, and sometimes my best ideas come when I'm lost in a reverie, or not thinking about a thing except whether a fat trout might be hiding beneath those rocks.

As the tug of my fly rod shook me back into reality, I realized what we had to do.

When I got home, Sharon was making her famous posole, one of our favorites. "We can't do layoffs," I told her. "There's got to be another way."

—◇—

When people ask me what makes The Container Store so special, I say it's our yummy culture. I know, chief executives don't often use words like "yummy" when talking about their companies. But it's a word we use all the time around here. When folks ask, "What do you mean by 'yummy'?" I say, well, it's the opposite of yucky. You see, I love good food, and my idea of a perfect vacation is going to the French countryside with Sharon, seeking out the most rural, ascending Michelin star restaurants with exciting, innovative chefs, drinking wine and enjoying the cuisine at one delightful spot after another. "Yummy" is simply the best way I know to express the deeply pleasurable sensation employees and customers get the moment they walk through the doors into our store. It was that delicious culture, built upon our Foundation Principles, that saved us during the Great Recession.

And we managed to do it without laying off a single employee.

That achievement, during the worst economic crisis since the Great Depression, ranks among our proudest moments. In all of our years, we have never had layoffs. It's especially remarkable because even though our sales continued to drop sharply—falling by 8 percent during 2008 and another 5 percent in 2009—our profits fell only modestly, bottoming out at about 8½ percent EBITDA during that time, and rebounded in stunning fashion.

How did we do it? The short answer is that thanks to the tremendous spirit and ingenuity of our employees, not to mention the calm, confident belief in us by our financial partners, we managed to cut expenses deeply enough to offset the drop in revenue. I mean, you have to balance your expenses with your now-lowered revenues. So quite simply, we had to cut our expenses by 13 percent. Once we made the solemn commitment not to do layoffs, the reservoir of goodwill we had built up over the years—among employees, vendors, and investors—created an enormous wave of positive feeling that carried us through the storm. It was living proof of what Melissa always says: "At the moment of commitment, the universe conspires to assist you." (That's a paraphrase of a quote usually attributed to Goethe, but Melissa will tell you that she got it from watching a television interview with her idol, Barbra Streisand.) I mean, everyone conspired to assist us—I joke that even our bankers and our lawyers conspire to assist us!

After our lunch, Sharon and I got on our conference call with Melissa. We talked about my fishing that morning, about that trout hiding under the rocks, and the importance of trusting our intuition—something we talk about a lot at The Container Store. All three of us knew intuitively that laying off people was not the answer. Instead, we had to work harder, be more creative. We also talked about being more Gumby. That's right, Gumby, that flexible, good-natured cartoon character. Gumby is our unofficial internal company mascot, and you'll see his image throughout our Dallas headquarters (we even call our cafeteria there the Gumby Cafe). That's because everyone at The Container Store is trained to be extremely flexible in adapting to any challenge they face. It's definitely a must in retail. If ever there was a time for us all to be Gumby, this was it.

———— ‹◦› ————

Once that decision was made, the next step, of course, was to try to figure out how to do it.

Quite simply, if we weren't going to do layoffs, we simply had to find a way to cut expenses. And that—just the way I had to look for that trout that was hiding behind a rock in the stream—meant looking everywhere to cut back.

In fact, that fishing metaphor became our rallying cry:

"Look under every rock!"

We put a temporary freeze on hiring and on all salary increases, and on our 401(k) company matching program, dramatic steps that were unheard-of at our company. Our vice-presidents and their teams found ways to work with vendors and cut costs on everything from store graphics to toilet paper. We strategically launched more promotions and discounts in our stores than usual to compete with the big-box retailers as consumers increasingly demanded to buy at a discount and refused to pay full price. We sent managers from our office to the front lines in our stores to be closer to our customers. And our loyal sales-floor staff redoubled their efforts to truly help customers solve their thorniest storage and organization problems. With Americans being very choosy about where they shopped and spent their dollars, our salespeople knew that every person stepping through our doors was there for a reason. And we needed to help them.

Perhaps more important than what we did was how we did it, with completely open, honest communication. We would never try to keep morale high by keeping employees in the dark—that's not our style. Instead, we kept everyone constantly informed about exactly how challenging the business climate was, continually restated how much we believed in them, and explained that freezing pay raises and 401(k) matches was necessary to preserve every single job. It's a moving testament to our extraordinary employees that they fully understood the need to do this. Their support was overwhelming—they knew these steps were saving people's jobs, their livelihoods. They also knew it was even okay to show their emotions, whatever those might be—fear, gratitude, relief. Like a family going through difficult times, we pulled together and worked harder than ever. At the same time, our vendors understood that we were simply trying to protect the business for all of us.

In the end, as the economy began to recover, we were excited to restore the 401(k) match, to lift the salary freeze, and eventually to go back to our prerecession policy of offering annual raises of up to 8 percent, about triple the industry average of 2 percent to 3 percent. Our vendor partnerships were stronger than ever—they had been inspired, too, by the open, honest communication. By the middle of 2010, we were back posting significant increases and had a banner year.

And no, there had been no layoffs.

2

Our Seven Foundation Principles

Over the years, many people have asked me, "Kip, when are you going to write a book?" I'm always flattered that people find our story inspiring enough to suggest such a thing, but I've always resisted the idea. I don't know, it just seemed presumptuous somehow. I've never been the kind of person who helps a little old lady across the street and then shouts about it from the rooftops. I always believed that those kinds of things, you did in private.

Also, I really didn't have a spare minute to take the time to put pen to paper, so to speak. But today, after more than thirty-five years as a businessman, I've gained some perspective and have come to realize that we're not helping anybody by keeping our business strategy—our magic, our "yummy recipe"—a secret.

Let me explain what I mean. During the depths of the 2008 recession, I attended a conference packed with the nation's top

CEOs. All the most famous names you can think of were there, the heads of big Wall Street firms, media conglomerates, and professional sports leagues. Even heads of state attended. One by one, these chief executives got up to speak.

But rather than offering words of inspiration or encouragement during a tough time, they began bragging about how many people they had laid off. It seemed to me like the biggest exhibition of braggadocio, a real testosterone overdose, to see who could lay off the most people. "A recession is a terrible thing to waste" was the rallying cry. Instead of trying to make this experience something positive and favorable, this was contorting a concept in the most jaded way. I couldn't believe it. It was as though each one of them was trying to outdo the others, the winner to be determined by how many thousands of people he had thrown out of work. I felt literally sick to my stomach. I left and didn't go back.

I just don't believe in that kind of approach to business.

The truth is, I know from personal experience that there are many great companies that operate in a conscious, ethical manner. I don't want to get into the legal and political debate about whether corporations are "people," but I'm convinced that companies do have certain tendencies, just like human beings. And, stunningly enough, they take on the traits of their top leadership. I just can't get over how true this is.

I'm proud to be a board member of Whole Foods Market, which is living proof that even large public companies can be highly profitable by operating in an inspiring and responsible way for the greater good. I am also in regular contact with many compassionate, innovative business leaders in my work with the Conscious Capitalism movement and as the incoming chairman of the National Retail Federation.

After thirty-six years in retail, you get to where you know most people in the industry. You hardly ever hear about all the great things these companies are doing—it's just not a headline-making story, I suppose, but we're trying to change that. These companies all have a powerful story to tell: not just that you can be hugely successful and be a good person at the same time, but that the two are inextricably intertwined. In fact, I would submit that as technology makes the world ever more connected, you won't be able to succeed in business (or any other area of life, for that matter) without doing the right thing.

One of my favorite quotes from a visit to the Aspen Ideas Festival came from Google executive chairman Eric Schmidt, who said, "Sure, there's always an evil person. But the other seven billion are good." That's surely how I see it, and so do many others. Whenever I give a speech about Conscious Capitalism or our Foundation Principles, people really go crazy—they love it! (It's the only time in my life when I feel like a rock star.) People come up afterward, so excited, and ask, "Why are you keeping this a secret?" That's when I knew we had been too modest over the years. We also figured out that it's good business to talk about this stuff. Increasingly, consumers are voting with their pocketbooks. They may like a service or a product, but when they become emotionally invested in a company, that's when you gain customers for life.

At The Container Store, every step we take is a reflection of our Foundation Principles. We realized we're not smart enough to teach each and every employee how to act in every situation. Retail is far, far too situational to force employees to stick to inflexible rules and policies. So instead of using a telephone-book-sized procedural manual, our seven Foundation Principles keep us on track, focused, and energized, and they provide the kind of guidance that our employees respond to, and then let them go to work. And with that—magically—employee decisions made in our Miami store happen exactly the way they do in our Minneapolis store. This liberates the creative genius of each individual employee, which results in better service, products, sales, and earnings, and, of course, a higher quality of workplace. And when that takes place, success happens naturally.

Here, then, is a brief summary of our seven Foundation Principles, which form the core of The Container Store's success:

Principle #1:

1 Great Person = 3 Good People^{SM}

This is our hiring philosophy.

We're wild-eyed fanatics when it comes to hiring great people. I mean, if you were on a golf team, wouldn't you want to have Jordan Spieth (a fellow Jesuit alum) on your team? That's who we're constantly on the lookout for—amazing employees who elevate the game of everyone around them to a new level.

Talent is the whole ball game. Our employees might not even have had any experience in retail. We've hired lawyers, PhDs, artists—people with talent and a passion for teaming up with other highly motivated employees to get the job done using their own creative genius. And once you find those great people, I liken it to puppy love, that feeling you got in grade school when you just couldn't believe that the coolest girl in school actually liked you back. There's just nothing more exciting than that genuine feeling of truly admiring the people you work around.

Another important aspect of our 1=3 philosophy: Since we're getting at least three times the usual quality and productivity from our employees (it's a purposeful understatement—you can actually get much, much more than three times the productivity at certain endeavors), we can afford to have the courage to pay the people closest to the customer—our salespeople—50 to 100 percent higher than the retail average, to communicate with them breathlessly, and to provide excellent benefits, hundreds of hours of training, and a happy place to go to work every day.

It's not just a win-win. .

It's a win-win-win.

The employee wins because she's getting paid twice as much.

The company wins because it's getting three times the productivity at two times the payroll cost.

And, most important, our customers win.

Principle #2:

Fill the Other Guy's Basket to the Brim. Making Money Then Becomes an Easy Proposition.^{SM}

This is a quote from Andrew Carnegie, the famous industrialist and philanthropist, who attributed all of his success to this simple adage. It has become our business philosophy, allowing us to creatively craft mutually beneficial relationships with the vendors who make the products that appear in our stores. New vendors are typically shocked when we explain this principle to them and ask them, "What can we do to fill your basket to the brim? How can we help you succeed?"

Many of our vendors are thriving small businesses who say they wouldn't even be solvent today without our support. And this is how a smaller retailer like The Container Store can compete on pricing with some of the giant mass merchants. Somebody has to get that last pallet of the vendors' hottest product—and it's usually us, because of our great relationships. Some businesspeople think they have to exploit the other party to succeed. Then they say, "Don't take it personally—it's just business."

I have never understood that way of thinking. How can you separate your personal and business values? Do you treat your business relationships differently than you would treat your friendships?

Simply put, the more win-win situations you can create, the more you'll succeed in everything you do.

Principle #3:

Man in the Desert Selling^{SM}

This is our selling philosophy. Imagine a man lost in the desert. He stumbles across an oasis, where he's offered a glass of water, because surely he must be thirsty. But if you stop to think about what he's just been through and what his needs really are, you know that he needs more than just water. He needs food, a comfortable place to sleep, a phone to call his wife and family, certainly a pair of shoes or a hat for the sun, and much, much more.

So when a customer comes into our store looking for shoe storage, we always ask questions to establish her needs first, starting with shoes, but then move to the rest of her closet. And maybe even the rest of her home, uncovering needs the customer didn't even know she had. Nobody wants to come across as a pushy salesperson, but if you fail to discover that your customer's closet is driving her crazy and her kids' toys are strewn all over the house, you're failing to help her in the true sense of the word. You're wimping out and doing her a great disservice. So that's what we focus on: discovering the customer's problems and solving them.

Sometimes the customer has a problem she doesn't even

know she has; our employees are there to help her discover it. I love this. It actually puts the moral imperative on selling versus not selling. Service and selling are the same thing. You can either help/help or hurt/hurt. You can help the customer by astonishing her and giving her the solution she actually needs and help the company at the same time. Or you can hurt the customer by not doing so—and also hurt the company.

Principle #4:

Communication IS Leadership^{SM}

Simply put, we want every single employee in our company to know absolutely everything. Out of respect, the only thing we don't talk about is individual compensation. But beyond that, we're fully transparent. Melissa is particularly passionate about this principle and created our definition of it: daily execution of practicing consistent, reliable, predictable, effective, thoughtful, compassionate, and yes, even courteous communication.

Doing this hard work takes time, but this has been critical to our success from the beginning, reflecting our "whole-brained" approach: Every employee is part of the company's cognitive process, and thinking together makes us far more powerful than the sum of our parts. We know that some information we share could fall into competitors' hands—revenue figures, upcoming sales, real estate plans, long-term strategic initiatives—but we're willing to take that risk because we consider open communication such a crucial part of our commitment in valuing one another and making sure we all feel appreciated, included, safe, secure, and empowered.

Principle #5:

The Best Selection, Service & Price^{SM}

In retail, being able to offer the best selection, service, and price is considered an impossible trifecta feat. It's the Holy Grail. Some stores have great selection and service, but their prices are higher. Some have low prices and great selection, but their service is poor. We work to hit the triple crown every day—offering a well-edited, carefully curated collection of 10,000 products, free expert advice and service that customers delight in, and prices competitive with the mass merchants.

How do we do it? Simple: We stick with what we know and do it better than anyone else (note that I said "simple," not "easy"). Don't forget, we saw lots of competitors emerge during the 1980s and '90s, but they all failed. Turns out that apparently none of them were as zealously devoted to every glorious nuance of this niche as we were (and none of them had Sharon Tindell as chief merchandising officer). Sharon and I often joke that we've somehow managed to make this "poopy" concept work. Meanwhile, the big chains may have two shoe storage solutions; we have hundreds.

I like to say it's kind of like the mom-and-pop convenience store that's across the street from the supermarket. Frankly, they can't photocopy the heart and soul we put into the business.

Principle #6:

Intuition Does Not Come to An Unprepared Mind. You Need to Train Before It Happens.[SM]

This is a quote I saw in a 1986 issue of the newsletter *Boardroom Reports*, in a piece by the author and journalist Roy Rowan that I dropped in that beloved file of mine. Roy was discussing Albert Einstein and the enormous role intuition played in his discovery of the theory of relativity.

One day, Einstein was sitting on a train that wasn't moving. As another train moved past, he felt as if he were moving backward. It's an experience most of us have had. But unlike the rest of us, Einstein used the experience, in a flash of intuition, to help him conceive the theory that would change our entire understanding of the universe. Einstein wouldn't have had this insight if he hadn't spent his whole life studying physics and mathematics. In other words, Einstein was *prepared* to have his breakthrough observation.

That's our inspiration for making a deep commitment to training. We train our full-time employees almost 300 hours in their first year, and the hours and hours of training for all of our employees continue throughout their careers. The average in the retail industry is about eight hours. This allows our fabulous 1=3 employees to practice Man in the Desert Selling masterfully, because they become organization experts who can intuitively understand the needs of our customers with an almost uncanny precision.

A wise person once said that intuition is the sum total of one's life experience. So why would you leave that at home when you come to work in the morning? I've only had one person disagree with me on that (I'll tell you who later).

Principle #7:

Air of Excitement!^{SM}

Three steps in the door and you can tell whether or not a store has it—a magical world of possibility that awaits you.

It's what I've always loved about retail, even as a kid. You can feel the Air of Excitement in our employees' smiling faces and genuine interest in a customer's needs; in the bright visual displays of elegant, clever, useful products; in our clean, well-organized shelves. In retail, customers can sense when employees are having fun, and this attitude is so contagious that customers end up spending hours in our stores. That doesn't just happen on its own. It's a total reflection of the pure enthusiasm our employees bring to our customers. The Air of Excitement is really the inevitable result of faithfully adhering to all the other Foundation Principles. It's a big reason why our customers don't just like The Container Store—they love it.

As one customer tweeted, "Going to The Container Store is better than a trip to Disneyland!" In fact, most of our employees are former customers who loved shopping in our stores so much they ended up working here. One of the smartest things you can do is hire your customers. They certainly bring the Air of Excitement immediately to your business. And if you do that long enough—hire your customers—they'll end up running your business.

Of course, when I talk about our seven Foundation Principles, or Conscious Capitalism, it's difficult for some people to get it. Some may think it's just a lot of New Age babble. Or a bit corny or old-fashioned.

Sometimes people ask me, "Well, if this approach works so well, why doesn't everybody do it?"

The answer is simple: Running a business this way is extremely hard work. It requires an open, generous heart, especially from those in top management, who must look for the good in human nature and must truly want everyone around them to succeed. It requires long-term planning, it costs real money in the short run, and it won't work unless you're completely devoted to your core values, even when the pressure grows intense to abandon them. You must check your ego at the door and truly not care about who gets the credit, as long as the results are achieved. And you have to constantly reinforce the principles your company holds dear—driving the points home every single day, so they become as natural to your employees as breathing.

It's also crucial to realize that in the long run, it's really about life, about the natural laws of human behavior. These principles weren't taught in business school until very recently, as we've worked diligently to change that. Because this is the way business will be done in the future. It's that powerful, and that contagious. Young people are demanding it, starting lots of exciting companies with a strong social mission. Companies are realizing that the old way of doing business simply isn't sustainable. Deep in their hearts, many other sector-leading companies believe that following the Golden Rule can lead to success—that nice guys can finish first. Companies that dominate their niche are this way. And yes, maybe there are a few cynics who say the real world doesn't work that way, that these are fairy tales. Well, I'm here to tell you this is no fairy tale. It is true. And we have the story to prove it.

——◇——

As I write this book, I'm continuing to run our business with Sharon and Melissa and all of the other fabulous folks here. But I do get back to our ranch in Colorado from time to time and manage to occasionally slip away for some fly-fishing (and to work on this book)—often with wonderful, beloved friends, or sometimes, just as gloriously, by myself. And when I get back, the first thing I do is unload my gear in the garage, making sure everything is put away exactly where it belongs: vest, waders, boots, rod and reel, fly boxes, flies, leaders, floatant, spools of tippet. My fishing equipment ranks high among my most treasured possessions. I have lots of it, for all types of fishing, and have been enthusiastically learning about it and collecting it for many years. My collection is special because much of it is secondhand: flies that belonged to a friend's father, an antique bass lure once owned by someone's grandfather. People who don't fish have frequently given me gifts like that because they know I'll appreciate them. Whenever I use a certain fly or lure, I think about that person, and what the fly or lure meant to him and his family. That can turn an otherwise ordinary fishing trip into a deeply emotional experience. So my fishing gear is pretty darn special. And when I really care about something, I like to keep it organized.

Maybe that's one reason I love this sport so much—to do it well, you really have to be very organized, able to find just the right fly in your vest at just the right time. I often say that there are two things I'm good at: fly-fishing and organizing closets (and if I couldn't do what I'm doing today, I'd probably be a fly-fishing guide somewhere in Colorado). Sharon always tells people that when we met, I had all the shirts in my closet arranged by color, from white to black, with all the colors of the rainbow in between. That's true—and my closet still looks that way. Getting organized is a form of meditation to me; keeping things clean and clear—whether it's in your mind or in your home—allows the space to be more creative and spontaneous. I'm finding that helpful even now, as I write.

Anyway, being out here in Colorado working on the book has given me time to reflect, and the memories are pouring back—opening our first store in the summer of 1978, meeting Garrett back when I was in high school, and of course all that makes me think about my mom and dad, and how I met Sharon. The truth is, I feel a little uncomfortable talking about myself. I'd rather talk fishing, or golf, or college football. I love talking about The Container Store, Conscious Capitalism, and the Foundation Principles, and I'll get to all of that in detail soon. But people who know about such things tell me the reader will want to know a little bit about the guy writing this book. So here goes…a story about a daydreaming boy from Louisiana who was good at sports and liked to organize closets.

3

Finding Love

When I was a boy growing up in Lake Charles, Louisiana, there was a field of clover near our house. I used to lie in that field for hours, daydreaming. Those are some of my happiest memories, just lying there by myself, studying the cumulus clouds floating by. Then I'd roll over to watch bumblebees buzzing around the white flower heads and look for four-leaf clovers. I don't have much time to lie around in clover fields anymore, but I still love to take a few moments now and then to just let my mind wander, take me where it pleases.

I had a real *Leave It to Beaver* childhood, extremely happy. For that, I'm grateful to my parents, who were kind, smart, fun-loving folks. Both were raised in New Orleans, so they had that special warmth and sociability found in people from that great city, and our house was always full of friends and laughter. My mom's name was Jacqueline, but everybody called her Jackie. She was from a middle-class French Catholic family, and her father, Bob Escousse, was a wonderful, larger-than-life character, a protégé of the legendary Huey Long. (People said I was a dead ringer for Grandpa.)

My dad's family was from the other side of the tracks—his father was a mechanic and shrimp fisherman who struggled to get the family through the Great Depression—but the two clans got along fabulously. My dad, Bill Tindell Jr., looked like Frank Sinatra and was a terrific dancer, so my mom's family loved it when he came to their fancy parties. They wanted to watch that handsome working-class kid jitterbug and foxtrot with beautiful Jackie, who also loved to dance. Until my mom passed away about seventeen years ago, my parents kept right on dancing, often taking vacations on cruise ships just to spend their days and nights twirling around the dance floor.

When they met, my parents were both students at Louisiana State University. They were married in 1952, soon after my mom graduated, and I was born ten months later, in Baton Rouge ("just barely legitimate," my dad likes to joke). My birth name was William Arthur Tindell III, after my dad and grandfather, but Mom said she didn't want yet another Bill Tindell running around, so she reached up into the sky and grabbed the name Kip, and it stuck.

We moved to Lake Charles when I was one, after my dad got his degree and landed a job as a petroleum engineer for Halliburton. In those days, there was a strong sense of loyalty between companies and their employees, and it was not uncommon to spend your entire career with one firm. Dad worked at Halliburton for twenty-seven years before retiring with a nice pension, then spent years as a consultant in the oil industry. Halliburton and the oil business are not universally beloved, of course, but despite my interest in business ethics, I don't like to go around criticizing other companies. Maybe it's because of my family's roots in live-and-let-live New Orleans, but I don't believe we were put on this earth to edit other people's behavior. I'd much rather try to offer a positive message for companies and entrepreneurs, pitching a big tent, with arms and heart open wide to saints and sinners alike.

I suppose I'm a lot like my mom in that way, always looking for the good in people, feeling positive about life. She majored in education at LSU and worked as a substitute elementary school teacher, but mostly she stayed home and took care of me and my brother, Tim, who came along three and a half years after me.

My mom was always there for me, and I could talk to her about anything. She read a lot—so in addition to being sweet and kind, she was well informed and extremely smart ("a near genius," my dad says). As I got older, she would listen to whatever problem I was struggling with, staying up until two or three in the morning if necessary, asking questions and hearing me out before offering her advice, never rushing to judgment. Those long talks were precious to me, and are probably why I've always felt that listening and good communication skills are critically important leadership qualities. Mom could always get to the heart of any problem and help me come up with an answer.

When I was in the fifth grade, we moved to Dallas after Halliburton transferred my dad there. His job was very demanding, and he was traveling somewhere just about every week, but he always found time for my brother and me. He coached our baseball and other sports teams, played catch in the backyard, took us golfing, and led our various scouting endeavors. I know it sounds corny, but I truly had the greatest mom and dad any kid could ask for.

My mom was very close to her sister, Janelle, who would drive with her husband and four kids from New Orleans to meet us in Dallas, after which we'd take two cars up to southwestern

Colorado for vacation. That's when I fell in love with the incredible beauty of that area, and those gorgeous mountains were such a
refreshing change from the flatlands of Texas. It took us two days
to get up to Colorado, and we'd spend a couple of weeks camping
and fishing on the Florida River at Lemon Dam reservoir.

By then, I was already a pretty good fisherman. My dad
wasn't much interested (he considered it work, since his dad was
a shrimper), so I mostly taught myself to fish—cold-water trout
in Colorado and warm-water bass back in Texas. I couldn't afford
real fly-fishing equipment, so I used stripped-down spin-casting
rods, very awkward gear that somehow got the job done. Instead
of artificial flies, I used live grasshoppers, which flew around
crazily when you cast your line. People like to say fishing is not
really about how many fish you catch; the most important thing
is just being out in the wilderness. I love that feeling of escape,
when your biggest worry is what to use to catch the next fish.

But like a lot of things in life, fishing is much more fun when
you're successful. What's better? Catching big fish or small fish?
I've always been very competitive—not a bad trait for an entrepreneur, I learned later—and I always wanted to catch more fish,
and bigger fish, than anybody else. And I usually did, much to
the aggravation of my cousins in particular. Once, I was on a
trip with my cousins and friends—there were about seventeen of
us together that time and everybody had a fishing license that
allowed them to catch five fish each. In any event, nobody else in
the group caught a single fish all day. They were all used to fishing for bass and bream, which you use big hooks for. Trout fishing
uses a hook about one-twentieth the size. After I caught my five,
I kept on catching more and more until I'd caught eighty-five in
all—five fish for each person times seventeen people—which left
everybody shocked and really annoyed. I know that sounds like a
tall fishing tale, but it's true.

I loved playing sports, especially baseball, and I'd spend all day on the dusty ball field with my buddies, guys like Pablo Escobar, Rett Hardin, and Jack Fraker.

I was a pretty good shortstop and pitcher—my dad says at ten years old, I threw the ball so hard it would make his hands sting—but what I treasure most from those days are the friendships. It's amazing that so many of the kids I met in school are still my closest friends. Over the years, I've spent endless hours playing golf and poker with those guys, and they're now part of my tightest circle of friends made in high school, college, and beyond. We still get together frequently for golfing and fishing trips. Those relationships, lasting through so many stages of life, have such profound depth and feeling, I really cherish them.

At one of the first Conscious Capitalism gatherings, the journalist Bettina Gordon characterized me for the audience. She told me I'm a long-term-relationship guy, and I guess it's true. I've been married to my beautiful wife, Sharon, for thirty-four years, and have known Garrett and Melissa for over thirty years each. I've had the same job since college and feel powerfully connected to those loyal employees of The Container Store who've stayed with us for ten, fifteen, twenty, twenty-five, thirty years. Every year we hold our Service Awards event and dinner at the Ritz-Carlton in Dallas—such a special time for all of us, full of teary moments of gratitude—for every employee who has reached another five-year milestone in their career with us. Those events drive home one of our core beliefs: Strong long-term relationships, built on affection, hard work, trust, and respect, are a huge key to success in business and life.

Even as a kid, I loved retail. Way back in the third and fourth grade, I would spend hour after hour hanging out in a dime store called Perry's. It was in a shopping center right behind our house in Lake Charles. Just about every day, I'd go to Perry's to wander around the store looking at the displays, see what products they'd added or replaced, and talk to the people who worked there. They were very kind, even though I didn't have much money and would spend a lot of time carefully studying the packaging of each piece of candy before deciding which one to buy. My teachers must have known about my fondness for Perry's, because whenever the classroom ran out of Scotch tape or paper clips, they sent me running to the store. I was always thrilled to be picked for that assignment—for me, being in Perry's was like being in a big circus tent with elephants and lions and tigers and clowns, full of beautiful color, excitement, and wonder. To this day, I have never lost that wonderful feeling.

The coincidence seems eerie now, almost like a foreshadowing, but I distinctly remember driving by the Preston Forest shopping center in Dallas and complaining to my mother that the shop owners had failed to replace letters that had broken off the store signs. "How can they do that?" I said indignantly. I just couldn't believe they weren't more meticulous about their appearance. Years later, I would finally get my chance to do it right when we opened our very first The Container Store in that same suburban center. Later, I read that one of my heroes, Stanley Marcus, the legendary merchant prince of Neiman Marcus, was like that as a child, too. He was so critical of customer service that his family finally refused to go shopping with him at all. I guess retailers are just a pain in the rear to shop with.

I had no dreams of becoming a businessman when I was a little boy, but in truth, I did want to buy a certain big white house on a hill outside Lake Charles that had a lovely lake in the front yard. I thought it was the most beautiful place I'd ever seen, like something from a fairy tale.

But first I needed some money. My family wasn't poor, but we were certainly lower middle class when my dad started his career, and I was determined to buy that big house with the lake—not to mention a good pair of waders, since my legs were always turning blue in those cold trout streams. So I started a rare-coin collection. There was an A&P grocery store in the same shopping center as Perry's, and those folks were nice enough to save their buffalo nickels and silver dollars for me. I spent endless hours on my collection, consulting my coin collector's bible—*The Official Red Book* by R. S. Yeoman—to grade each coin: good, fine, very fine, extremely fine, etc. My aunt Janelle and uncle Bobby would say, "Kip, we just know you're going to be a millionaire."

Collecting coins also satisfied another powerful urge: my desire to organize things. Even as a kid, I loved the challenge of finding just the right place for everything, and coin collections are pretty much worthless if they're not well organized. Yes, that penchant for being organized came early. When my parents went out to dinner or a party, I would proudly reorganize their pantry or linen closet. I wanted to please them with this. Give them a gift. When they came home, I'd say, "I have a surprise for you— come see!" and *voilà!* There it was: the world's most incredibly well-organized pantry. Later, in college, I couldn't study for an exam until the apartment was completely clean. I would organize everything until one o'clock in the morning, making the whole place perfect, before I could sit down and start cramming.

It was thrilling to watch my coin collection grow in value over the years. But making money for its own sake wasn't interesting to me. There had to be a strong reason for making it—some greater cause, even if it was just having a good time with your friends. When I was a child, it was the vision of buying that house with the lake. When I became an adult, it was to create an ideal life with Sharon. At The Container Store, the goal is to make customers happy by helping them get organized, while also working with a fabulous team of employees, vendors, and investors who approach every challenge with enthusiasm and joy.

The cause also has to be more important than my own financial gain. Not because I believe in sacrifice for its own sake—honestly, I don't. I'm an epicure, a big believer in all the pleasures of life, and I have some very nice suits in my well-organized closet. I truly love making money and have always found it a satisfying process, ever since those coin-collecting days. But making money is a lot more fun when you're also helping the people around you become successful. That's what we mean by "cause before self." Sharon and I have always lived according to that principle. It's a blast to make money for yourself *and* all the people around you simultaneously. It's like those rare moments when you and your friends take over a roulette table in Vegas and everyone is winning. It's a thrill. A blast. It's much, much more fun than sitting by yourself winning. That just pales in comparison.

I didn't fully appreciate it at the time, but a big factor in shaping that community-oriented view of life was my school, Everette Lee DeGolyer Elementary, in Dallas. It was an extraordinary place, especially for a public school, and mostly because of the principal, the late Wade Thompson. He insisted there be no locks in the school, as a way to build community—not on bikes, on lockers, or anywhere. You would hear Mr. Thompson on the loudspeaker saying, "Today, John Smith lost twenty-seven cents on the playground, a quarter and two pennies. That was his lunch money. If you found it, please return it to John. It's important for you, and important for John."

When something bad happened, Mr. Thompson would seize upon it as a teachable moment. One day, two kids started throwing rocks at the gym and broke the windows. A car came by with three high school kids, who got out and said, "Hey, why did you do that? Where do you live?" The two younger kids said they were fifth graders who had just moved to the neighborhood from out of town. "Well, you're lucky because you get to go to this very special school," the older kids said. "And you don't want to break these windows, because it's a fun place with a great gym teacher."

They found the janitor and took the boys to the hardware store to buy new glass and putty and spent the afternoon helping them replace the windows.

Now, you might wonder, "Why would a group of cruising teenagers stop to do such a thing?" In some neighborhoods, they'd be the ones throwing the rocks. But these kids used to be students at DeGolyer and had once been caught breaking those same windows. The janitor and Mr. Thompson had helped them fix the windows, telling them, "Whenever you make a mistake, it's your job to make it right." So the teenagers lent the kids money to buy the glass and told them how to earn money around the neighborhood to pay them back. "That's how we learned to feel okay about a mistake we made," the older kids said. The fifth graders mowed lawns, walked the neighbors' dogs, and got their hands dirty gardening until they paid off the debt. Even as a kid, I got the message: You are part of a community where people care about doing the right thing, and you have an obligation to carry on that tradition.

My art teacher in the fifth grade at Everette Lee DeGolyer was a wonderful woman named Ann McGee-Cooper, who had a sign on her classroom door that said IMAGINATION'S GROWING PLACE. She was creative and fun, and really let our imaginations run wild. In one of those amazing coincidences you could never make up, Ann went on to become a professor, an author, a consultant, and a leading expert in the creative approaches to business pioneered by companies like Southwest Airlines, TDIndustries, and The Container Store. Ann is a passionate advocate of Servant Leadership, a term coined by the great management thinker Robert K. Greenleaf to describe something we've been practicing instinctively since we opened our first store. After our company was well established, we learned about Greenleaf's work and realized that it perfectly described the way we do business: placing the highest premium on listening, empathy, humility, and serving others rather than the old militaristic command-and-control style.

Recently, Ann told me a moving story that illustrates well how our principal, Mr. Thompson, was the very embodiment of Servant Leadership: One morning, she dropped off her eighteen-month-old baby at day care and pulled into the school parking lot twenty minutes late—not for the first time. When she saw Mr. Thompson running up to her car, she thought she would be fired on the spot. Instead, he said, "How can I help you?" He had immediately sized up the situation: She was in a very difficult marital circumstance that was often chaotic. So he helped carry her box of art supplies into the school, got the class started with the Pledge of Allegiance, and said, "Ann, I would love to take your class for a while. I'll bet you would like a cup of coffee and a few minutes to yourself."

Ann washed her face, tried to pull herself together, and went back to her class. A few hours later, she went to Mr. Thompson's office, still expecting to get fired. "I am so sorry that I was late— I know it's not the first time, and it won't be the last time. I just want to get this over with—"

Mr. Thompson stopped her, sat her down, took her by the hand, and said, "Ann, I'm a grandfather and I grew up on a farm, so I get up early. You're a young mother, and the most important thing for you is to get your boy up in the morning, get a good breakfast in him, and get him off to day care. So I tell you what: We'll be partners. I want you to know that whenever you can get here, you will be the teacher every child in this school needs. You will find ways to reach into their hearts and create miracles in their lives. This school needs you. And I will watch your parking space. If the bell rings and I don't see your car, I want you to know that I will be in your room teaching until you get there."

"And at that point," Ann said, nearly in tears as she told me the story, "I wanted so badly to be the person he saw in me. I

knew I wasn't that person yet, but I really, really wanted to be."
Ann says her father taught her, "Don't trust until a person proves
he is trustworthy." But Greenleaf had a different approach with
Servant Leadership: "There are times when you trust a person
and help them grow into the person they want to be." And that's
what Ann did after her meeting with Mr. Thompson. Eventually,
she very much became the person Mr. Thompson saw in her.

That's about the best description I've heard of how we treat
one another at The Container Store—constantly motivating
one another to be the best we can possibly be, especially in the
face of the daunting challenges all of us face at some point in
our lives, both personal and professional. And I'm amazed that
the universe conspired to bring Mr. Thompson and Ann to me
at such an impressionable age, when messages like that really
sink in, however subtly and indirectly. I was especially lucky that
both of these inspiring leaders took a special interest in me. Mr.
Thompson would come into the art room and say, "Ann, I have a
boy in my office who defaced the tiles in the bathroom. We need
someone to mentor this young man." And they would inevitably
choose me. They once asked me to help a boy with no friends, so
I made the bullies leave him alone and got the kid involved with
other kids in playground games. For whatever reason, other kids
followed my lead. Whenever my friends created a new club, I was
always the leader. Honestly, I wasn't *trying* to be the leader, and I
can't fully explain why that role came to me. It just always somehow worked out that way.

————◇————

When it was time to move on to high school, I told my parents
I wanted to go to Jesuit College Preparatory School in Dallas.
My dad was Methodist, but we were raised Catholic at my mom's
insistence, so she was happy I chose a parochial school. But they
were worried about being able to afford the tuition—$1,000 a

year, which was a lot of money in 1967. There would be no girls and you had to wear a beanie, but I was determined to go there because the school provided a great education, wonderful athletics, and a well-rounded learning environment. Curiously, I found myself becoming more involved in philosophy.

Philosophy was my adolescent equivalent of lying in the clover fields, daydreaming. I loved getting lost in a volume of Kierkegaard or Nietzsche and debating big ideas. Our teachers, and especially my favorite, Ben Smylie, constantly challenged us to question our most cherished beliefs (including Catholicism), but rather than descend into nihilism, as some kids did, I was exhilarated. That's when I began keeping my Philosophy Epistle File, my folder of "great ideas and inspiring quotes" that would evolve into the seven Foundation Principles our company's culture is based upon.

As I said earlier, that name, Philosophy Epistle File, scrawled on the folder tab, sounds a bit pompous (and very Catholic) to me now. But I was very earnest in my devotion to that plain manila folder, because it contained the most profound pieces of wisdom I knew, heard, or wondered about—bits from magazine articles and books, and comments from teachers and friends, as well as ideas I dreamed up myself. I was very selective about what went into that file; it had to be something truly exceptional. I could never have imagined how powerful those ideas would become in my own life and the lives of others, of course, but I knew it would relate to my future career path somehow. I was convinced that a person has to understand some basic truths about life before he can accomplish anything.

Though business wasn't a career goal, I nevertheless found myself wrestling with big questions about business ethics. I would drop notes into my Philosophy Epistle File: "How can someone have one set of values in their personal life and a looser set of values in their business? Why shouldn't they be the same, since business is just one aspect of life?" As I thought about money and social status, it seemed very important that everyone should be treated the same way, whether it was the checkout guy at the 7-Eleven or the president of the United States. Looking around, I didn't see enough people behaving like that. Even today, my favorite moment in interviewing people for a big job is to take them to lunch or dinner and watch how they treat the waiter. If they don't treat the restaurant staff well, I won't even consider hiring them. I don't care how phenomenal you are at what you do—if you do not possess basic human kindness, you won't fit in at The Container Store.

For as long as I can remember, I enjoyed pleasing people, treating them well, because you never know—they may have big problems you don't even know about. In my view, we were put on this earth to enrich the lives of people around us, and everything we do comes back to us in some way, good or bad. Maybe that shows the influence of my Catholic upbringing—somebody up there is watching us—but I've never thought about this in a religious way. It just seems clear to me that our wake—the consequences of our actions—is much bigger than we think.

Later, I realized this might sound a lot like the idea of karma, but I'm no convert to Eastern religions, either (though I have great respect for the wisdom of those traditions). I've simply always rejected the whole zero-sum approach, the notion that anytime I give to someone—my time, money, love, whatever—I've lost something. Instead, my experience is that we always benefit from our giving, either now or in the future, and life is brimming with win-win propositions. The same is true for business transactions: There's no reason why every deal can't be creatively crafted for everyone's benefit, and that's how we approach every negotiation at The Container Store.

Anyway, one night when I was a senior at Jesuit, I was driving down the highway with my girlfriend when we stopped at the scene of a terrible traffic accident. A man was badly injured, with head wounds, and there was blood everywhere. I remember the ambulance taking forever. It was a very messy scene. We waited and waited for the ambulance to get there, but I just couldn't wait any longer. We somehow got the injured man into my car, bleeding all over the backseat, and we drove him to the nearest hospital. Incredibly, the emergency room staff rejected him because he didn't have health insurance. They said they'd have to transfer him to another hospital—"the charity hospital."

After much pleading, I convinced the hospital staff to treat him. "At least stop the bleeding, for God's sake! This man is gravely injured!" More time went by. They finally transferred him to that other hospital, which was far away but accepted everyone. I don't know if the man survived, but the coldness of the hospital staffers had a huge impact on me. How could people treat a human life with such disregard? That was, and remains, absolutely mind-boggling to me. That cruel moment stays with me.

◆

Around this time, my interests in philosophy and the retail business, and my passion for organizing things, all began to come together. After my first year at Jesuit, I was looking for a summer job when I saw a HELP WANTED sign at a Sherwin-Williams paint store near our house. The manager wouldn't hire me because I wasn't sixteen yet, but that's when I learned my first business lesson: the value of persistence. I kept coming back, over and over, telling him how badly I wanted the job. Finally, he said, "Okay, to heck with that rule. I'm gonna hire you anyway—you'll be great."

Now I had to live up to his expectations, so I restacked and dusted all the paint cans to make the store displays look perfect. That's what I loved so much about Perry's back in Lake

Charles—those neat product displays—and working on visual presentation is still one of my favorite things to do at The Container Store. When you create a display that looks just right, you can stand back and watch the product leap off the shelves. That's probably the most gratifying part about retail, because the payoff is immediate. Working the stock room, meanwhile, was a lot like organizing my parents' pantry. When the store manager was on vacation, I would completely reorganize all the boxes and paint cans, lining them up as straight and beautiful as possible, with all the labels showing, then proudly show it all off when he got back. The boss loved it, of course. Who doesn't like to be organized?

I just loved getting paid to work hard and have fun at the same time. But after two years at the Sherwin-Williams paint store, I got restless and decided I wanted to work in a bigger store. So the summer before my senior year, I strolled into the Montgomery Ward at the mall and met a man who would change my life: Garrett Boone.

Garrett was the manager of the paint department. He saw that I had experience and good references and hired me on the spot. He was twenty-seven, ten years older than I was, and had his own apartment, so I thought he was pretty cool. We soon became friends, and he told me he'd never dreamed he'd end up in retail. He originally aspired to be an architect, but switched to a degree in European history at Rice University. Then he got a master's degree in history at the University of Texas at Austin and thought about becoming a teacher. When he returned home to Dallas, the only job he could find was at Montgomery Ward, and he was surprised to find that he loved retailing from day one. "Every day, you wake up and wonder, 'How will this day go?'" he told me. "I love the physical activity, the emotions, the creativity of solving whatever problem the customer walks into the store with."

That was exactly how I felt! Clearly, Garrett and I were kindred spirits. He was a warm, caring person who shared my philosophy about the right way to treat people. We were alike in other ways, too, starting with our physical appearance—a couple of tall, skinny guys. In fact, the store manager, who always walked with his head down, said he couldn't tell us apart—all he saw were these long, thin legs in bell-bottoms. We both loved the excitement, unpredictability, and social aspects of the job. For us, retail was like theater, the chance to put on a show. But more than anything, we loved selling. To us, "selling" was simply another word for helping people.

I started at the minimum wage of $1.60 per hour and did so well they moved me into clothing and appliances. We also got a commission, so I was thrilled to get an extra check when I sold a refrigerator or washing machine. I worked with Garrett at Montgomery Ward during summers and school vacations until he left in 1972 to manage the Dallas store of a regional chain of furniture stores called Storehouse.

By then, I had finished my first year at the University of Texas at Austin. Back in Dallas for the summer, I decided to swing by the company's warehouse to say hello to Garrett and found him high up in the dusty rafters, vacuuming. It must have been 110 degrees in that building, an old military barracks, and Garrett was really suffering. So I offered to help, and while we were cleaning up, one of the owners of Storehouse, Fred Currey, walked in. He just couldn't believe we would be working so hard in that Texas heat. We got to talking and Fred seemed impressed and offered me a job.

Storehouse had a great concept, importing original Thonet bentwood chairs from Europe, which we would assemble with drills and screws. In fact, the company transformed the furniture industry by bringing in some of the most innovative and value-laden sources to the United States for the first time. Since

I was still in college, I really couldn't take on a full-time job, but regardless, Storehouse asked me to open its new store in Austin. So I hired the best manager I could find and got the store launched. We did spectacularly well—the smallest store in the chain racked up the second-highest sales volume—and I found myself making what seemed to be phenomenal money and having a lot more fun than in my classes.

But after these positive signs, I still didn't consider retail a real career path. My plan was to go to law school. Becoming a lawyer would let me indulge my love of big ideas and challenging arguments and help people with their legal problems while also making a lot of money. The only problem was I really didn't like going to class. I was still that kid in the clover field, letting my mind wander wherever it happened to go. I wanted to major in philosophy, but my dad said he wouldn't pay for it if I did, so I became an English major (which is pretty much the same thing). I read a lot of everything: literature, philosophy, economics, politics, sociology, psychology—whether it had anything to do with my classes or not—and, of course, I continued placing the most inspiring bits of wisdom in my Philosophy Epistle File.

Learning that way was so much more fun than going to a class every Monday, Wednesday, and Friday from nine to ten, listening to dull lectures and cramming for tests. But I was worried that a low grade-point average would ruin my chances for law school. So anytime it looked like I'd get anything lower than a B, I'd drop that class, even if it was right before the final exam. Meanwhile, I aced my English classes because the grade was almost entirely dependent on writing papers—something I was very good at—but I wasn't accumulating enough hours to go into the prescribed buckets toward graduation. As you might imagine, my parents were not too happy about this, since they were paying my way. "Trust me," I told my mom, "I'm learning more than I would if I really applied myself!"

That was true. It was also true that I wanted to fully enjoy the paradise that was Austin, Texas, in the 1970s: warm weather, beautiful women, honky-tonks where you could hear Willie Nelson play all night for a dollar and Bob Dylan would show up at a Joni Mitchell concert. I played a little guitar and harmonica, liked to sing, played poker all night, went fishing, shot pool, and played golf.

By my third year, feeling restless, I decided to take a semester off to work on an offshore oil rig. I needed some adventure and wanted to learn more about my dad's business. So my dad helped me and a friend get jobs in the Gulf of Mexico with the Ocean Drilling and Exploration Company of New Orleans. We served as roustabouts—basically gofers, the lowest guys on the totem pole. It was tough physical labor. If you were sleeping and a supply boat came in, even if the seas were high and dangerous, you still had to unload the cargo right away. It was like doing bench presses all day. In one semester, I went from 6'3" and 150 pounds to 185 pounds, all muscle.

We often worked a hundred hours a week and then took a week off. After all that overtime pay, we felt like millionaires. My buddy and I had only one rule—that we had to spend our entire weekly earnings during our week off. So we would fly to Colorado and go skiing. But we quickly discovered why the job paid so well: We were among the few roustabouts who still had all ten fingers. Once, I turned around and saw a whole wall of drill pipe sliding toward me—somehow, I was able to leap high enough that it went under me; otherwise, I would have been crushed for sure. Another day, there was a serious blowout on the next rig over. We grabbed binoculars and watched a coast guard helicopter land on the rig as it was going down. The twelve biggest and strongest guys climbed aboard, fighting off the others, who didn't make it. A number of people died that day. That had a real impact on us. The next week, my friend and I quit and went back to college.

One skill I hadn't expected to develop during that semester was poker playing. In our free time on the rig, we played a Southern Louisiana game called booray, and I won almost every time. I can't really explain why, but I've always been very good at gambling. One guy I was with in college was John Mackey, now the co-CEO of Whole Foods Market. In 1975, John was just another University of Texas student who happened to move into the apartment on 25 ½ Street in Austin that I shared with three other guys. It was a duplex with a little deck where we would all hang out and talk and play poker. I'm pretty sure John was the most interesting person at UT. We never talked about business, though we sometimes talked about the big thinkers we both loved to read, since John was a philosophy major. But mostly we talked about girls and music and played an awful lot of poker. John could never figure out why I always beat him. Later, he said, "I kept thinking, 'Is this guy smarter than me, or does he cheat, or what's the deal?'"

—◇—

John and I didn't always do the same things in college. He didn't like hanging out in smoky nightclubs, as I did, because he was beginning to develop the health consciousness that would fuel his mission in life. "You probably enjoyed college a lot more than I did," he told me later. "For me, it was a very serious business of trying to figure out who the heck I was and what I wanted to do in life." John moved out of the apartment after a year, but after college we followed each other's business quite closely, with pride. (It's funny and ironic now as I look at a letter in my Philosophy Epistle File from my old friend and roommate Bill Parrish in 1985: "Dear Kip, remember John Mackey?" Bill attached an article from the August issue of *Texas Homes*. "The philosophy behind John's store reminds me of you and The Container Store. Both emphasize quality products and good service and are based upon an underlying moral and ethical philosophy. It is really heartening to see two such businesses not only survive but flourish.")

It's fascinating to consider the mysterious ways people move in and out of our lives, and the powerful wake they leave. Because no sooner had one remarkable person vanished from my life than another one materialized, in the form of a lovely young woman named Sharon Fiehler.

It was the summer of 1976, and I had taken a part-time job as manager of our small apartment complex in Austin, the Oak Tree Apartments—four apartments and a duplex. Sharon moved into one of the units. She was studying landscape architecture at LSU and had landed an internship with the City of Austin. The tenants all hung out together and became great friends, gathering for barbecues and shrimp boils (I loved to cook Louisiana food). It wasn't love at first sight—we were friends first—but I was immediately fascinated by this very bright, slim, pretty blond girl. Nothing happened romantically for a while—but my friend Pablo kept reminding me how cool she was, and our first date was to a concert by Commander Cody and His Lost Planet Airmen at the Armadillo World Headquarters, Austin's famous music venue. That's when Sharon and I really clicked, and we ended up swimming in Lake Travis that night.

For the rest of the summer, we were together constantly. Then Sharon had to return to Baton Rouge for her final year of school. Smitten, I visited her often. Since Baton Rouge was my birthplace and LSU is where my parents met, it felt very natural to make the eight-hour drive, across the huge Baton Rouge bridge over the Mississippi. During those visits, we realized how much alike we were—logical and analytical but also creative and playful. We realized we were both daydreamers and analyzers, which is how we later approached our work together at The Container Store. Sharon and I have always felt comfortable being this way together, even back in our college days, when we hung out in the old Catfish Town section of Baton Rouge, where she lived, eating oyster po'boys, listening to music, and dreaming about what we would do with our lives.

Like any couple, we have our differences, too. I'm a filer and she's a piler. Where I made sure everything was neatly in place, she had big piles in her apartment—stacks of books, clothes, records, you name it. She's not like that anymore—nobody works at The Container Store long before realizing that being organized is really a fun habit anyone can learn—but she still likes her small piles.

Another big difference is that Sharon studied constantly in those days, while I never did. Sharon's demanding program required six years of study and 180 credits, while I joked that I was cramming four years of school into my six years at UT. Sharon graduated in 1977 right on time—but that was the year my dad's patience finally wore out. He cut off my funding and I returned to Dallas to live at home.

The truth is, I never did get my degree—I'm just a few hours short, I think, in math and science courses—but I later discovered that John Mackey didn't get his, either, after six years of unstructured intellectual exploration at UT. Sometimes we talk about the irony that we're often asked to speak to MBA programs, since neither of us would have been caught dead in the business school when we were in college. I loved retail but never thought of that as business. Business was banking or oil, which in the early '70s were very uncool. Now Conscious Capitalism is being taught in business schools; academics have written books about Whole Foods and The Container Store; John's brilliant book, *Conscious Capitalism*, was recently published by Harvard Business Review Press, and I was touched to recently receive an honorary doctorate from Babson College, a top business school near Boston, and deliver the 2013 commencement speech. Funny how life works out.

Many successful businesspeople dropped out of college, of course—Steve Jobs, Bill Gates, Paul Allen, Richard Branson, Mark Zuckerberg, Sam Walton, Henry Ford, David Geffen, Ralph Lauren, Walt Disney, Ray Kroc, Barry Diller; the list goes on and on. Entrepreneurs are usually too impatient to sit through classes and are anxious to get on with their passion. When young people ask me for advice, I say forget about grades and making a big salary—follow your dream. If you really want to go to business school, get it done as quickly as possible and then get back out into the real world. If you really want to be an entrepreneur, don't get settled into a career and get used to making six figures—before you know it, you'll be married with kids and will never give up that job security to start something. Do it right out of the gate, throw yourself into it 100 percent, and never look back. If you wait, you'll never have the courage to create something special.

But back to reality. There I was, twenty-four years old and unemployed, living at home with my parents. My mom was far more worried than I was. She insisted I register for courses at the University of Texas at Dallas, so I did—but, of course, I never went to class. I was happy spending time with Sharon, who had moved to Dallas so we could be together while she planned her own next career move. Meanwhile, I was reading a lot and adding to my Philosophy Epistle File. I played golf and fished with Sam Adams, a buddy from Jesuit and UT, who by then had gotten his degree, had a job for a while, and was already looking for another. When he came over, my mom would shake her head and say, "Sam, what are we doing to do with Kip?"

My main idea was to become a writer. I always loved composing those English papers in college. I figured that if I could get a few short stories published, maybe I'd eventually find a way to make a living. So I landed a job writing a syndicated newspaper column about the richness of Southwest regional literature.

I loved interviewing authors, reading their work, and being published in newspapers across the South. But writing that column
made me realize how hard it is to survive financially as a writer. If
I took that road, I was sure I'd starve to death.

So I began thinking about what else I could do to earn a living, figuring I would maybe get back to writing later. My mom
thought I was daydreaming again—and I was—but I was also
doing some serious thinking: about how my pal Pablo and I used
to come up with crazy business ideas in college based on social
trends we noticed. I remembered how much I loved playing with
numbers, analyzing them, and assessing the risk-reward ratios of
my poker playing. I noticed that more of the ideas I was drop-
ping into the Philosophy Epistle File had to do with leadership,
management, and marketing. And I thought about how much
I'd always loved being in retail stores, from the magic of Perry's
dime store to my jobs at Sherwin-Williams, Montgomery Ward,
and Storehouse.

As all those ideas and impulses swirled, I started hanging
out with Garrett again. He had returned to Dallas about two
years earlier and was considering starting his own business after
quitting Storehouse—a gutsy move, considering he had risen to
become regional director of Texas stores and was probably on his
way to becoming president of the company. Fortunately, his new
wife, Cecilia, a customer he met at Storehouse, fully supported
his decision to follow his dream. Her job as a manager support
representative at IBM kept them afloat while Garrett researched
his concept—a handmade furniture store called Basics.

Garrett had learned enough about woodworking to make
a few prototype products but was starting to realize that buying and selling furniture made meticulously by hand would be
prohibitively expensive. So he began searching for other ideas.
That's when he and I started talking seriously about going into
business together.

Over the years, we'd talked about opening our own store, but those weren't much more than idle fantasies. Now we were both in a position to actually do it. Garrett was thirty-four years old, with lots of management experience, and I had been working in retail for years and was full of youthful energy and ideas. I was glad to hear that Garrett was losing interest in the furniture store idea. That sounded incredibly boring to me. Retail is done best with a lot of theater, and I saw no theatrical potential in selling furniture. All I could imagine were couches gathering dust on the sales floor and listening to the drone of the air conditioner as we waited for customers to arrive.

So I suggested a grocery store. I'd always been fascinated by the grocery business—in fact, the only class in college that inspired me to study hard was a graduate-level course on the subject at UT's LBJ School of Public Affairs. I'd always considered grocers the best retailers on the planet, because they had to have the right product at the right time or it would spoil. It had an expiration date, which made the merchandising strategies highly interesting to me. And I've always enjoyed good food, gardening, and cooking, and loved the excitement and energy of grocery stores. But Garrett wasn't interested in a grocery store—it seemed like a risky proposition to him, too far from his experience at Storehouse and Montgomery Ward. So he and I kept tossing ideas around.

My mom, dad, and friends were still worried about what I was going to do with my life, but I wasn't—by that time, I knew. I might not have been able to clearly articulate it, but all the pieces of my life were coming together at this moment. I've always been a big believer in intuition, and my intuition told me that I had found what I was looking for: a way to explore and share the wisdom in my Philosophy Epistle File. In a way, I was still that boy lying in the clover field, but now my daydreams were in search of ways to unleash the power of entrepreneurship to create value and wealth for everybody involved—customers, investors, employees, vendors, and the community at large. I began dreaming about what the perfect store might look like—with no broken letters on the signs or trash on the front steps, with every display perfectly organized. I imagined the fun, crazy products we could sell, the thousands of ways we could improve the lives of our employees and customers—by giving them an exciting experience and spreading kindness and inspiration to everyone who walked through our doors. Finally, I had a cause that would transcend my own strong desire to succeed. The answer had been there all along, I just hadn't seen it.

Retail was like the girl you were best friends with but never considered marrying until you realized that she was stunningly beautiful, everything you always wanted, and that you were really in love with her all along.

4

1 Great Person = 3 Good People

Talent is the whole ball game.

It really is. When you surround yourself with hugely talented, passionate, dedicated, and genuinely kind people, you will succeed in whatever you do—there's no doubt in my mind about that.

This first Foundation Principle is our hiring and payroll philosophy: One great person is equal to three good people. We really believe that. It's not much different than trying to build a basketball team to win the NBA championship. We're trying to get the very best people we can, in the stores, in the office, and in our distribution center. No one is overqualified. If a retired Federal Reserve chairman wants a job in our accounting department, that's great with us.

We absolutely want our employees to be the very best. We love and are compassionate to everybody, but we want excellence.

I think life is too short not to try to do anything and everything with excellence.

My feeling is that we all have to go to work and we have to be there all day anyway, so we might as well do something we really feel proud of, something we get to go home at night feeling really good about. And it's really important to work with people who are great at what they do.

So we say that one great person can match the business productivity of three good people. Then we say that one good is equal to three average, and one average is equal to three lousy. So by that logic, I guess one great is actually worth twenty-seven lousy. Right?

I'm being somewhat tongue-in-cheek, of course, since such multiples are impossible to quantify. But I would say that our 1=3 ratio vastly underestimates the value of extraordinary people to any endeavor. One great employee can easily generate seven or eight times—even, sometimes, twenty times—the productivity of the merely good employee. I think the two most important things about the Foundation Principles—and The Container Store's culture—are, number one, you get to work with great people you respect and who really have your back, and number two, communication. Nothing makes people feel more like they're a part of a true team than real communication, and nothing makes people feel *not* a part of something than being excluded. So we think that great people and communication are the two most important aspects of our culture.

Now, just to clarify, I certainly don't believe that any one human being is better than another—that's not what our 1=3 philosophy is about. My belief is that everyone is to be treated the same way, from the janitor to the chairman. If you're not treating the cabdriver and the waiter with the same respect you give your doctor, say, or the town mayor, there may be some real ego and insecurity issues that you need to take care of.

But when it comes to productivity, some people are just head and shoulders above the rest—and that's the kind of person we want on our team. That may sound a tad Darwinian, but at The Container Store, we don't let the high premium we place on love and compassion suggest that we'll ever settle for anything less than the best. That's why, as I mentioned earlier, I'd want Jordan Spieth on my golf team. I would be thrilled just to be around him, and he would inspire me to play better. Working alongside people of that caliber makes you go home at night feeling great about everything you accomplished that day and thrilled to get up out of bed and go back to work the next morning to reach for the stars again.

Being on a great team, in my opinion, is one of the most rewarding of all human experiences. And our team has a clear goal: to be the best retailer in America. That's probably my competitive nature talking, but I can't think of a single downside to relentlessly striving for perfection—all the while doggedly and joyfully ensuring that everyone associated with the business is thriving.

Of course, we understand that people make mistakes. That's why we create a warm, safe, nurturing workplace that allows employees to take chances without fear of reprisal when they fail. Allowing people's individual creative genius to flourish benefits the entire team. I don't think we're the best retailer yet; being so close to the business, I often feel as if we still have a long way to go. But amazingly, I do get told pretty frequently by some wonderful business leaders that we're sure headed in that direction.

Another key point: We try to pay our people really well. In fact, I'm very proud of our payroll philosophy. Our compensation policy is one of the things we do best, one of the many areas of our business that is applauded by other companies. We've found a very business-minded and efficient way to do it. We know that by *not* doing it the way we do it, we could lose our best people.

Our store payroll as a percentage of sales is quite high. It's a very healthy ratio, though, at about 11.5 percent of sales, far above most retailers. As a result, our people generally feel mildly tickled about their compensation. I would guess that most employees can't say that. That is, most businesses have people who don't feel good about their compensation. And in the aggregate, the totals for those companies don't look good, either. The key is, our totals look very good and people are generally pleased with their compensation because we pay in accordance with each employee's contribution.

For as long as I can remember, we've tried to pay our salespeople 50 to 100 percent above the retail industry average, a policy that really comes into play with roles closest to the customers. Our average full-time salesperson makes almost $50,000 a year. While $50,000 is not an enormous amount of money, it's an enormous amount for a retail salesperson and easily double the industry average. The top positions don't get that 50 to 100 percent, but we've tried hard to make sure our vice-presidents are at, or slightly above, industry average.

Contribution isn't only about an employee's volume of responsibility or tenure; it also has much to do with the manager "praying for wisdom," so to speak, and trying to assess the contribution an employee makes to the company while also being aware of industry averages for that position.

If there are fourteen employees reporting to a department head, for example, we want the person with the highest/greatest contribution to the company to also receive the highest compensation. And the employee with the fourteenth-highest contribution has the fourteenth-highest compensation. That's why The Container Store is a meritocracy: Compensation is directly commensurate with contribution. We must carefully and painstakingly manage every employee's contribution and career every single day. This is one of the things we're doing with our people—working hard to make sure that the number one person in contribution is the number one person in compensation.

Managing someone's compensation and career is something we take very seriously. Compensation is a very important part of the whole picture; so is culture, and being surrounded by great people, and everything else we do to make The Container Store a place where people look forward to getting up in the morning and coming to work, rather than dreading it. What a responsibility it is to manage someone else's compensation and career!

How employees perform has so much to do with how we manage them and communicate with them, being mindful of our wake, and our impact on the life of each wonderful, devoted, hardworking person. We don't ever want to think that compensation is not important. Spouses and children depend upon it, and people who are great at what they do deserve to be paid well. We're not advocates of paying mediocre people well, but we're huge advocates of paying great people well.

Sometimes there are aberrations, and a situation is inherited where the top contributor is the third in compensation. This may take a while to correct—it might even take two to four years to fully correct—but we have to be patient. It can't be fixed in one performance review, probably not even in one year. The problem is that if we try to fix it all at once, we'll end up with a situation like what we see in Major League Baseball's free agent compensation. Currently in baseball, as soon as one person makes X, everyone who thinks he's comparable believes he should also make X. That's not the way to do it.

———◇———

In the case of a store employee, the general manager, store manager, regional director, area director, and VP of stores are all involved and can collaborate and help to make sure that compensation and contribution are equated. We make certain all of these people understand our payroll philosophy and work hard to ensure that every area of our business is making decisions the same way.

A company has to be extremely self-confident and knowledgeable to pay great people well. It takes more bravery to pay great people well than just about anything else. Again, the proof is in the bottom line. We have superb productivity and terrific numbers, and as I said before, our payroll as a percentage of sales is very healthy. This is so rare. The leaders of the organization— probably including someone in my position—have to be brave enough to pay great people well.

Our approach to payroll is easy to justify because we're convinced that our 1=3 approach really works. Our employee wins, because she's making far more than anyone else in another company is likely to pay her for that position. The Container Store wins, because it gets three times the productivity at only 50 to 100 percent more cost. And the customers win because they have this superb salesperson who actually cares about working in the store. I think the reason most managers are afraid to pay people well is that they just don't believe in 1=3. But we really do believe in it.

People say, "Oh, it's culture that matters." No, it's not just the culture. It's pay that matters, too. That's part of the culture. We've had some of the best companies in America ask us about our compensation strategy; about how we divide up that pie and how we go through this painstaking process. We really work hard on it. I think most Conscious Capitalist business leaders do. It's what makes their companies unique. It boils down to the fact that we really work it to death.

Even after more than three decades as a businessperson, I am still astonished by how magical this process is. I use the word "magical" deliberately because I realize this approach contradicts the usual, superrational way of doing business, the number-crunching mind-set that blindly tries to cut costs everywhere and assumes business is really about spreadsheets, not about people or the vast, complex energies of life sustaining itself. The coolest part is when you're doing a performance review and give an employee a much bigger raise than she was expecting. She starts crying, you start crying, and the magic spreads across the company, and out into the world.

When we launched The Container Store, I was incredibly fortunate to have a partner like Garrett, who embodied the 1=3 principle—and just shortly after, Sharon officially joined the company. We eventually attracted a stellar team of sales-floor employees and executives, all of whom also personify this core value on a daily basis. We didn't use the phrase "1=3" in those early days, since our seven Foundation Principles were still in the gestation phase, but the idea of surrounding yourself with terrific people was always very important to me.

Once we decided to start our own store, it wasn't enough to have a strong partnership of shared values—we still needed a viable business idea. So every day, we would spend long hours at Garrett's house researching and tossing ideas around. Garrett's original idea of a handmade-furniture store was still under consideration, but we couldn't figure out a way to get the products made cheaply enough—and I still thought that concept sounded too boring. We agreed we could sell other household products like elfa, the ingenious component system we both loved. I was still inspired by the grocery store idea but finally said, "If we can't do food, let's do function." Whatever we sold, we agreed, the store should be lively and fun, creating that sense of theater that we both loved so much about retail.

We began poring over the *Thomas Register of American Manufacturers*, a giant set of reference books listing hundreds of thousands of industrial products. Flipping through it, we became fascinated by the "Material Parts & Handling" section, which described things like Akro bins, commercial Metro shelving, cutlery holders, and bus tubs. We knew that customers could use them for, well, something. Even back then, we knew you had to be reasonably organized to accomplish the things you wanted to in life. Those were the days before fax machines and the Internet, so we spent long days and nights typing out hundreds of letters to manufacturers requesting catalogs and samples. We were ignored or refused by some of them—even laughed at a bit when we told them our concept. They were commercial vendors who sold their products by the thousands and had never dealt with retailers before; in any case, they couldn't be bothered with young entrepreneurs like us.

But most did send us samples, and we began dreaming about how they might be used. Why couldn't that mason's tool bag become a rugged overnight bag? Parents could use those big wire leaf burners to store pool toys and soccer balls—the wire construction allowed you to actually see what was being stored. Perfect! Egg-collecting baskets could be used for gardening tools.

The process was exhilarating—and discouraging at times. While Garrett's wife, Cecilia, was being incredibly patient and supportive, her parents were wondering how long it would take their son-in-law to get his act together. So Garrett began looking through the help wanted ads but kept getting sidetracked by other ads for products like modular drawer units. Instead of going on job interviews, he wrote asking for samples for our new store, which we were still calling Basics.

Garrett says his "Aha!" moment came in January of 1978, when he went to a home-improvement show in Dallas and got excited about Lundia, another shelving system from Sweden. We were both familiar with Lundia from our days at Storehouse, and we agreed it would be a great product for our new store. "Suddenly a lightbulb went off," Garrett recalls. "I was driving down the highway in Dallas and thought, 'That's it! We could create a store that sold the resources for people to organize all the stuff in their lives.'" In truth, my own recollection is a more gradual process that evolved after countless conversations with Garrett, John Mullen, and scores of other folks.

We only dimly realized it at the time, but as we began to focus more and more on storage and organization products, we were tapping into several powerful trends of the late '70s. Our funky collection of products echoed the famous *Whole Earth Catalog* of the late '60s—the main difference being that our target market was not hippies, but homeowners who had busy lives and a desire to shop for items that would help them gain more order in those lives. Encouraging people to organize what they already owned using super-high-quality products that would last a lifetime appealed to a growing environmental awareness. The look and feel of these commercial products fit well into the modernist "high-tech" architecture style of that period and what was later called industrial chic but also worked well in all types of environments. And while the information revolution was still in its infancy, there was already a sense that living more efficiently, simplifying your life, and saving space and time would become increasingly important, thanks to pop-culture books like *Future Shock* that warned of the quickening pace of technological and social change.

We rarely discussed our ideas in such lofty terms, of course. Mostly we said things like "Wow, these European canning jars are cool!" "And what if we actually sold those colorful dairy crates that people are stealing from behind the grocery store to help organize their record albums?"

We especially loved the idea of indulging our love for organizing, that Zen feeling you get when everything is neatly in place. Everybody knows the frustration of searching around the house for the car keys, hunting for hours and still not finding them; or when you can't find a favorite shirt, or pair of shoes, because your closet is such a mess. It's such a colossal waste of time. Studies show that the average American spends nearly an hour a day looking for things—a bit more than fifteen days a year that could be spent on happier, more productive pursuits.

When customers see the orderly way we showcase the products, and feel the positive energy generated by our organized space, they become inspired to do the same in their own homes. I'm not talking about encouraging obsessive-compulsive behavior—that's a stressful state of mind (although I've always said a tiny bit of OCD is actually a very good thing). Rather, our goal is to relieve stress, making people's lives simpler, easier, calmer. The positive energy in our stores would make that case better than any form of advertising.

Now, though, we needed an actual store. As an architect, our investor and partner John Mullen was knowledgeable about the real estate market, so he helped us search upscale neighborhoods full of elegant homes with big closets and lots of possessions to organize. Finally, we found just the right spot—a small, 1,600-square-foot storefront in a shopping center at Preston Road and Forest Lane, right next to the Hockaday School in Dallas. Our shopping center cotenants weren't the most glamorous—a country-and-western clothing store called the Horseman's Mart, a New York–style delicatessen called the Cheese House, and a hair salon. But rent was only two dollars per square foot per year, or $3,200 a year—a truly stunning deal considering the area's demographics.

We also needed a name. We agreed that Basics would not do. A store with a name like that could sell just about anything, and the name didn't begin to describe our company's mission. So we brainstormed and asked everybody we knew for suggestions. The result was a long list with several hundred names, which we laid out in triple columns: The Box Company; The Box Store; The Storage Store; etc. Nothing seemed right, but we were too busy ordering products to really focus on it.

By late May, the date we picked to open the store—July 1, 1978—was fast approaching and we still didn't have a name, just a blank sign on the front of the store. So one day, Garrett and John and I met in the empty storefront, sat cross-legged on the floor, and stared up at the wall, where we had posted collages of photos of our favorite products from the manufacturers' literature. We read aloud from the list of names, testing each one to see whether it matched the feeling we got when looking up at the pictures. "Nope...no...negative...definitely not."

Finally, on page three or four, in the middle column, was a suggestion John had received from Bob Wilson (the father of actors Owen and Luke), then CEO of the Dallas public television station, KERA, whose background was in advertising and public relations: The Container Store.

We all looked at one another and said, "That's it! That's the name!" The word "container" implied utility and function, perfectly describing what we were selling, and, as Bob pointed out, didn't come with any strong associations, allowing our brand to fill in the blanks. Our store would "contain" everything customers needed to get organized and save space and time. We could even use the phrase "Contain yourself" in advertising campaigns. We wondered if "The" would sound arrogant—who are we to call ourselves *The* Container Store?—but quickly realized that since there were no other container stores, it wasn't like saying "The Restaurant." Nobody had ever tried anything like this before. We were (and are) the one and only, The Container Store!

As we ordered products, our small store began to fill with bins, tins, baskets, barrels, bags, busboy tubs for dishes, cans, chests, trunks, totes, towel bars for tie racks, drawers and shelving made of wire, and hundreds of other products we thought were cool, interesting, useful, or all of the above. A few of our products could be found elsewhere—like garment bags and hangers—but the intrigue of our concept was that you couldn't find most of them in any retail store (except perhaps in what used to be called the notions section of some department stores).

Other products had the unvarnished feel of something you'd find in a hardware store. That's why Sharon began calling The Container Store a hardware store for women—because it's a place to discover things you didn't know how to use, or didn't even know about, in your search for solutions to improve your home or office. Many products didn't come in retail packaging—and we stripped off the packaging from those that did—allowing us to create displays that were propped, show the products in action, and let customers play around with the items to get ideas about how to use them.

To get people talking, John Mullen even built a pine coffin, which we displayed in the store, and which I guess is the ultimate container. That created quite a buzz in Dallas, but after a while it began to freak people out, so we got rid of it. By the time the store opened, we had amassed an enormous inventory of 800 products—and, remarkably enough, we still carry many of those items today.

It was the oddest collection of retail products anybody had ever seen. Lots of people were questioning our business savvy. When my parents attended a dinner party with my dad's oilman friends and their wives, there was lots of chatter and shaking of heads: "How are Kip and Boone's boy gonna make a living selling empty boxes?" A rep from the Metro shelving company (another best seller we still offer today) was also incredulous when he came by our empty space to show us his products. "Let's face it, guys. This isn't going to work," he said, giving us his card. "But it's a nice space, so gimme a call when you're ready to sublet it." My old high school pal Phil Lenihan, who was managing local rock bands at the time, came over with some musician friends to see what was going on. When I explained, they looked at one another like I was nuts. "We thought it was one of the most crackpot business ideas we had ever heard of," Phil told me later. "I remember thinking to myself, 'Well, I'm just glad I have something solid to fall back on, like managing punk bands.'"

And yet we simply had no doubt that The Container Store would be a hit. Call it youthful naïveté, or a "we can conquer the world" positive spirit, or just intuition based on the decade of retail experience that we had accumulated by that time, but we knew we had a winner. When students or aspiring entrepreneurs ask me how they can tell if their business idea is any good, I always use the analogy of musicians who made a hit record. Almost every time, I'm sure, they knew they had a winner while they were recording it and listening to it in the studio. They just knew. There was no doubt it would be a huge hit from the moment they walked out of the studio. We certainly didn't feel that way when we were wandering around in the wilderness with a handmade furniture concept called Basics—that one just never felt right. But once we developed the storage and organization concept and came up with the name The Container Store, we were so excited that we knew customers would feel the same way. We just knew.

I've never subscribed to the notion that just because a business idea has never been tried, or successfully executed, that means there must be no market for it. Some people like to say, "If it's so great, how come nobody's ever done it before?" Or, "There's nothing new under the sun." But that assumes a perfectly rational market, and any behavioral economist can tell you that markets, like people, often behave irrationally. There are literally and truly millions of original, sustainable business ideas out there right now, just waiting for the right entrepreneurs to bring them into being.

On the other hand, it's not enough to have a great idea—you also have to execute it. We set our grand opening date for July 1 at 9 AM and plastered the entire area with flyers and newspaper ads. (I smile now in hindsight, thinking about that opening date—just before the Fourth of July. Brilliant! We'd have to close for the holiday right after we opened the doors!) In any event, by mid-June, our little storefront was a mess. Products were still streaming in, stacked up everywhere, and the place looked like an attic full of junk. How could we open a store that promised to help people get organized when our own store was in total chaos?

The answer, we would discover, was to surround ourselves with 1=3 people. Like Sharon, for example. By then, she had started her career as a landscape architect at a small firm in Dallas. With her little spare time, she plunged right in to help. Using her excellent architectural design skills and her expertise in art and printing, she created the handwritten signs for all 800 products, our GRAND OPENING banner, and other signs around the store. Sharon didn't officially join the company until a year or so later, but she was a tremendous help in those early days with her creative ideas and positive spirit—and, of course, her emotional support for me during such an exhilarating but challenging time.

Just as I could never have predicted how big our company would become in those days, I never would have imagined how critical Sharon would be to our success. Garrett and I usually get all the credit, but in my opinion Sharon soon became the most important person at The Container Store—selecting just the right products (keeping us focused when it was tempting to diversify our selection) and learning every facet of the business, from operations to finance. Because Sharon prefers to avoid the limelight, she has never received the credit she deserves. I know, people always say that about their spouses, but there's a simple reason why I don't believe I'm being biased when I say Sharon is the best merchant in retail today: So many of the retailers

I admire most in the world just carry on and on about her—far more than they carry on about me, for that matter. And rightfully so.

Sharon was not the only 1=3 person who helped out as the clock ticked toward opening day. Everyone who knew us and loved us was there. Garrett's wife, Cecilia, pitched in heroically as we were setting up the store, even helping with bookkeeping after we opened, until their first child was born. Garrett's parents, his sister and brother, and John Mullen and his wife, Anne, also helped enormously. I was proud to see my dad hauling boxes and my mom stocking shelves, supporting me as only my parents can—and my brother, Tim, jumped in, too. It was inspiring to watch our family and friends roll up their sleeves to help out, like an old-fashioned barn raising or like putting up the timber-frame home Tim built out in East Texas. A house raising with friends and family and neighbors.

If great teammates are defined as people with talent who work hard for the greater good, then we had an incredible 1=3 team. Nobody was getting paid yet—heck, Garrett and I didn't get paid for many months before and many months after the store opened—but we were all bound by love for one another and a belief in a great idea that would truly make people's lives better.

I should add that nobody thought this store was going to make any of us rich. Sure, we wanted to be profitable, but like most entrepreneurs, we were motivated by passion, not money. In fact, nearly every successful entrepreneur I have ever known was not motivated primarily by money—from John Mackey of Whole Foods to Herb Kelleher of Southwest Airlines to Gordon Segal of Crate & Barrel. The reason is simple: None of us would have lasted through so many years of long, stressful days, working for no pay, if we hadn't been fueled by some higher calling—the same noble purpose we always talk about at Conscious

Capitalism gatherings. That's why we never hesitate to use the word "love" at The Container Store—from those earliest days, as our family and friends pitched in, the company was founded on love. And those feelings still drive us today.

————⟨○⟩————

On the night of June thirtieth, our fear was that the store would still be a mess by the time we opened at nine o'clock the next morning. The shelving installation had only been completed the day before, and there were so many products jamming the aisles that it felt like a gridlocked intersection at rush hour. Today, we talk to our customers about making the most of their vertical space. Well, we certainly did a good job of that back then, with products stacked to the ceiling. In fact, we had to haul stuff out into the back alley to make room to create displays inside. There were so many decisions to be made: What style should the store have? What should it look and feel like? Where should the signs go? Our helpers would hold up merchandise, yelling, "How much is this?" We would shout "Four ninety-nine!" (by then, we had all the prices memorized) and they would scribble the price on the sign.

We worked right through the night, and by the time the sun came up at 6:30 AM, Garrett and I were the only ones left. We stood near the front door and scanned the store. The early-morning sun filtered through the big front windows, lighting the place with a beautiful glow. By some miracle, each display was perfectly organized, the floors free of debris, each sign neatly in its place. That Zen-like feeling of peace and positive energy we loved so much pulsed through our empty store. It felt like the stunning culmination of Santa and his elves making gifts for the entire freaking world and delivering them before all the children woke up on Christmas morning.

But there was no time to revel in our accomplishment. Garrett's house was nearby, so we ran over to shower and change clothes. We arrived back, with minutes to spare, for the grand opening of The Container Store.

———◇———

What an amazing sight: As soon as the doors opened, customers came streaming through, dozens of them! Admittedly, most were family and friends, but we were touched to see their excitement as they wandered the aisles, inspecting the merchandise. We still have the receipt from our first customer—Garrett's sister, Nancy Word, who bought a bamboo trunk and a jewelry box for $143, including tax. The total take for our first day was about $550, with close to 80 percent of that coming from people we knew. But each day was a little busier than the last, and by the second week, the store was jammed. Everybody was so curious: They didn't know what they were looking at, what they should buy, or how to use it. That's where Garrett and I—these two tall, lanky guys—came in, standing nearby to give them ideas. Next to the dairy crates, we posted a list of dozens and dozens of possible uses, and wives would say to their husbands, "Look, honey—toy storage!" You could hear people reading the lists out loud.

It's amazing how many things have stayed the same at The Container Store since that first day. One of our mottos is "We sell the hard stuff"—unlike Bounty paper towels or Coca-Cola, which can just sit on the shelf and sell themselves. That's always been our competitive advantage. We sell items most retailers won't even carry—because they don't have the highly trained staff to explain them to the customer. Our 1=3 people are so talented, so well prepared, and so free to use their intuition, they can suggest even the most unlikely product to solve whatever organizational issue a customer has. They can tell the stories behind the products. For example, they explain that the Nalgene travel bottle—originally created for laboratory chemical storage—absolutely, positively won't leak in your luggage on the airplane. You could even say we're as much a service business as a merchandiser, though of course the service is free.

Take elfa. It's remarkable that elfa is our number-one-selling product, because so many other retailers couldn't sell it—they tried to sell it as a "closet in a box" without the service and customization (we know, because we used to wholesale it to other retailers). It's component based (metric based, for God's sake; talk about complex), made in Sweden, and salespeople at other stores were not sufficiently trained to explain why elfa is the greatest closet system ever devised: elegantly designed and strong and flexible enough to solve any storage problem. Basically, our salespeople had to be like interior designers, helping to design your closet (in those days, by hand-sketching on a piece of grid paper). Before we came along, nobody had ever heard of a salesperson being able to do that. We have enhanced this further so that now customers can have their closets designed with our experts at our Custom Design Center.

By the third week, our aisles were so crowded, we thought the displays would come crashing down from people bumping into them. We had obtained the parents' association directory from the nearby Hockaday School and the directory from Dallas's 500, Inc. Club—the leading contributors to the arts in Dallas—and we used both mailing lists extensively. It has become increasingly apparent that "trickle-down" may not always work in economics, but it sure works in marketing: Those affluent, influential, and buzz-generating customers were struck by what they saw in our store, and they quickly spread the word to the masses. "It's the most amazing place, right over there in Preston Forest," we heard people saying. "You won't believe it, you gotta go see it!"

When somebody came into the store and didn't buy anything

(which didn't happen often), we were shocked. All the products were so useful, and since everybody wrestles with some kind of organizational problem, how could you possibly not buy anything? Most often, people left with shopping bags stuffed with far more merchandise than they'd ever planned to buy, leaving the store excited to get home and get their space organized.

Another factor in our success—and I don't know how to say this without sounding full of myself—is that if Garrett and I could do anything reasonably well, it was probably, first and foremost, that we were really good at helping customers on the sales floor. We love the spontaneous banter, the flash of inspiration when you come up with a solution to a customer's problem, and the adrenaline rush when you close a sale.

———◇———

Looking back on those days, it's remarkable that we never had to deal with the usual entrepreneur's fear that we'd go out of business. We had positive cash flow immediately, and never spent more than half of our $35,000 initial investment. We were very frugal, because we were truly terrified of running out of cash and needed to make sure we had enough money to buy new products. We ordered products really, really frequently in really, really small quantities (to the amused aggravation of our vendors). We didn't even buy a cash register until we'd been open more than a year. Instead, we used a wooden box to keep our money in.

At the end of the night, we would hide it somewhere in the shop. Since we didn't have a distribution center yet, every time a new shipment came in we had to work until dawn reorganizing the store, and sometimes we got so sleepy we forgot where we'd put the money box.

This made for some interesting moments. Whenever a customer bought a large container, we'd have to inspect it to make sure our cash box wasn't inside. Some of my scariest memories are about searching for that damn wooden box—and the day it did officially go missing was the day we finally decided to invest in a cash register. Today, in honor of those crazy days, when employees reach their fifth anniversary, we give them a replica of that original cash box.

We didn't realize the full impact of what we'd achieved until we got a couple of surprise visits during those first few months. The first came when the then president of the housewares giant Rubbermaid walked in unexpectedly, saying he'd heard about this weird store in Dallas and wanted to learn more. When we showed him around, he was dazzled and said it was one of the most innovative business ideas he'd ever seen. We were already carrying some Rubbermaid products, but that visit helped create a much deeper relationship.

Later, we got a visit, and then many visits, from Stanley Marcus of Neiman Marcus, who was also astonished at what he saw and offered to help us out in any way he could. Until his death in 2002, he was a constant source of advice and encouragement—a true mentor for me—and I will never forget his generosity and kindness. It's hard to convey how much his interest meant to us, since Stanley Marcus had always been my hero and was a man of great taste and refinement, the true gold standard in retail for his commitment to quality and service. (His book, *Minding the Store*, is a classic and a great primer for anyone considering a retail business—or any kind of business, for that matter.)

My point is, if you really believe in your life's mission, and the principles that fuel it, you will want to achieve excellence (if you're satisfied with mediocrity, in my opinion, you have not found your calling). And we realized early on at The Container

Store that the only way to fulfill that ambition is to work with talented people who share your passion for greatness. As the sales volume grew during those first few months and years, Garrett and I realized we could no longer rely on the generosity of our friends and family. We had to start hiring people!

By 1979 we had hired some phenomenal 1=3 employees. One of our key early employees, who blazed the trail of career advancement at The Container Store, was a young woman named Barbara Anderson, who came into the store one day with her two kids. We all knew Barb as a regular customer. "Do you guys ever need any part-time help?" she said as I was ringing her up, her children embarrassed that their mom was asking for a job. "Well, you know, we just might," I said, tearing off the corner of a piece of paper. "Here—write down your phone number."

Turned out Barb had been a statistician at a medical school in Portland, Oregon, before moving to Dallas in the early '70s when her husband, Dick, a cell biologist (who was later on a Nobel Prize–winning research team) got a job at the University of Texas health science center. "I had never seen a store like this before," she told me later. "It was very earthy, organic, and had all these weird products that were so cool, things you couldn't normally buy. There was so much energy and passion, such down-to-earth folksiness, that it reminded me of the Pacific Northwest. It was like, 'Oh my gosh, I'm home!' "

On her first day of shopping at The Container Store, Barbara bought Akro bins—modular, stackable plastic bins, which we still sell—to hold clothespins and odd socks in her laundry room. She found herself coming back to the store every chance she got—for wedding gifts, birthday presents, whatever. "I was so surprised when I heard those words coming out of my mouth, asking for a job," she said, laughing. "I had no time for a job, we weren't having financial difficulty, and I'd never worked in retail before. I guess some part of me just wanted to be part of that great energy you guys had in that store."

Even then, we believed that passionate customers make the best employees. So I called Barbara to ask when she could start. "Well, I have two children in elementary school and I need to be home by three PM. And I really can't work weekends, because that's family time." That kind of talk is not usually considered a great way to land a job, but it didn't bother me a bit; it showed she also had passion for her family! "Okay, how about weekdays, nine AM to two PM?" I said. "Can you start tomorrow?"

Though we didn't know Barb well, our intuition told us she would be perfect—and she was. She learned to use our new cash register and found she loved helping customers and organizing display cases. She was quickly promoted to full-time and later became the store manager. She went on to become an important champion of our corporate culture as director of community services and staff development in the mid-'90s and then became one of our first vice-presidents of stores. After thirty years of tremendous service, Barb retired in 2009 and returned to her beloved native Portland, where today she often drops in to work part-time at our Bridgeport Village store, and frequently speaks at company events. We like to call her our Honorary Employee #1.

———◦———

Clearly, Barb Anderson was a 1=3 employee—and certainly much more. But you may be wondering, "How do you define a great employee?" It's an important question, because the answer guides our decision-making in hiring, performance reviews, pay raises, and promotion.

Our definition of "great" is the same for every job at the company. You have to be secure enough to hire people better than you. That's how you create a team of all-stars. You have to be dedicated to excellence. The owner of that NBA franchise is not afraid to strive for excellence when building a basketball team. But for some reason, some people don't understand it when building a business. You want to put the best people you can in every position. So many folks set the standard for 1=3 in our company. John Thrailkill pops into my mind at the moment— John T., as everyone calls him. It's pretty much been that way since he joined the company in our stores straight out of college as a part-time salesperson more than twenty years ago, intending to work with us until he found a "real job." He's been everything from what we used to call a "Super Sales Trainer" to elfa wholesale representative, store manager, and marketing manager, and he is now our vice-president of store metrics & systems, customer support & business development. He's so beloved by all—positive, devoted, and trustworthy, and has been responsible for instilling that ethic in what I'd bet are thousands of employees over the years. I'm actually not sure you could ever create a colleague and friend who's more reliable than John T. That's who you want on your team.

First, the CEO has to believe it's possible. At The Container Store, whether they work the sales floor part-time, run the forklift at our distribution center, or are part of our executive team, all truly great employees must demonstrate the following seven characteristics, which we use during our annual performance review process:

• **Commitment and Accountability:** Great employees show responsibility and a selfless commitment, doing whatever it takes to get the job done completely and successfully. They take initiative, make things happen, and are dedicated to the company's goals, from sales to recruiting. They take responsibility for their own actions, feel a loyal obligation to the company, and constantly seek out ways to improve their job performance.

- **Planning and Organizing and Attention to Detail:** Great employees plan and organize their work effectively. They make good judgments about time allocation and know how to set priorities, asking for help when necessary. They take a whole-brained approach to business by understanding that "everything matters" affects the quality of every aspect of their work and directly affects the entire company.

- **Communication IS Leadership:** Great employees understand our company vision and whole-brained approach to communication. They keep supervisors and coworkers informed through necessary, courteous, and beneficial communication. They have strong written, verbal, and interpersonal skills and a passion for knowledge, staying aware of internal and external communication and industry trends and news to support their own professional development. As president Melissa Reiff says, "We must practice consistent, reliable, predictable, effective, thoughtful, courteous, and compassionate communication every single day to successfully sustain, develop, and grow our business."

- **Professionalism:** Great employees display professionalism in their approach to work through their appearance, social interactions, and ethical approach to business. They deal with anger, frustration, and disappointment in a mature and professional manner. They are conscious of coworkers' time and are always ready for scheduled shifts, meetings, and responsibilities. They respect the opinions and perspectives of others.

- **Problem Solving:** Great employees anticipate and identify problems and recommend solutions while bringing opportunities and challenges to the attention of the appropriate people. They solve problems by creating an action plan that utilizes all available resources.

• **Teamwork/Wake:** Great employees understand the value of working together to produce the best results. They motivate, inspire, and encourage fellow employees, share credit and opportunities, and help others when needed. They work diligently to connect with all types of personalities, build new connections throughout the company, and keep long-standing relationships strong. They create a sense of community in their own department and other areas of the company. They know the power of wake—that every decision can have an effect on the team, the customer, and other stakeholders.

• **Ability and Attitude:** Great employees handle changes in working conditions or responsibilities with grace. They are courteous and respectful and understand the importance of being Gumby—that is, remaining flexible to get the job done. They embrace new opportunities to grow and develop, and they set a great example for others with contagious enthusiasm and a positive, consistent, can-do attitude.

This may seem like a daunting list of star qualities, but we would never say our employees have to be perfect. Instead, we work hard to create an environment where people feel unafraid to make mistakes. A place where they know they won't get yelled at or punished. Go ahead, take chances and make mistakes, we say— as Sharon puts it, "What's the worst that can happen?" You realize it's a mistake, you fix it, and you start over. It's human nature to want to feel safe and protected, so we go to great lengths to let everyone know it's okay to fail—in fact, we'll probably love you more than ever because that usually means you're trying something new or reaching further than you've ever gone before.

When I'm skiing, if I'm afraid to fall, I'm not pushing myself and maximizing my potential on the slopes. When I'm fishing, if I'm only casting in the middle of the water, not getting too close to the brush for fear of getting my line hung up, I'm really decreasing my chances of catching the most fish. We honored Tadashi Yanai, founder of the übersuccessful Japanese retail chain Uniqlo, at the National Retail Federation several years ago. And I remember him talking about his book, *One Win Nine Losses*, and how he counts on failures to help fuel his success, using experimentation and risks to uncover breakthroughs, and noting that with experimentation comes mistakes along the way.

As John Mackey and Raj Sisodia point out in their book, *Conscious Capitalism*, the average level of engagement that employees have with their work has remained at 30 percent or less for the past ten years, according to Gallup Strategic Consulting. And my friend and author Lou Carbone puts it this way: "Someone in your position or mine should have, I think, a moral obligation to create a place where people love coming to work." He says only the first 25 percent of employees' effort is mandatory, and the next 75 percent is completely voluntary, based on their boss and culture.

This view acknowledges the true essence of the human spirit—people don't want to goof off; they want to achieve and work with great people and go home at night feeling wonderful about what they've accomplished.

Carbone did a session at our company a few years ago and said he'd never seen a higher level of volunteerism than at The Container Store. Why? Because we hire truly unique employees who only know one way of performing: at the very highest level possible. For our folks, it's just second nature.

Now that we've defined a great employee, how do you find one? We spend a lot of time thinking about that question, because the only thing harder than motivating and retaining talent is the ability to identify and develop talent.

The first place we look is among our own customers. They're people like Cricket Stewart, a suburban mother of three who, before coming to work for us, shopped at our store in Tysons Corner, Virginia, so often she felt like Norm in the TV series *Cheers*. Remember how everybody yelled "Norm!" whenever he walked into the bar? Well, at The Container Store, they shouted "Cricket!" She got to know everyone so well, her employee friends finally said to her, "Cricket, why don't you work here?"

So she applied, got the job, and took the "mommy shift" when her kids were in school. This year, we'll fly Cricket and her husband to Dallas for our 2014 Service Awards dinner to say "Thank you!" for giving us fifteen wonderful years (and counting), all part-time. Cricket's children are grown now, but she's still a big customer of The Container Store. At her ten-year anniversary at the Ritz-Carlton in Dallas, her husband, Craig, a financial adviser, stood up to make an announcement as we all dined on celebrated chef Dean Fearing's famous tortilla soup and buffalo tenderloin: Even with her 40 percent employee discount, Craig told the crowd, the family is only just about breaking even on the deal! Everyone laughed because we could all relate: Being able to pay only sixty cents on the dollar for the incredible selection of merchandise at The Container Store is actually a big reason why some of our most loyal fans come to work for us.

Our employees are so enthusiastic about The Container Store, in fact, that they're also our best recruiters. We only have a few "official" full-time employees in our recruiting department in our Dallas headquarters, mostly to fill specialized job openings. Instead, we train every employee in the company in how to recruit new members of our team, and we offer constant reminders about the importance of always being on the lookout for talent. It's not the recruiting department's job to recruit. It's the recruiting department's job to make sure everyone takes on the personal responsibility of recruiting—that we all do it. We all carry recruiting cards to give to friends or that extra-attentive waiter at a restaurant or that mom we meet at a birthday party who looks like a perfect fit for our culture. It's not easy getting a job at The Container Store—we hire only about 3 percent of all applicants—but we're always looking for 1=3 people. If we don't have an opening at that moment, we'll contact the best candidates later, as soon as something opens up.

We also tell our employees to approach family members who share our company's values—brothers and sisters, parents, children, and cousins. As you might expect, Sharon and I are big believers in married couples working together (and, of course, we accommodate employees so they aren't reporting directly to their spouses). In fact, dozens of couples have met and fallen in love at The Container Store. Take John and Amy Urbin, for example. They were both in their midtwenties when they met as employees at our Chicago store in 2004, and they were married a year later. "We became good friends, and I think the entire Chicago store was rooting for us to get together," Amy told me at the 2012 Service Awards dinner, when John was honored for ten years at the company. "I finally said to him, 'Why aren't we dating?' "

John, sitting next to her, laughed. "We often credit our successful marriage to the Foundation Principles," he said. "Especially Communication IS Leadership." Amy leaned over and put her hand on John's arm. "We both came from families that were very good at communicating," she said, "but it really helps to be constantly reminded how important it is. Sometimes John and I will have a disagreement and I'll find myself rephrasing things to explain it better, like I'd do in a training session. Or I'll try to look at it from John's point of view. Even something as simple as the way I put the trash in the trash can, to make it easier for him to take out. Because on the job we're always thinking, 'How can I help the next person do their job better?' "

We get those kinds of comments a lot, and I'm humbled and astonished every time I hear them. It's an incredible feeling to hear your employees talk that way—far beyond anything we dreamed of back when we opened our first little store. We started the Service Awards dinners years ago to show our long-term employees how much they mean to us. But at some point, quite spontaneously, these events became much more than the wonderful keepsakes and trips, extra vacation time, and money the employees receive with each milestone: These events have become a forum for employees to take the microphone and to talk about how much the company means to them.

It's always an emotional, memorable night: Kids get up to rave about their parents, husbands about their wives, managers about their staff, all speaking from the heart about how working at The Container Store has made them better at everything they do, or helped them during a difficult or painful moment in their lives, or simply created so much joy and happiness—especially during the recession, when everyone was elated not to have to worry about losing their jobs. Of all our accomplishments, those heartfelt, often teary speeches are among the ones I will always treasure most.

———◇———

In training our employees to recruit, we always encourage them to keep their minds open to anyone and everyone, regardless of their professional background, even those with no experience in retail. You need only look at the origins of our company to see why. Remember, back in 1978, Garrett had a master's degree in history, Sharon was a landscape architect, and I was an English major dropout. None of us really knew the first thing about running a business, which actually freed us up to create our own way of doing things. We soon adopted many industry best practices, of course, but it's clear that our unique corporate culture—and our success—is a direct result of our unconventional backgrounds.

Since we want the best of the best, our interviewing process is quite thorough. There's an online application, then a phone interview, then a group interview with homework assignments, and then various personal interviews (the number of personal interviews varies based on the position). We train our employees on the best way to interview to find great people. We ask questions about their life experience, how they've overcome challenges in other jobs, how their last manager would describe them, to describe a recent experience where they had good service (and to explain what "good service" means to them), and more.

As I mentioned, for us, there's no such thing as an over-qualified employee. John Urbin, whom I talked about earlier, for example, got his degree in architecture, but once he started working professionally in that field, he realized it just wasn't what he wanted to do. So he took a part-time job on the sales floor while he figured out what was next, and told his manager, Terri Williams, that this would be temporary employment, that he would never consider a career in retail for the long term.

But Terri saw something in the new young employee and kept offering him greater challenges and more responsibility until John realized that not only did he love retail, and love working at The Container Store, but he could also actually envision a thriving career with us. Now he is an outstanding general manager of our Minneapolis store.

Daniel White, a Columbus, Ohio, store manager (who has a degree in anthropology), once put it this way: "On the sales floor, I have worked alongside rocket scientists, teachers, doctors, lawyers, homemakers, students, chefs, executives, government employees, bakers, and small business owners. These individuals with diverse backgrounds have come together with a common passion for the Container Store culture and an understanding that they can make a difference in our customers' lives." And our fabulous, educated customers notice. They love interacting with lively, interesting, smart people who give them highly focused, individual attention.

———◅◦▻———

As The Container Store grows, even some of our longtime employees wonder if we'll be able to find and keep enough 1=3 people to maintain and expand our unique culture. This makes me chuckle, because people have been worrying about that since 1981, when we opened our second store. The truth is that the bigger we get, the stronger our culture becomes. Our culture is stronger than it was one year ago, five years ago, and on and on. I only have to point to larger companies like Southwest Airlines, Costco, and Whole Foods Market—Conscious Capitalists all— to show how a corporate culture can get deeper and stronger as it grows. We're expanding faster than ever today, but when I go to a new-store opening, I am amazed that each group of new employees is the best I've ever seen—until the next grand opening, when I find myself saying the very same thing. Our employees just keep getting better and better.

———◅◦▻———

Once we've found our 1=3 employees, how do we keep them? Simply put, we make life so wonderful that they wouldn't dream of going anywhere else. It's amazing that our turnover rate is so low in a revolving-door industry that usually assumes every single employee will eventually walk or be fired—that's why for the average retailer, turnover is around 100 percent. One reason we're so different is that we offer enormous potential for advancement. Even after thirty-six years of phenomenal growth, The Container Store is still expanding rapidly, with hundreds of still-untapped markets across the United States and abroad. That puts us in stark contrast to companies that treat employees as a mere cost of doing business rather than as treasured assets who can help the company grow.

The tremendous emphasis we place on training—nearly 300 hours in a full-time employee's first year, compared to the retail average of 10—also builds loyalty. When employees see how deeply we invest in them, they reciprocate by investing in us. It's that simple.

The Container Store also has the highly evolved compensation/contribution philosophy I described earlier that ensures employees know exactly how they are doing at all times—where they're performing well and what they need to work on. That creates tremendous trust, a positive work environment, and few surprises when it comes time for raises. Our performance review process is quite elaborate, requiring many hours from both employees and managers, using the seven characteristics of a great employee outlined above. They discuss their contributions and opportunities for growth, along with our Foundation Principles, and agree to a set of goals. We also ask about what the employee's supervisor can do. All those hours are well spent, because the process ultimately guides us to a fair decision in measuring each employee's contribution.

As one young employee wrote to me after reading a newspaper article about employee perks:

> I thought this was a really great article from *USA Today* that points out that the special perks (pool table, beer Fridays, nap pods…etc.) don't actually correlate with employee satisfaction. They call out that even though Google is one of *Fortune*'s Top 100 Companies and provides more "perks" than any other company, that alone won't lead to long-term employee satisfaction and contributes to an average-to-high turnover rate. The article would've been better if they had pointed out that at

The Container Store we give hours and hours of annual reviews that will knock any employee's socks off! And through our Foundation Principle, Communication IS Leadership, we let ALL employees express what they want in their career and what is or isn't motivating them, which all contributes to the LOWEST turnover rate in retail!

Wow. I was just blown away by this millennial's observation.

Of course, we're not perfect when it comes to hiring and retaining 1=3 employees. Sometimes we mutually agree that an employee and the company's goals are not aligning and that we need to part ways, or, in extreme cases, let an employee go after ample warning that something is awry. Some people may be highly qualified or may be really nice people but are simply not a good fit for our culture. "This is a highly energetic, communicative, positive place, so if you take a jaundiced view of life, you're probably going to hate it here," says Eva Gordon, our vice-president of stores, training, development, and recruiting. Other employees have seemed great during the interview process but slacked off on the job. Melissa coined a memorable term—"bobbers"—to describe folks who float along on the efforts of others. Fortunately, our communication-rich approach, performance review process, and peer-management environment usually catches such issues before they develop into big headaches. As Amy Carovillano, our vice-president of logistics and distribution, puts it, "Do you want to work here because it's a great place to work…or is it a great place to work because you work here?"

There are many, many touching stories from our employees (which you can find on our blog at whatwestandfor.com) that are great examples of the great people we hire and the love they, in turn, give back to our company and their colleagues.

Yes, I know, that word again—"love"—often creates confusion in a business context. That's because the English language, lovely as it is, is surprisingly limited when it comes to talking about love. We often end up using one word to describe many different kinds of affection. As the noted scientist and author Paul Zak pointed out during a wonderful presentation he delivered to our company in 2011, the ancient Greeks distinguished between four types of love: *eros* (romantic, sensual love), *storge* (the love of parents for their children), *agape* (later used by Christians to mean love of God), and *philia* (brotherly love, or love of humanity, of community). When we talk about love at The Container Store, of course, we're talking about the last one—*philia*. That's the feeling that infuses every company that follows the principles of Conscious Capitalism, and I would submit that no business can reach its full potential unless it takes advantage of the boundless human capacity for such love in every decision it makes.

Philia. That's the type of love that has produced the sales growth we've enjoyed throughout our company's history, not to mention our astonishing, historic average 21 percent compound annual growth rate since inception. Some might find it odd to discuss love and profits in the same breath. But we are, after all, a business. Conscious Capitalism has nothing to do with religion, and yet we're evangelical about harnessing the power of the free market to improve the state of humankind.

Contrary to the popular view of business, we don't seek profit for its own sake. Our Foundation Principles wouldn't work without a higher purpose. To borrow from Aesop, that would kill the goose that laid the golden egg. On the other hand, creating profits with a powerful purpose creates an incredibly powerful force for good. Our company doesn't exist to make a profit; it makes a profit so it can exist. And it exists to bring happiness and prosperity to every life we touch. That way, in the end, everybody wins.

5

Fill the Other Guy's Basket to the Brim. Making Money Then Becomes an Easy Proposition.

I once heard a story that Andrew Carnegie, the famous industrialist and philanthropist, was lying on his deathbed in the Berkshire Mountains of Massachusetts when a cub reporter from New York paid him a visit.

"Mr. Carnegie, you are perhaps the most successful industrialist of all time," the reporter said. "I'd just like to ask for posterity: Is there anything you attribute your incredible business success to?"

Carnegie thought for a moment, then replied, "Actually, yes, there is one beacon, one guiding light that I attribute all my business success to: Fill the other guy's basket to the brim. Making money then becomes an easy proposition."

I have no idea whether this story is true. But I can tell you that the underlying business principle is right on target. That's why "Fill the other guy's basket to the brim. Making money then becomes an easy proposition" is our business philosophy. It reflects our commitment to creatively crafting mutually beneficial relationships with our vendors to help them produce and provide the kind of useful, fun, well-designed, high-quality products that delight our customers.

What does that mean, to creatively craft mutually beneficial relationships? Well, it starts with spending a lot of time getting to know our vendors, learning about their business and the issues they face, and constantly searching for ways to help them, make them happier, more productive, more profitable. We also help them get to know us by explaining our culture and Foundation Principles so they understand we're not just being altruistic but are following a deliberate business strategy that yields tremendous results for everyone.

The better you get to know someone, in my experience, the more you can care about them. And we love our vendors as much as our employees. Around here, it's really hard sometimes to tell a vendor from an employee. They're all part of our family, and our vendors have been known to turn up at a trade show wearing our employee buttons celebrating our annual appearance on *Fortune* magazine's list of 100 Best Companies to Work For. That just makes us beam with pride.

———◇———

Our vendors are overjoyed when we show an interest in them and say, essentially, "How can we fill your basket to the brim?" We help them develop products our customers are asking for, place orders during their slow periods so they can keep their factories running, pay them on time (sometimes early when they have cash-flow issues), and invite them to company events.

Many of our vendors are small business owners who've been with us for decades, so they're happily accustomed to our style, but a new vendor will sometimes wonder what the catch is. That's when we stress the second half of this Foundation Principle—"Making money then becomes an easy proposition"—to help them understand that there is no catch, that we are absolutely also acting in our own interest as well. Conscious Capitalism and our Foundation Principles are unashamed about making money and being profitable—after all, without that you can't take care of your employees and other stakeholders.

It's hard to overstate how crucial these close relationships are to our success—it's why our vendors give us exclusive, custom-made products, fast delivery, and high quality. And it's why they give us great pricing. We can't beat the mass merchants on volume, but we can always beat them on relationships.

The vast majority of our products are either exclusive or proprietary. That's because we work so closely with our vendors to make sure we get their most special designs. And we wonderfully partner to develop the most innovative products to fill what we think are holes in the market. We would have no reason to exist if we were just selling the same thing as everybody else. Stunning, differentiated product development and innovation is key to our customers' getting products they can't get anywhere else.

When it comes time to sit down and negotiate with our vendors, there's a simple reason why they agree to so many things: They understand that that's what pays for our amazing company culture, which sells their products so well. Once vendors see that we're genuinely interested in their well-being—and that our success is their success—a warm, trusting relationship develops, and

they're ecstatic to be part of our team. These are relationships
that we've had for decades, and that's where the most marvelous,
innovative, and differentiated products come from.

Our great relationships with vendors wouldn't be possible
without the deep familiarity we have with each one. Some of our
dearest friends over the past thirty-plus years have been vendors—
wonderful people like Paul Bilsky, who helped us create our
hugely successful Gift Wrap Wonderland section during Christmas, and Rich Klein of Lynk, Inc., a former elfa distributor with
whom we've enjoyed creating many products over the decades.
And many more, too numerous to name. We socialize together,
play golf together, even take vacations together.

I have been very proud to team up with Mike Gusdorf of
Storage Solutions in St. Louis, a vendor for twenty-five years, in
the time-honored bass fishing tournament at the Little Sandy
Hunting & Fishing Club of Hawkins, Texas. I waited twenty-five
years to get into Little Sandy. When you go through those gates,
it's like driving into East Texas of the 1920s. Our fishing partnership is just as successful as our business partnership, since we've
won that tough tournament twice over the past several years,
which is pretty hard to do (by the way, I find that the Scum Frog
lure and buzz bait work best if you have the patience for it, which
I do).

I can't for the life of me understand why people caution
against developing close personal relationships with business
associates. If you love your work, how could you not also grow
to love all the incredible folks you get to work with? The reverse
is also true: Some of my dearest friends have become employees and partners in the business. To me, it just seems like common sense to do business with those you love and trust the most.
After all, if your values at home and at work are the same, and you
enjoy treating people with affection, honesty, and respect, you
have nothing to fear.

As close as I feel to our vendors, the person who really deserves the most credit for beautifully executing our "Fill the other guy's basket" Foundation Principle is Sharon, our chief merchant. When you enjoy your work as much as I do, it's an incredible feeling to have the love of your life also be your most trusted business partner. We sometimes have to make an effort not to talk about work too much at home, to give ourselves a break, but most often the relationship between our business and professional life is seamless.

I use an analogy from the art world: The true artist of life blurs the lines between work and play. Was Claude Monet working or playing when he was painting the water lilies? He was doing what he wanted to do.

In much the same way, that has been the same approach for nearly all of my thirty-seven years with Sharon, since I had only known her for a couple of years when we developed the store concept. By the time Sharon and I were married, in November of 1979—I was twenty-six and she was twenty-four—the store was just sixteen months old.

Sharon and I didn't have a lot of money for an elaborate wedding (and neither did our parents), so we held our reception at the Louisiana Tech University Alumni Center. Her dad, a retired English professor at Louisiana Tech, wrote editorials for the local newspaper and asked the paper's photographer to shoot the wedding to keep the costs down. It did save a lot of money, but in truth, it turned into one of those wedding disasters (word to the wise: Photos are not a place you want to cut corners when planning a wedding!).

But Sharon and I never needed a lot of money to have a great time, and we still remember that day as one of the greatest of our lives. Anyone lucky enough to have experienced a wedding like that knows what an overwhelming feeling it is to have everyone you love in one place to celebrate—parents, siblings, relatives, and friends. My high school buddies still talk about ol' Uncle Bobby telling wild stories at the rehearsal dinner. Since Sharon's parents were devout Lutherans, we had a Lutheran minister. But we had a Catholic priest there, too, making the sign of the cross throughout the ceremony and blessing everything, which made my mom very happy. For our honeymoon, we went to Puerto Vallarta, Mexico, for five days before scrambling back to Dallas to help keep the store running.

As I mentioned, Sharon was involved in and had an influence on The Container Store even before the original store opened, but "officially" joined the company in 1980. Before that, she was a landscape architect. She had zero interest in retail and would stay to help the "family business" for only a short time, she said. That was more than three decades ago.

Sharon quickly got swept up in the passion and energy of our little store and was surprised to find she enjoyed some of the more mundane aspects, such as taking inventory, working the cash register, even unloading trucks. It reminded her of being a kid "playing store" and was much more fun than working in an office.

Sharon immediately began to gravitate toward merchandising. Garrett and I had our hands full working the sales floor, creating displays, supervising employees, and managing the financial aspects of the business. We really needed someone to focus on buying products and working with vendors. As it turned out, that's what Sharon loved doing best, yet another case of the universe conspiring to assist us. Her extensive background in art and design allowed her to collaborate beautifully with product designers.

Sharon has the rare gift of knowing what the customer wants before the customer actually knows she wants it, and Sharon loved the adrenaline rush of watching products fly off the shelves. She also has superb analytical skills and is good with numbers. A rare left- and right-brain person!

But the moment it became crystal clear that Sharon was running circles around us was during a meeting with Garrett and me about what kinds of products we should carry. We were debating how far we could stray from our core business: Should we carry traditional housewares like extension cords, lights, and clocks, or stick to storage and organization products? The conversation went on and on and on, lasting for five hours, and got very heated at times, until Sharon finally said, "You know what? We really don't need to talk about this anymore. I've got it, just let me take it from here." That was when Garrett and I knew we needed to give that merchandising thing up.

From that moment on, merchandising was Sharon's job, and what a tremendous boost for the company that turned out to be. She kept us focused on our mission, even when it was extremely tempting to diversify. We know we could probably have made a whole lot of money selling bubble gum at the register or carrying shower curtains, soft drinks, and thousands of other products. But we have just as surely brought in much more by not doing that—by instead devoting ourselves solely to being the best storage and organization destination on the planet. Customers have to know what to expect from you, and you have to know what's outside your guardrails. Drifting too far from our core competency would have diluted our brand and made us too much like all the other retailers who end up competing on price and convenience alone. Where's the magic in that?

Sharon also brings an unerring eye for what constitutes a product worthy of The Container Store. It has recently become fashionable in retail to use the word "curate" to describe what the best merchants do, but the term truly applies to Sharon and her team of buyers as they come up with just the right mix of the astounding 10,000 products we carry in stores—2,000 of which change every year (and she can discuss each one intimately). It certainly helps that Sharon has an incredibly talented, deeply experienced team of buyers who average fifteen years of tenure at The Container Store. They frequently work directly with vendors to create our exclusive products, often based on direct feedback from our customers.

One of the very special buyers who enriched our lives, helped fuel our company's growth, and executed the Fill the Other Guy's Basket principle beautifully was Mona Williams, whom Sharon hired in 1981. Like Sharon, Mona came to us young (twenty-four years old), newly married, with no interest in retail (she had dreams of becoming a journalist). Sharon and Mona used to joke that neither one knew the difference between gross margins and oleomargarine—and yet both ended up embodying our business philosophy.

As a negotiator, Mona was tough but fair, firm but sweet. "I think it's always important to remember that being friendly and cordial and polite does not mean that you are a pushover," she liked to say. Vendors loved her, thinking of her as a protective mom who could be forceful or nurturing, depending on the situation. When Mona got excited, she would say "Fan-TAS-tic!" or "Wheeeeeeee!" and had such a playful personality you could often hear her humming a tune, even if it was "Deck the Halls" in the middle of April. She touched virtually every area of the company in her thirty years with us, becoming vice-president of buying in 2005 and a respected leader in the housewares industry. She was fiercely devoted to her family—her husband, Marty (who was also an incredible leader in our distribution center), daughter, Megan, and grandson, David—and inspired us by the way she bravely faced every challenge, treating obstacles as if they simply did not exist.

That's why so many of us were devastated when Mona died suddenly in November of 2011, after a brief illness. More than sixty employees took a bus to Shreveport, Louisiana, on a rainy Saturday morning for the memorial service, and Sharon delivered a moving eulogy. We still miss Mona so much and continue to celebrate her life and contributions.

Mona and Sharon had many conversations over the years about how we should decide what products to carry. We've never had any written rules about that, because Sharon believes (and I agree) that rules would limit the imagination, creativity, and intuition her team brings to the job. But it's safe to say that we place a high premium on clever, well-designed items that are, most of all, extremely functional. "Form should follow function," Sharon likes to say, and "Aesthetics are important, but secondary to functionality." The ideal product has multiple uses, like a laundry bin that can also be used for toy storage or trash recycling.

———◇———

Whenever Sharon and I travel—to trade shows, meetings with vendors, or visits with our elfa team in Sweden—we're on the lookout for quirky, fun, multifunctional products. But the bottom line is: Will this product make life easier or better for our customers? Will it help them get more organized and, ultimately, save them time?

The reason our devoted customers know that the answer to those questions will always be a resounding "Yes!" is that all our products are created by vendors who are passionate about what they do. That's why, from the very beginning, we did whatever we could to help our vendors channel that passion into their work rather than get distracted by all the worry and foolishness that businesspeople often have to deal with. We didn't actually use the phrase "Fill the other guy's basket" in those early days, because we didn't start formalizing our Foundation Principles until 1988. But we didn't have to. I was a Boy Scout, Sharon was a Girl Scout, and our parents taught us the Golden Rule. Maybe we were naïve, but it really did seem that simple. None of us had a formal business background, so we didn't have to unlearn bad habits about how negotiations were "supposed" to be done. But we did have a sense that what we were doing was a bit different, and that we might very well, in our own humble way, be rewriting the rules of business.

———◇———

In those early days, Sharon went to trade shows looking for vendors and found herself constantly trying to explain our concept. "At first, people didn't understand why anyone would want to buy an empty box," she recalls. "We'd go to a booth and say, 'Do you sell that container?' They'd look at us strangely, so I'd say, 'Right there, that box that's holding the other things you're selling.' And they'd simply say, 'No, why do you want that?' We had a lot of conversations like that."

At one such trade show, we found our wonderful AMAC boxes, which have become one of our signature products. The boxes come in all sorts of sizes and fabulous colors. AMAC already had a cult following among artists since the late '60s, when Andy Warhol silk-screened the images of various artists on its model #522 plastic boxes for a piece called *Portraits of the Artists*. Today, AMAC boxes are enshrined in the permanent collection of the Museum of Modern Art in New York, but from the beginning we understood their aesthetic appeal. "Other retailers would just dump our boxes into a bin," says Steve Catechi of AMAC. "But The Container Store displays showed customers how beautiful and useful they could be."

In the mid-'90s, AMAC's #105 box became the container of choice for Beanie Babies when those stuffed toys became a national collectible craze, doubling AMAC's sales in one year. They had to build a new factory in Petaluma, California, just to keep up with demand. Grateful for our role in that success, AMAC filled our orders immediately, while other retailers had to wait for the company's usual eight-month turnaround. Sales for both our companies skyrocketed—another classic win-win.

The added value our talented sales staff brings to our vendor relationships was also clear early on, when a representative from a company called Art Wire Works came into our stores. He wanted to know why their organizer for storing cookie sheets was selling so much better at our little store than at the big chains. We told him we were suggesting that customers use it for things like organizing children's puzzles and file folders on desks. He was absolutely amazed—he'd never thought of his product that way—and the company later changed the packaging to suggest other uses. That kind of thing happens a lot. Vendors often tell us, "Your people know our products better than our own employees do!"

Because many of our vendors started as entrepreneurs, we filled their basket with encouragement, product ideas, and, when times got tough, deep loyalty. We did all those things for Andy Van Meter, who was in his first year of law school in 1982 when he teamed up with his sister, Alice, a college senior, to create a wire mesh basket for college kids to carry their toiletries to the bathroom (the only alternative on the market then was a plastic paint bucket that didn't drain, so their slogan was "No more mucky slop!").

Andy and Alice met Sharon and Mona at the national housewares show in Chicago while stationed at their booth, which was tucked away near the women's restroom. Mona loved the basket and ordered a gross on the spot. Andy and Alice were excited but still so green they didn't know what a gross was (it's a dozen dozen, or 144 items). When that product sold well, Sharon asked Andy and Alice for a meeting to discuss what other product ideas they had. "The problem was, we didn't have any other ideas," Andy says. "But Sharon and Mona did, so that became our business model—listen to Sharon and Mona and write down whatever they say."

He's exaggerating, of course—Andy and Alice are amazingly creative, hardworking entrepreneurs who built their company, Design Ideas of Springfield, Illinois, into one with nearly $50 million in sales and eighty employees. But every young start-up needs a helping hand, so that's what we try to give. Since we were creating a new retail category, we needed companies that understood our vision and could develop exciting new products.

I love the story Andy tells about the time when one of our trailers full of his product had been stolen and left on the side of the road. It was full of items that were to be featured in advertising in our back-to-school campaign—foam drawer dividers. When the FBI found the trailer, only about eight of the boxes had been opened, with the rest of the trailer untouched. The entire inventory was still there. Andy jokes, "The Container Store has products that are so hard to sell, people won't even steal them."

And we stayed with those vendors when they ran into trouble. In 1988, a typhoon destroyed the Design Ideas factory in Taiwan. It happened right in the middle of their back-to-school manufacturing season, so most of their retail customers canceled their purchase orders. Andy and Alice thought they were finished. But we assured them we would not cancel their order, or replace their products with those from another vendor, and would take their products whenever they could deliver. "It was a six-figure purchase order, and that was enough for us to get financing to rebuild the plant," Andy says. "Without The Container Store, there is no doubt we would have gone out of business. You helped us get started, stayed with us when times were hard, never canceled a purchase order—even during the recession!—and were never late on a payment. It's been just extraordinary support the whole way. We'll never forget what you've done for us."

I get chills hearing our vendors talk this way, and I have to confess, I'm still a little embarrassed about sharing these stories in public. You know, "There he goes, bragging about helping a little old lady across the street!" But I truly hope these stories will inspire other companies to realize that treating people well is not just altruism, it's good business. It's true that sometimes we have no choice but to do things that are not in our vendors' immediate best interests—like switching to another supplier who might offer a clearly superior product at a significantly better price. But even then, we'll see if there's some creative way to figure out how to do a new piece of business with that old vendor. Ninety-nine percent of the time, we succeed. That kind of loyalty feels good, for sure, but it also helps us. It gives our vendors the confidence to invest, expand, hire more employees, and create better and more products for our stores.

As John Mackey likes to point out, many people mistakenly think that Conscious Capitalism means that companies must try to "balance" the interests of their various stakeholders—that in treating vendors well, for example, you must compromise some other part of the business. But that assumes a zero-sum game, which business most definitely is not.

One of my favorite people, Ed Freeman, the professor at the Darden School of Business at the University of Virginia who is often called the father of the Conscious Capitalism stakeholder model, prefers the word "harmony" to "balance," because your goal should be to harmonize the interests of all the stakeholders. Perhaps Ed uses that word because he is a stunningly accomplished musician; the image of a band or an orchestra working together to create beautiful music is a great metaphor for what a company can accomplish when it harmonizes the interests of its various stakeholders. If a company is making stark and dramatic trade-offs between stakeholders, that usually means it's not working hard enough, or being creative enough, to find a better solution that benefits everyone.

In some cases, it's simply a matter of loyalty. Allan Goldstein, who has been selling us garment bags since 1986, loves to talk about what our loyalty means to him personally. In 2002, he came to the opening of our Paramus, New Jersey, store and introduced me to his two kids, then in middle school. When we had a quiet moment, I told him, "I'm not telling you we're going to buy from you forever, but at least until you get your kids through college." Allan, who is still a cherished vendor, recently reminded me of that conversation—adding wryly that now that his kids have graduated, he wants an extension. "That meant so much to me, to hear you say that when my kids were younger," he says. "How could I not remember and appreciate somebody like that? That's the kind of company culture that doesn't exist in today's world. That's why we need more employers like The Container Store."

Sometimes even the smallest gestures can mean a lot. Anne Bergl, a vendor since 1985, said she received a call one day from our accounting department and braced herself for bad news. But we just wanted to thank her for doing her invoicing paperwork correctly, making our job so much easier. "You just fall over when somebody does that," Anne says. "I'm always so amazed at your employees' attitude and general niceness. Some people think if you act like that, other people will think you're a pushover and take advantage of you. But that doesn't happen because The Container Store is so rare and precious in this industry, everybody wants to do business with you."

In short, people don't try to take advantage of us because we don't try to take advantage of them. I believe that one of the worst business moves a company can make is to overnegotiate its position and be tone-deaf to the concept of cooperation between two companies.

What we're trying to do is create synergy. That's the most pleasurable, joyful way of doing business. Those who make the most money for the longest time adopt this form of capitalism—creating these mutually beneficial, long-term relationships. So why don't people seek out win-win situations more often? I'm convinced it's because of their own insecurity.

If you're secure in yourself and your own abilities, you won't feel threatened by filling the other guy's basket. You won't worry that someone else will succeed more than you will, or somehow will use your own spirit of fair play against you.

On the contrary, you'll be openhearted and supportive. You'll realize that helping other people succeed is actually the best way to succeed yourself. That's why it's so important to be mindful of our wake, as I mentioned earlier. With every action we take, we're not just affecting other people far more than we realize. We're also creating powerful waves and endless ripple effects that ultimately find their way back to us.

Other early vendors and now great friends are Paul Rowan and Les Mandelbaum, who had just started a Canadian company called Umbra when Sharon met them at a trade show in the early '80s. We felt an instant connection to Paul and Les, who were also in their midtwenties and interested in adapting industrial designs for consumer products. We shared an aesthetic of simple and functional yet beautifully designed housewares, far different from that of our parents' generation, and saw this as part of an important cultural shift. Today, Umbra is one of a handful of vendors—including AMAC, IRIS, and Casabella—that we market and promote under their own brand names, which gives both of us valuable cachet. Umbra also has a product in the permanent collection of the Museum of Modern Art: the Garbino swing-top plastic trash can (named after Greta Garbo), designed by Karim Rashid—a trash can that really can make you smile.

One way we filled Umbra's basket was through our commitment to "sell the hard stuff." "With a lot of our products, people didn't get it at first," says Les. "Those products would die at other retailers that didn't have educated salespeople to explain them and answer questions." A good example is Umbra's Flip Hook Rack, which attaches to a wall. The hooks lie flat against the rack until you flip down only the ones you need for your coat, umbrella, or hat, which makes the rack extremely useful but also sleek and stylish. "That product failed at some of the most esteemed retailers in America, but now it's one of our biggest-selling products," says Les. The same thing happened with Umbra's Conceal Book Shelf, an ingenious L-shaped bracket that makes your books appear to float on the wall, with no visible means of support. "It's a huge seller because The Container Store goes the extra mile to display it beautifully and train employees to explain how it works," says Paul.

Umbra is an extremely successful line for us, but its value transcends the bottom line. Paul happens to be an awesome harmonica player, singer, and showman, and Les is an accomplished bass player. Both have performed at company events. It's impossible to quantify how much those happy moments mean to us, how important they are to spreading our values and culture. It's always inspiring to see our vendors showing up at company events with so much energy and enthusiasm. Vendor Jayne Norwood, aka the Bag Lady, has come to just about every store opening since she started selling us shopping bags in the early '80s, and today those events just wouldn't feel complete without her. She's always the first one on the dance floor (well, after Garrett).

As you can tell, I could talk about our vendors all day. There's Hardeep Melamed, CEO of in.bag, maker of the amazing in.bag purse organizer, who often tells us excitedly that she feels like "an extension of your family." There's Charles Tsai, who has always expressed deep thanks for our role in 1984 in encouraging his little start-up company, Unicorn, which made magazine racks and paper towel holders and eventually allowed him to put his three children through college and retire comfortably. And there's Jan Macho of Dial Industries, whose partnership with us helped Dial expand from just a handful of products to offering over two hundred items.

Back in the early '80s, we were very happy to be able to help our friend Lee White with an $18,000 loan so he could buy a shrink-wrap machine for a jewelry box his company made. He paid us a nickel an item until it was paid back.

When he retired, he wrote me a moving letter that described his company's humble beginnings: "[We] were very short on money. I remember on more than one occasion that I would phone you a week or so after you picked up a shipment and ask if there was a chance we could get paid early and you would let me come over and give me a check.... Good people like you, Garrett, and Sharon are so rare in business today.... In closing, I'll mention that my wife still uses the wooden jewelry box you gave to your suppliers one year."

Another great vendor friend is Bruce Kaminstein of Casabella, which makes kitchen and cleaning products for us. Bruce still talks about the time he sent us 1,000 mops but only billed us for 800—and didn't realize his mistake until we sent him a check for the difference. "You don't forget something like that," he says.

———<o>———

At The Container Store, some vendors are so tightly integrated into our company that it's hard to tell where one starts and the other ends.

Take IRIS USA, for example, a Wisconsin-based firm whose

parent company is in Japan. When we were designing Our Clear Storage Boxes together, they suggested two options: Either we would enter into a three-year exclusive contract or we would pay for the cost of the molds (the proprietary design that makes the boxes so special). We discussed with them how basic this product was to our customers, how they would build collections around it and would not want "something new" in three years, which is the norm in Japan. We discussed our sales volume and what it could become. We expressed our commitment to proprietary products and how we would so proudly, perfectly, and boldly feature it in our stores, in our catalogs, and on our website. We talked about how these boxes would be the perfect complement to elfa, our best-selling product.

After a lengthy negotiation, they agreed to a lifetime exclusive on these products and didn't charge us for the cost of the molds. That was remarkable enough, but in 2002, IRIS decided to build a new factory near our distribution center in Dallas to save freight costs. Now we can just load the boxes from the IRIS factory directly into our trucks and immediately take them to our stores.

"If another retailer came to us and said, 'If you build a new facility near our warehouse we'll give you thirty million dollars in business,' we'd probably say no," says Chet Kaiser, president of IRIS USA and our dear friend since he joined the company in 1997. "Because doing a high percentage of your business with one retailer puts you in a pretty weak position if you happen to lose that business—a lot of lives depend on those jobs. But we have such a great relationship with The Container Store, we don't have to worry about that. In fact, there was so much trust that when we did this deal for Clear Storage Boxes, we didn't even get lawyers involved. It was basically done on a handshake. We knew they would follow through, and they have done that and then some."

A good old-fashioned handshake! The result? IRIS is our second-largest vendor and we've sold millions of those Clear Storage Boxes. So many boxes, in fact, that we needed more molds to meet our needs. And the "turn" on our IRIS products—a measure of how many times inventory turns over—is stunningly higher than for our other vendors. Building IRIS's new factory so close to us, in nearby Mesquite, Texas, allowed us to do what we call cross-docking, where the inventory never has to go into our distribution center. It's expensive to ship big empty storage boxes, so having that facility nearby helps us maintain the retail prices we need for our customers. Our relationship with IRIS has continued to grow even stronger.

We have tremendous respect for and trust in each other, so when we're discussing costs, we can develop solutions that are beneficial and profitable for both companies. For example, we've seen many ups and downs in the cost of injection-molded plastic. An increase came right before the drop of our Back to School catalog a few years ago—a catalog that prominently featured some of those Clear Storage Boxes. That could have meant our customer would see higher prices online or in our stores than what was printed in the catalog. But because of the respect and trust we'd developed with IRIS, we were able to work through the timing issues to ensure that our costs could remain as they were quoted in the catalog.

Soon after we finalized this, Japan was struck by the tsunami of 2011. IRIS Japan was affected, and many of their workers were left without homes; some even perished. Three employees who happened to take the day off were killed when the floods hit their homes.

The IRIS factory sits up on a hill overlooking Sendai, so it was spared, but employees' homes and the city itself were devastated.

As you can imagine, our hearts broke for our friends in

Japan. We wanted to help. We decided to involve our customers by donating a percentage of the sales of every Clear Storage Box to the relief fund. Our goal was to raise $100,000 during an eight-week period, and we did it.

Our 500 home office and distribution center employees ended up surprising Chet when he came to our offices for a meeting—and we presented him with a $100,000 check.

"I turn the corner and see all these Container Store employees standing there clapping and cheering," says Chet. "They handed me this huge check, and oh my goodness, I got choked up. I had just gotten back from Japan and saw the area that was devastated. You could just feel the love and genuineness as all the employees stood there smiling and cheering. It had such a profound effect on me; I'll never forget that as long as I live."

———◇———

The phenomenal growth of The Container Store in our first few years—which continued for the next three decades—is a direct result of these incredibly close relationships with vendors.

We sold so many elfa units in those days that the only way we could be assured of getting enough supply was to become an elfa distributor ourselves. We had to compete against much bigger companies, but in the early '80s, elfa awarded us its five-state south-central US territory because it was clear that we understood its products better than anyone else. In fact, our relationship with elfa became so close over the next two decades that we actually acquired the company in 1999 when it came up for sale, again beating out much larger competitors against very long odds.

When our company sales reached $1.6 million in 1981, we began to talk seriously about opening a second store. But we reasoned that many of the best restaurants in the country have just one location. So why not just continue to refine this single store, making it as big and successful as possible?

Then there was the financial risk. Our strategy has always been to fund any expansion with our own profits rather than borrowing or accepting investors. But what if we stretched ourselves too thin? Could we open another store without jeopardizing everything we'd achieved?

In many ways, we could have been content to spend the rest of our lives running one perfect store. But customer demand was so intense, and sales were rising so quickly, that it seemed silly not to at least try. When we found a great spot, a 7,600-square-foot space on Mockingbird Lane in Dallas, we made the leap of faith and moved in during August of 1981.

It was a stressful time leading up to our grand opening, of course, but also incredibly joyous, and the new store did even better than the first. Then, in 1983, we opened our third and fourth stores in the Dallas area—about 15,000 square feet each—and each one did better than the last, aided by our first computer system and electronic cash registers.

But in truth, opening two stores in one year was a real stretch. So we eased off the accelerator, letting three years go by before opening another store, this one in Austin, our fifth location, in 1986. (In the interim, we moved our original store to a much bigger location, the bowling alley across the street. I just knew that real estate would somehow become available—it was just too good. And since it was in a dry area and the bowling alley couldn't sell beer or wine—it couldn't possibly make it.)

I've always been focused on the fact that some of the best retail specialty stores/chains eventually overexpand themselves to death. We were determined not to do that.

Not that we weren't tempted. Stanley Marcus approached us with an opportunity to open a store within a store in the famous

Harrods of London and with the original family who owned it. It was the most incredibly flattering invitation we'd ever received— and coming from the beloved Stanley Marcus, for goodness' sake. It sure would have been fun flying back and forth on a private plane, but it was outside the guardrails of our core business.

We would have had to remerchandise the store design with European resources. I'm convinced we wouldn't be here today if we'd done it. I learned early on that business has a superabundance of opportunities and the most important thing is to judiciously select them based on the finite supply of human and financial resources you have. Good management is the wise allocation of those resources.

I'm glad we had the discipline and the courage to say no. Very few people would have passed up the allure and the glamour of that offer.

—⟨◇⟩—

Meanwhile, during the '80s, big-box discount retailers and super-stores were spreading across the landscape. Service and quality were deemphasized in many cases. Vendors were left with fewer places for their wares and less negotiating power. We stepped into that void to offer customers a far more personal touch with our highly trained staff and gave vendors a partner who treated them well and assisted in their success. We also benefited from a revolution in the plastics industry: Manufacturers developed resins that made plastic more transparent, making it easier to see what was inside when storing things.

Plastic used to be very brittle—if you dropped a shoe box, it would shatter into a million pieces—but these new injection-molded plastics made them unbreakable. We loved it and so did our customers. You got visibility, durability, and sustainability with these new products, which last a lifetime. The same is true for the many wire products we sell, and the bamboo used to make items like drawer organizers, file holders, and compost pails. Wouldn't it be great if everything were made so durable you never had to replace it?

I'm very proud that virtually everything in our store is designed to last a lifetime. I just think it's wasteful to buy poorly and inexpensively designed and produced flimsy products. Our goal is that when you buy an item in our store you'll never need to replace it. Quality. Function. Durability. Shouldn't at least most products be that way?

◦

As we opened one amazing store after another in our first decade of business, our success was truly beyond our wildest dreams. It was also inevitable that serious competitors would emerge. After all, we had created an entirely new retail category and hardly expected the housewares industry to stand idly by and watch us dominate the market.

As I mentioned, we saw hundreds of specialty-store knock-offs—retailers who tried to emulate our business. Even the big department stores tried their hand at storage and organization sections. We saw everything, from local retailers like Dana's Containers and regional chains like Organized Living to national retailers like Williams-Sonoma's Hold Everything, all eventually went out of business.

Why did all these competitors fail while we kept growing through the 1980s, the 1990s, the 2000s, and beyond? I think it's because nobody else was willing to commit to a truly solutions-based form of retail that requires hiring great people and training them to offer unheard-of levels of service while selling an amazing collection of differentiated products developed with incredible vendor relationships. You can copy a company two-dimensionally, but you can't copy its heart and soul. That, to me, is the key. No one wants to build a business that's so hiring- and training- and people-intensive. That's usually the last thing people want to deal with in business.

The late Howard Lester, Williams-Sonoma's CEO, and I were friendly and had a lot of dialogue, and he expressed interest in combining our two companies. He called me up one day and said, "Kip, I gotta hand it to you. We are just bad at this, we can't do it. We give up. We copied you to begin with, but we couldn't do it. You know we've never failed at anything, but we failed miserably at this. Congratulations."

Our vendors have their own theories about why our competitors have all pretty much vanished. "Nobody else stuck with the formula," says Andy Van Meter. "Everybody else wandered off into toaster ovens and things. And nobody else had the creative intuition. We have never felt this kind of product-development creativity with anybody else."

We discovered that potential competitors were out there during our first six months in business, when interested investors stopped by. Some offered to buy a minority stake, others wanted majority control, and a few even proposed a path to going public. For more than twenty years, we politely said no. We loved what we were doing and knew we were onto something special.

One day, a group of men from a large Texas company came by to say they really admired what we were doing and wanted to form a financial partnership. When we told them we weren't interested, one said, "I don't think you understand. We are either going to buy you or copy you and put you out of business."

As he heard this threat, Garrett smiled. "Well, if you're so good that you can copy us that easily, then we should either come to work for you . . . or we should just go do something else. Best of luck." That was the last we heard from them.

As competitors and potential investors came and went, we just kept on filling the other guy's basket—not only because it felt good, but also because it worked. In that way, we're not much different than most mom-and-pop entrepreneurs who became successful by just naturally treating others well.

Leveraging mutually beneficial relationships and investing time and effort to learn a lot about them is easy, pain free, and joyful. Rarely does someone, in any walk of life, just take, take, take, and not reciprocate. Most people instinctively know to try love—it will come back to you in spades. The tricky part comes when a company starts to grow—when outside investors with different values come in, when the founders lose control of the business, or they get so distracted by expanding that they don't place a high priority on developing a strong culture inside their growing company, making sure everybody understands and puts into daily practice the generosity and higher purpose that made them so successful in the first place. That's when a small business can morph into a different creature altogether, one that the founders may not even recognize.

That almost happened to us in 1988, when we started growing faster than ever before. In the next chapter, I'll explain how we got back on track, and how the Foundation Principles have guided us ever since.

6

Man in the Desert Selling

All retail salespeople really want is to just go through life without ever being accused of being pushy salespeople. That's what they're all secretly worried about.

So I came up with the Foundation Principle "Man in the Desert Selling," which addresses this problem by putting the moral imperative on selling versus not selling.

We often illustrate this principle with short skits that Garrett and I perform while training new employees before each new store opening.

Our goal is to make these training sessions enjoyable while communicating the philosophy and strategies behind the Foundation Principles. In doing this, we tell a story about a character living in an oasis in the desert. One day, I look out and see a barefoot man (Garrett) staggering toward me in a tattered shirt, crying, "Water!...Water!...Water!"

That's the Man in the Desert. He sees me and gasps, "Is that a mirage?"

"No, sir," I say, "I'm real. Come on up here to my oasis. Here, have some water. Take the whole bottle!"

"Okay, thank you very much." He gulps down the water, looks around, and then says: "I'm gonna go wander in the desert some more. See you."

Problem solved! I pat myself on the back and yell after him, "You're gonna make it, you'll be fine. Bye!"

"Yikes, I'm out of water again!" Here comes the Man in the Desert, staggering back into the room. Our new employees laugh.

Great—this is my chance to really help the guy. "Here, have some more water. Now, let's go underneath these palm trees" (which is typically my beloved assistant, Karla, holding a palm-leaf-decorated umbrella over Garrett's head).

"Oh my goodness, shade!" the Man says. "I've been looking for shade for so long. And my feet turned purple out there in the hot sand! I feel terrible—"

"Wow, this is hard work," I say. "I'm trying to intuit your needs here."

"Do you have a hat?" the Man says. I give him a hat and a pair of sunglasses and then say, "I know you've had enough water, but here—I think you might need some electrolytes."

"Oh, Gatorade, yes, I need it desperately. Mmmm, yum."

"You've stumbled upon a pretty stylish oasis," I say, presenting him with a CONTAIN YOURSELF T-shirt from The Container Store. "I've also got some cool clothing here. I see your shirt is tattered. And if you wear these flip-flops, your feet will quit turning purple. And here's a first-aid kit—we're gonna get a little aloe vera going here..."

"Thank you. Gosh, I've got so many needs—"

"You know what? We need to call your family and tell them you're okay!"

"Oh my God, you're right! I told my wife I was going to the home improvement store and would be back in thirty minutes and now I've been lost for days."

I go on and on about how hours later, the Man in the Desert is delighted, having a margarita, and floating in the pool in my oasis.

Yes, it's a silly skit, but it illustrates very well our selling philosophy, which is one of our most important Foundation Principles. It means that when a customer comes into our store looking for something—shoe storage, for example—we try to equate her with that disheveled man who wanders in from the desert in desperate need of a complete solution. We start asking questions about her needs, starting with shoes, then moving to the rest of her closet.

While other retailers might simply help a customer find a shoe rack—that simple glass of water—we don't stop with the obvious. We try to truly help her by anticipating her every need, even helping her discover needs she didn't know she had.

Over the years, we've found Man in the Desert to be a very useful metaphor. Because when you think about what that poor fellow has just experienced and what his needs really are, he truly needs more than just water. He needs food, a comfortable place to sleep, a phone to call his wife and family, maybe a pair of shoes and a hat.

Just to be clear: We're not trying to train employees to "sell up"—that is, trying to sell a customer the most expensive product in the store, regardless of whether it solves her problem. Some salespeople in clothing stores are trained to say, "Come over here to the Armani section," even if the guy is short and stocky and doesn't look good wearing Armani. That's not real service. That kind of approach will hurt the retailer in the long run because the customer is eventually going to realize that Armani was not the best choice and he won't come back. That purchase didn't make him feel good because it wasn't the right solution.

Instead, we say, "Don't sell the customer the more expensive item—just sell her the item that's most appropriate for her problem." That's why we're a solutions-based form of retail, not items-based. Our customers don't typically come in wanting that $9.99 item they saw in the newspaper. Instead, we often hear them say, "Oh, my kid's toy storage area's driving me nuts. Can you help me?" Our products have a thousand uses. You can use a dairy crate for that, or stacking bins, or dozens of other items we carry. And once you get this problem solved, our customers get so excited, their heart rate goes up and then they go home and become even more excited.

They love that space so much, they do a little dance every morning when they open the door. They don't curse you every time they go into their kids' storage area—now they love you. And they invite their sister-in-law and their neighbor over to see it. They're proud. That's how we build our business, especially in a new market—one customer at a time.

In fact, if we don't do Man in the Desert Selling, everything we're doing is wrong. We have the wrong products, because our products are very hard to sell. We're hiring the wrong people, we're paying them too much money, we're training them too much.

We explain to our employees that if they don't do Man in the Desert Selling, we will not survive as a company. On the other hand, when we really do it right, we have an unassailable advantage that no competitor can match. I mean, nobody can come close to it. Because now you have all these great products and this amazing service and this customer experience that causes them to dance and say, "I don't just like The Container Store, I love The Container Store!" It all comes back to helping one customer at a time because they leave the store so excited they tell everybody about it.

"So don't wimp out," we tell employees. Wimping out is saying, "I don't want this customer to think I'm a pushy salesperson." You know what I do when I'm in one of our stores? I get customers to put their arms out, give them a basket or a shopping cart, and say, "This will probably help you buy more, too." They laugh and say, "Thank you!" The reason it's okay for salespeople to say things like that to our customers is because we're trying to help them in the true sense of the word.

The more customers buy, the happier they're going to be. Because selling and service are the same thing. We tell our salespeople they can either help/help or hurt/hurt. They can help the customer by astonishing her and giving her the solution she really needs and help the company at the same time. Or they can hurt the customer by not truly helping her—and also hurt the company.

Our employees know that a mutually successful outcome only occurs by developing a warm, trusting relationship with the customer. Just as we get to know our vendors well to figure out how we can help them succeed, we also make a big effort to learn as much as possible about our customers so we can help meet their needs.

The reason that most salespeople offer customers only that figurative glass of water and then pat themselves on the back, believing that they've just offered great service, is because they're embarrassed by the whole idea of selling—and, quite candidly, they fear that people will look down on them.

Just consider all the negative connotations of the word "sell": You sell your soul to the devil. You sell someone down the river. You sell out. Ironically, most of our 1=3 employees, many of whom are well educated and came from different professions, never imagined themselves as salespeople, because that often conjures images of someone like Willy Loman riding on a smile and a shoeshine (or worse, those snakes in Mamet's *Glengarry Glen Ross*).

So in thinking about how to train our employees, we decided to change that view of salesmanship. We wanted to liberate our salespeople to feel truly great about selling, to see it as a virtuous activity that improves people's lives—yes, the lives of both the buyer and the seller.

That's why we say we put the moral imperative on selling versus not selling. We know our customer really wants to fix that closet that's driving her crazy—after all, she's in our store. She came into The Container Store, stood in our closet section, and had a shoe rack in her hand. So we have a deep obligation to discover what it would take to make her as delighted as humanly possible.

Since we're a solutions-based form of retail, we think there's no reason why every business shouldn't see itself as existing primarily to solve people's problems, to make the world a better place. That's the "higher purpose" we talk about in Conscious Capitalism. When our customer gets home and we've installed her new elfa closet system, we expect that she'll be so excited she'll come back to the store and say, "Great, now let's do the pantry!"

———◁◦▷———

Let me give you a real example of great Man in the Desert Selling. Not long ago, a woman came into our Houston store asking for help with paper clutter. Jene, a part-time salesperson, could have easily sold her some letter trays or desktop filing systems—in other words, a glass of water. Instead, she struck up a conversation with the woman and learned that she had three grandchildren, and when they came to visit, they did all their homework on her dining room table. The paper always seemed to pile up on the table, so she needed a way to neatly organize it so there was room to use the table for its actual purpose—eating dinner.

Jene said she'd be happy to help the woman organize those homework papers, but she could see there was a bigger challenge here. "What if I could give you your dining room table back?" she said. Surprised and curious, the woman listened as Jene began talking about elfa, our shelving system. What if each grandchild got an elfa desk with shelves—the woman could put them in the bedrooms they slept in when they came to visit. The woman loved the idea, so Jene said, "Let's get you an elfa desk solution, too," and later suggested Bungee Office Chairs for each desk. By the time the woman checked out, this small issue of organizing paper clutter had turned into a $1,700 elfa sale—and the woman was thrilled to get her dining room table back.

Of course, Man in the Desert Selling doesn't work unless we follow the other Foundation Principles, too. We need to have 1=3 employees like Jene who are smart and creative enough to think well on their feet, connect with the customer, ask questions, and actually listen to the customer's answers. They understand that "intuition does not come to an unprepared mind. You have to train before it happens." More on that training later.

No amount of advertising and marketing can buy the kind of trust we have with our customers, who know we truly have their best interests at heart. Again, this is not altruism, it's just good business. Today, with social media, such happy customer encounters are regularly tweeted far and wide, posted on Facebook, and written up on shopping comparison sites and in blogs, deepening the emotional bond we have with our customers across the country. And, of course, it feels great for everyone. Since our earliest days, customers have actually come into our stores bringing cookies or ice cream for employees. We get to know them and their families—exchanging hugs when someone gets married or tears when someone dies—and that's why our customers so often come to work for us. Loyal customers and employees of The Container Store are both so proud of our culture that they're eager to share it with everyone they know. There is a huge trust correlation with Man in the Desert Selling.

Amy Carovillano, a beloved employee since 1987, tells a story that provides a dramatic illustration of how much our customers trust us. One day, she was at Dallas's Love Field Airport waiting for a flight to Houston. Amy noticed a woman talking in a very animated manner with the airline's gate agent. When the woman left the counter, she was clearly unhappy and began looking around as if searching for someone.

There were more than a hundred people in the waiting area, but she headed straight for Amy, passing at least fifty other people closer to her. "Excuse me, are you on the next Houston flight?" the woman asked.

When Amy said she was, the woman asked for a favor: Her husband had flown to Houston on an earlier flight but was stranded at the airport's rental car counter. He had forgotten his wallet and couldn't rent a car without his driver's license (he was able to fly without the photo ID because airport security was not as tight back then). The woman had come to the airport with the wallet, hoping that a crew member would take it to Houston on the next flight. But when the crew was not willing to do that, she walked over to Amy. Remember, she didn't know Amy at all.

Amy was happy to help but had a question: Why did the woman single her out? The woman said it was because Amy was wearing a jacket with our iconic CONTAIN YOURSELF! logo on it and a watch with The Container Store logo on it and she assumed Amy was an employee. The woman added that she was a loyal customer and knew from firsthand experience how nice and willing to help all the employees at The Container Store are. And that's why she approached Amy in the airport.

After landing in Houston, Amy met the woman's husband and gave him the wallet.

During her flight, and for a long time afterward, Amy kept thinking, "What an amazing company I work for—talk about the power of a great brand!"

———◇———

After our skit about Man in the Desert Selling, Garrett gives a more formal presentation on the subject to new employees because it's a particular passion of his. And he truly is a master at it. Garrett is in his early seventies now but says he still feels like twenty-five—and when you see him dancing at our grand-opening parties, you'll understand why. He loves passing on his lifetime of retail selling wisdom to the next generation.

After all the training and parties are over and the new store finally opens on Saturday morning, Garrett usually dons an apron and works the sales floor to demonstrate how it's done under real conditions. The new salespeople are amazed to watch him interact with customers in his warm, affable way, helping them solve their problems, and to see them leave so excited to get home to try everything out. They marvel that the company's cofounder and chairman emeritus still enjoys roaming the sales floor. "I really do love it," Garrett tells the employees. "If it weren't for the selling part, I would have never gone into retail in the first place."

As we explain it, the most important part of Man in the Desert Selling is getting to know the customer well enough to propose a solution. There are three steps: Approach, Connection, and Sale.

Let's start with the two questions you almost always get from an approaching salesperson when you walk into a store:

1. "How are you doing today?" To which people usually reply, "Fine, thanks," and keep on walking.
2. "Can I help you?" To which customers almost always respond, "No thanks, just looking."

Both of these questions bother us. The problem with these approaches is that they're so general and so meaningless that they elicit equally meaningless replies from the customer. They're halfhearted overtures that create little chance of a genuine connection (variations include: "Let me know if you have any questions," "Find everything you need?" and "Anything in particular you're looking for?").

Instinctively, we all know this doesn't work, but salespeople across America keep asking these same banal questions because they live in mortal fear of coming across as pushy. They walk away thinking, "Nobody really wants my help. I tried, but they really just want to be left alone."

Sure, they want to be left alone. They want to be left alone by people asking, "How are you doing today?"

On the other hand, it's our fervent belief that every customer would welcome a salesperson who can really engage them in a meaningful way. How many times have you said reflexively, "No thanks, I'm just looking," then realized you actually do have a question, turned around, and there's no salesperson in sight? That store just lost a big opportunity because its employee didn't make a real effort to connect with you.

At The Container Store, we don't immediately try to sell something to a customer; we can't, because we don't know enough about her yet. We simply start a conversation first, to open the door a bit, and earn her trust so we can begin exploring how to help her. We've found that the best opening lines are usually statements about the customer or what she's doing. She's often revealing lots of details about herself without saying a word—what she's wearing, whom she's shopping with, her facial expressions and body language, which products she's looking at or has already put in her cart.

Because we trust the intuitive genius of our employees, we don't give them specific approach lines. But a compliment—"I love your hat"—often works well as an icebreaker, as long as it's genuine (people can spot phony flattery a mile away). If she's holding a product, we might say "Let me show you how this works" or "Let me take it out of the package." (Customers are always astonished when you go to the trouble to take something out of the package.) Questions can work if they contain important information, like "What closet are you going to use that shoe rack in?" because that can jump-start a conversation about a specific issue. It takes some intuitive genius, of course—you have to read the customer. Is she a hurried, busy mom with two kids in tow? Or a proud customer who has done her research and is handy with projects?

Humor works, too. We tell a story from one of our salespeople in our Houston store who once saw an elderly woman with perfectly coiffed hair holding a poodle puppy and said, "So I see you've taken advantage of our puppy sale, how about our travel sale?" The woman stopped and laughed, then said, "Actually, I just came to buy a box." Then the salesperson said, "Do you do any traveling?" Turned out she was getting ready to go on a cruise, and she ended up walking out of the store with $600 worth of Eagle Creek travel products—plus the box she originally came for. That's Man in the Desert Selling.

Once the approach has been made, we go to step two: connecting with the customer by asking questions in a helpful way. What space are you trying to organize? What does it look like? Who uses it? One customer came in looking for pushpins, but during the conversation we learned that she wanted to pin papers that were cluttering her desk onto the wall. She ended up buying a complete home office system.

Finally, the sale comes when we devise a solution that makes the customer excited about conquering a problem in a way she probably never would have imagined on her own (after all, she's not the storage and organization expert—we are). Our employees are like the friend you go shopping with because you trust her judgment: When we say a solution will work and looks great, the customer trusts us.

So it's the Approach, the Connection, and then the Sale. But to do this takes confidence. In training we remind our salespeople what it means to be a confident salesperson:

- I believe this customer needs and wants my help.
- I know I am capable of helping them.
- I want to do everything I can to help them *today*.

If the sale is nearly completed but the customer is wavering, our generous return policy often helps. If you're not 100 percent delighted with the product for any reason, we'll take it back. "So why not give it a try? You have nothing to lose." We actually appreciate it when people return something—there's no guilt, shame, or suspicious questioning—because we want them excited about absolutely everything they buy at The Container Store. It doesn't help anybody if we sell a trash can that makes the customer think badly of us every time they throw something away. The possible loss on that item is irrelevant compared to the damage that would do to our reputation. By the same token, the joy of selling someone just the right product, the one that solves a problem and lasts forever, does wonders not only for our customer, but also for our brand name and, ultimately, our profitability.

But, as we never tire of pointing out, you can't practice Man in the Desert Selling without making that great initial approach. Garrett once delivered one of the greatest opening lines of all time. When he worked at the Storehouse furniture store in Dallas in the early '70s, he saw an attractive young woman walk into the store.

"Would you like to dance?" Garrett said.

"No thanks, I'm just looking."

The woman kept walking, then stopped and turned around. "What did you say?"

"Would you like to dance?"

"Oh, no thanks," she said. "But I do need a new sofa and some chairs."

Garrett and the woman began talking, and he sold her a chair. But it turned out she had other needs as well, which he recognized because they were so similar to his own. Fortunately, she paid with a check that had her phone number on it. A month later, he finally mustered the courage to call her, asked her out to dinner, and Garrett and Cecilia have been happily married for nearly forty years.

Now that's Man in the Desert Selling.

———◇———

I came up with the crazy, corny story about the Man in the Desert the night before one of the biggest turning points in our company's history—a meeting with the employees of our Houston store in 1989. It was a powerful moment for me personally because it was the first time I had ever attempted to articulate my deepest, most heartfelt beliefs about life and business before a large group. And it was a crucial moment for The Container Store because that's when our cherished Foundation Principles were born.

The meeting was urgently necessary: After more than ten years of fairy-tale success, our rapid growth had begun to spin wildly out of control. In most respects, we were doing extremely well. We had six stores—four in Dallas and one each in Austin and San Antonio—and were selling so many products that our 75,000-square-foot distribution center was nearly full and we would soon need to move to yet another larger space. But in August of 1988, we were plunged into a real crisis the day we opened our seventh store, in Houston.

The grand opening on August 6, 1988, was the culmination of a longtime dream. We had searched for years for just the right spot in the large Houston market and were ecstatic to finally find it at the coveted corner of Post Oak and Westheimer, near two of the city's most exclusive neighborhoods, River Oaks and Memorial. It was one of the largest and highest-sales-per-foot retail centers in America. Our store was right across the street from the Galleria, one of the nation's premier shopping malls, which today attracts millions of visitors to its hundreds of stores, restaurants, high-rise hotels, and office towers.

We thought our Houston store would do well, given that this was our first location in a truly urban area, unlike our other stores in cozier, suburban neighborhoods. And we knew the Galleria would bring in lots of regional and tourist traffic. But without today's sophisticated techniques to estimate sales volume, we could make only an educated guess about how much business we might do. We hoped we might do 10 percent more than our very successful San Antonio store.

When the doors finally opened, we were stunned by the huge crowds streaming through. There were traffic jams in the aisles, long checkout lines, and empty shelves as customers snatched up products. Many Houston residents, we realized, had shopped at our other stores and were just waiting to pounce. Over the next few months, the traffic did not abate and sales skyrocketed, averaging three to four times higher than we'd expected. Amy Carovillano (yes, the one from the earlier airline story), our store manager, needed to triple her staff overnight. She began advertising, interviewing people coming in off the street, and basically grabbed every available warm body she could find. She would literally interview people in the morning and say, "Can you start this afternoon?"

With sales off the charts, we couldn't keep shelves stocked, irritating customers. We had no time to train employees, so our service was terrible. At our other stores, nearly everyone had worked directly with Garrett and me or had been trained by someone who had. Now dozens of employees had no clue about our approach to selling, our culture, and our values. We flew employees in from other stores to work the sales floor, unload trucks, and rally the troops—but that was hardly a sustainable strategy. I would often hop a Southwest Airlines flight to Houston myself to help out and send Amy home to get some rest, sometimes personally stocking shelves until dawn.

Amy performed heroically. She found herself running to the bathroom to show an employee how to plunge an overflowing toilet; then to the register to explain that flathead screws, not the panhead kind, went with the hooks the customer was buying; then to the shelving department to explain which shelf could hold fifty pounds. "Help! I need help prioritizing," she pleaded to me one day by phone. "I'm running around just stomping out fires all day and I feel like I'm not being effective."

"What's your number one priority?" I asked her.

"My number one priority is taking care of the customers," she said. No, I said, that's not it. "Okay…my number one priority is running the business efficiently and profitably?" Nope, I gently prodded, try again. "What do you want to hear?" she cried, frustrated. "I'm the store manager and I don't even know what my number one priority is!"

"Your number one priority," I told her, "is managing the values and attitudes of the people who work for you."

Amy wrote that down, and it's still taped to her computer

monitor to this day. In fact, we often use that statement in our training. In any event, I reassured Amy that she was doing an amazing job in an incredibly difficult situation but told her she couldn't keep running around doing other people's work for them. That meant training and delegating, of course, but it was and is more than that: "As a manager, you need to help our employees understand the values our company is based on, then help them develop attitudes and behavior consistent with those values."

Easier said than done. Amy tried her best to explain to her employees the values that made The Container Store culture so special, but she struggled. I understood why. It is hard to explain, especially to sixty new employees in a chaotic new store. Until then, our culture had been transmitted in small ways, through personal conversations, over lunch, by watching one another work, in small-group meetings. It happened almost by osmosis. But at the Houston store, dozens of brand-new employees were convinced they worked for some large, generic retail company. It was a fun place to work, they said, but The Container Store seemed just like any other chain.

This was not good. At her wits' end, Amy asked me to come down to Houston to have a talk with the employees at her home, where she often held Staff Meetings (you'll read more about Staff Meetings in Chapter 10). "We don't need a sales meeting, or an elfa meeting," she said. "I just want you to talk about what makes The Container Store different, why we're not like any old retailer." Hmm, interesting idea. "What should I say?" I asked her. "I don't know," she said. "Just talk to them."

Amy was right. The days when we could handle a personnel problem by taking an employee out for Mexican food and having a little chat over a margarita and tacos were past. The Container Store wasn't a little mom-and-pop shop anymore. With Houston out of control, the viability of the entire company was now at stake. Any entrepreneur who achieves sudden success recognizes the symptoms. Because we were in such a hurry-up mode, we weren't necessarily hiring the right people. But even when we did, those employees weren't getting the training and perspective they needed.

Our new location didn't even feel like The Container Store— it felt like another company altogether. All that being said, sales were still strong in Houston—Christmas shopping and our annual elfa sale in January went through the roof—but it was only a matter of time before the wheels came off the speeding bus.

The night before the meeting at Amy's house, I was a nervous wreck. What made The Container Store special was a very personal matter to me, very difficult to talk about. So I even took out my old, battered Philosophy Epistle File and began reviewing the articles, quotations, and scrawled notes I had collected. That was when I came up with the Man in the Desert story. I've always loved dreaming up analogies, and that goofy image seemed like a good way to dramatize the modern approach to selling we needed as the world moved rapidly toward a service economy. It was raining when I arrived at Amy's place. Everyone was gathered around her fireplace in the living room, snacking on pretzels and chips and sipping beer and soda.

Unsure of where to start, I thanked everyone for coming and began talking the way I normally would to my family of colleagues, glancing occasionally at my Philosophy Epistle File. I spoke from the heart about the things that mattered most to me—why I've always believed in kindness and in treating people well, the importance of having the same values in your business and personal life, why our wake is much more powerful than we can ever imagine. Anyone lucky enough to be somebody else's employer, I said, has a moral obligation to make sure their employees look forward to getting out of bed and going to work in the morning. I told the Andrew Carnegie story about filling the other guy's basket to the brim, after which making money becomes an easy proposition; and about how Albert Einstein used his intuition to discover the theory of relativity.

I explained why one great person is worth three good people, about the importance of paying those people well, and why customers should feel an Air of Excitement three steps after walking into The Container Store. This may sound ridiculous and a bit dramatic, but there really was a big storm that night, and every once in a while there were bursts of lightning and thunder (some quite loud) after I'd made an important point. For whatever reason, the whole night had a surreal feel.

When it was over, I was convinced that this hip, urban crowd would be bored with my absurd, corny spiel. I half-expected rotten tomatoes to come flying in my direction. But to my astonishment, they went crazy! Applause broke out and tears appeared in grateful eyes, after which there was a round of hugs. "We can do that, brother!" one man yelled. I felt like a preacher who had roused his congregation, and everybody was genuinely swept up by a new spirit of joy and hope. It was an incredible experience, one I'll truly never forget.

That night was really the birth of The Container Store as we know it today. Garrett often says, "I think that moment was as important to the company as opening our very first store." Houston eventually righted itself as we committed ourselves to hiring and training great employees according to the principles we talked about that evening. And over the next few years, our staff helped us wade through all these disparate philosophical ideas to arrive at the six Foundation Principles that would guide us until 2008, when we then added, "Communication IS Leadership," for which we have Melissa to thank.

And yet it's not enough to simply write down your values, put them on a plaque, and hang them on the wall in the lobby so everyone can marvel at how principled you are. That's what many companies do—even when they behave in exactly the opposite way.

But here's the real challenge: How do you bring these lofty ideas down from the clouds so everyone in the company actually lives by them, turns them into a reliable habit, feels them so deeply in their bones that they would never dream of behaving any other way?

Here's a little exercise to drive home how difficult this challenge is: Everybody knows the Ten Commandments, right? Okay, so take out a piece of paper and write them down. Go ahead, I'll wait...take your time...no hurry...finished yet? How many did you get? Four? Maybe five...six tops? Studies show that a substantial majority of Americans who grew up going to church every Sunday can't name even half of the Ten Commandments. Remarkable, isn't it, that we can't remember a universal set of values that most people believe we know by heart?

So no wonder employees forget those so-called wonderful values their company was founded on back when Mom and Pop got started. As a company grows, people forget the higher purpose that made their company successful in the first place, the great spirit and energy that drove the founders to endure hardship and long hours against impossible odds. The company gradually becomes all about profit, and employees tend to do anything to achieve that, even when betraying the noble values on that plaque in the lobby.

After our Houston meeting, we embarked on a journey—one we're still on today—to make sure every one of our employees understands and practices our Foundation Principles. The fact that these principles actually work certainly helps. It's much easier to get people to buy into an approach that has been shown to be successful. But we never try to force-feed this material to anybody, a mistake some companies make when trying to create a strong culture.

In our case, other managers heard about the meeting at Amy's house and asked me to give the same talk at their stores, and those employees went nuts over it, too. And why not? After all, the Foundation Principles really empower them. "We're not smart enough to tell you how to handle any given situation that comes up," I like to tell employees. "Retail is like real life—it's far too situational to use the typical phone-book-sized procedural manual. Instead, just use these principles to guide you. Once we agree on the ends, you are free to choose the means to achieve those ends."

Employees are at their most productive when they use their own unshackled, intuitive genius to handle any situation. That goes for everybody in the company, whether it's our finance people negotiating with a bank, a salesperson helping a customer, or a distribution center employee talking to a truck driver in the 110-degree Dallas heat. All employees can make decisions based on the same set of values, principles, and information as everyone else.

We're not following a rote, arrogant suggestion of how to do things, but instead are liberating salespeople to be genuine, creative, and productive. Amazingly enough, a situation in the Boston store usually ends up being handled the same way as in the Seattle store. When someone asks, "Why do we do this?" a colleague might answer, "You know, that's Man in the Desert Selling." It's our own shorthand—like in the joke about the guys in prison who've heard the same joke so many times, they don't even bother to tell the whole joke. They just say "Number Twenty-Seven!" and everybody laughs.

———◇———

Over the years, we've made sure everyone in the company knows it's their responsibility to point out why we do this. And we expect them to reinforce and coach when their colleagues aren't doing it. It does start with the leader of the organization doing it. That's a core tenet of Conscious Capitalism—a conscious leader. But it can't just be one person—everyone has to be doing it.

Even today, we're constantly on the lookout for new ways to teach and reinforce our Foundation Principles. New employees learn about them from the very beginning, when they go to our website to apply for a job, then again at their job interview. They get a full week of "Foundation" training on our culture, Foundation Principles, Conscious Capitalism, and company philosophy and goals before ever setting foot on the sales floor. We've put our Foundation Principles on our shopping bags and T-shirts, and we even named conference rooms in our Dallas headquarters after them. We explain them to everyone we do business with and discuss them in nearly every communication with employees, and during the daily "huddle," a morning meeting of the store staff before the doors open.

This constant reinforcement is necessary because sometimes a Foundation Principle can be misinterpreted and the new version can take on a life of its own—a mutation of the culture, I call it. Someone will thank a colleague for getting them coffee by saying, "Wow, you really filled my basket!" That, of course, misses the point that this principle is really about creatively crafting mutually beneficial relationships with our vendors. Or an employee will help a customer who locked herself out of her car and will say, "That was Man in the Desert!" That was a great gesture, and something we encourage, but it had nothing to do with selling products. We keep talking about the principles, over and over, so their true meaning is understood by all.

Our Foundation Principles reveal our higher purpose by motivating our employees to do whatever they can to help the company thrive. In that sense, the moral imperative of Man in the Desert Selling is about more than just helping the customer.

It's also about ensuring that a company that does so much good for so many people—from employees to vendors to customers to investors to the community nonprofits we support—can flourish and reach its full potential.

In recent years, as we began publicizing our Foundation Principles and what we stand for, we've been surprised by how much customers respond to them, too. That's part of a larger trend of consumers increasingly insisting that brands reflect their own values and make a positive contribution to the world. They're definitely voting with their pocketbooks. And that's not just about donating to charities—though we do plenty of that, too. Consumers also want a company's basic DNA, how it feels and operates, to be based on positive values.

So we began explaining our Foundation Principles to customers in our catalogs, on our website, via social media like Facebook and Twitter, even on the sales floor. Audrey Robertson, our vice-president of cultural programs, community relations & social media, has really helped me champion this effort. She's really a kindred spirit. We always talk about "doing our jobs" and making each day great for everyone around us. We do that well together, and apart. She's motivated me to work to do that even more often and better. And in doing that, it inspired the whole company. In fact, I'd say she's helping to raise the consciousness of doing that throughout our company, bringing even more positive energy and helpfulness to my life and those of others. And she has really been the cheerleader for our *What We Stand For* focus. We created our *What We Stand For* blog, which gives customers an inside view into our culture—with wonderful posts by employees, vendors, our community partners, etc. We have devoted entire campaigns to our principles, with full-page ads in the *New York Times* and direct mailers to our customers. The response has been overwhelming. Here's a small sampling of the thousands of positive comments we've received from customers:

"I love the stores, and now that I know the principles upon which the stores were founded, I am even more impressed. Thanks for letting us know. I'll shop there more now."

"If all companies in America were run like The Container Store we wouldn't be in the economy we are in. The banks that are too big to fail would never have made the loans they did or bet on derivatives the way they did. Ethical behavior by all companies would create a solid foundation from which to grow our economy. Unfortunately, not every company is a Container Store."

"Your foundation principles show in the attitudes of your employees! I have always been greeted with a smile and assisted with the same level of courtesy no matter what the size of my purchase."

"The idea that you can enrich the entire supply chain, rather than squeeze a vendor dry and destroy their profitability, is one of the main reasons I shop at The Container Store....Another huge and often underrated benefit is that a quality product is better for our environment—there are too many 'cheap' disposable products for sale these days, filling up landfills for no reason. I'm proud to be a Container Store customer and am impressed by all your principles!"

"I wish every business out there had your principles. What a world this would be."

It's hard to express what it meant to me to read these comments. To think that these deeply personal ideas that I was so shy about explaining to a small group of employees twenty-five years ago could get this kind of reaction throughout the country today, well, that's really amazing. It just shows how hungry people are to live in a more just and ethical world, and how it can only help companies to embrace such universal values, and that we shouldn't be timid about sharing them with the world. It's stunning to me that some of the best business schools in America are teaching the Foundation Principles and the best and brightest MBA students are coming out of school talking about how business is not a zero-sum game and are taking a long-term view of business.

That's why the Conscious Capitalism movement has gained such traction since it began a few years ago. In truth, the Foundation Principles are Conscious Capitalism. There just wasn't a name for it back when we were getting started. But it's gratifying to see that there are so many other companies running their businesses the same way: Southwest Airlines, Whole Foods, Zappos, Starbucks, REI, Life is good, Tom's Shoes, Panera Bread, Google, Union Square Hospitality Group, Patagonia, Eaton, TDIndustries, the Tata Group, Costco, Wegmans, UPS, Joie de Vivre Hospitality, POSCO, Bright Horizons, GSD&M Idea City, Medtronic—the list goes on and on.

What these companies know is that following the tenets of Conscious Capitalism actually results in higher profits than the old way of merely putting the interests of shareholders above everything else. It's ironic, really—not making profit your number one goal actually makes you more profitable. Seeing all these companies thrive by doing the right thing inspires other entrepreneurs to run their businesses in a conscious way. Of course, the landscape is littered with the remains of promising start-ups that failed to make the transition into large, thriving companies—becoming, in essence, victims of their own success.

But I hope that our story, and the story of so many other Conscious Capitalism companies, will help entrepreneurs realize that creating a strong culture by defining a set of values, and then truly living out those values and constantly reinforcing them, is the key to making that difficult transition.

And the more I meet the leaders of Conscious Capitalism–focused companies, the more I realize we're all simply using different words to describe the same basic principles. When I met Danny Meyer, the legendary New York restaurateur (and now a member of our board of directors), I realized there was another important concept implied by our Man in the Desert Selling philosophy, one we could do a better job of emphasizing: hospitality.

I met Danny in 2011 at a dinner at his fabulous Gramercy Tavern in Manhattan. It was a dinner with Billy Shore of Share our Strength, the wonderful nonprofit with the No Kid Hungry campaign. We were joined by my friends Walter Robb, co-CEO of Whole Foods, and Jon Sokoloff of Leonard Green & Partners (both of whom are now on our board). The moment you walk into any of Danny's restaurants, you understand how deeply he understands hospitality, because you instantly feel relaxed and at home. As we talked, we hit it off immediately. "It felt like a business version of a first date," Danny said later, "the kind where you could stay up all night talking."

It was eerie how similar our views about service and hospitality were—and later, I devoured his wonderful book, *Setting the Table: The Transforming Power of Hospitality in Business*. Hospitality has always been very important to me, being from the South and raised by parents from New Orleans, who created a warm, gracious home that was a real magnet for friends and family alike. Somehow, I think my fondness for hospitality found its way into the atmosphere at The Container Store, something Danny said he noticed during his very first visit to our first Manhattan location in Chelsea years ago. "The brilliance of The Container

Store, and the reason I want to go back, is that I totally trust that everyone who is working there is on my side," Danny said. "That's how I define hospitality. I feel like they are trying to do something *for* me, not trying to do something *to* me. I'm not just a transaction. I am a human opportunity to solve a problem."

I couldn't have said it better. That's Man in the Desert Selling—the essence of our Foundation Principles. That's the animating spirit that drives Conscious Capitalism. Hearing Danny talk about hospitality made me realize that, as great as our commitment to Man in the Desert Selling is, we can probably bring it to an even higher level. In fact, I think our culture is far stronger today than it was five, ten, or even twenty years ago. Stronger today than it was even yesterday. People are always asking me, "How can we keep the culture so strong as we grow and have more stores?" The truth is that it keeps getting stronger every year. Each new crop of employees is more aware of and in tune with our culture and Foundation Principles like Man in the Desert Selling than the previous one. That's what drives the value of the business. Even as we grow into a multi-billion-dollar company, our culture is still what will drive it. As the management guru Peter Drucker famously said, "Culture eats strategy for breakfast."

And if our RPM needle ever gets in the red and our precious, yummy culture is in need of a bit of a hug, we'll stop and give it the love it deserves and needs. For there is no doubt in my mind that love is what The Container Store's past, present, and future are built on.

7

Communication IS Leadership

It's true. Communication and leadership really are the same thing. After all, how can people trust their leaders if they're not being fully informed about what's at stake? At The Container Store, we often quote a wonderful line Melissa came up with, quite spontaneously, during a media interview years ago to explain how we communicate with our employees: "We must practice consistent, reliable, predictable, effective, thoughtful, compassionate, and even, yes, courteous communication every single day to successfully sustain, develop, and grow our business."

We want to communicate everything to every person. Sometimes that's not possible, but we're thrilled that we come closer to doing this than anyone else because we put more value on it than anyone else. As I said earlier, out of respect, the only thing we don't talk about openly is an individual's compensation.

So what *do* we share? Company goals and objectives,

financial details, daily sales results, real estate expansion plans, marketing plans, major initiatives, sales campaign results, companywide leadership meeting notes, product information—truly, the list goes on and on. And this communication comes in many forms: scheduled meetings, off-the-cuff encounters, voice mail, video, company conference calls, e-mail, and old-fashioned written memos—any way possible. And, of course, the daily ongoing communication that happens between employees— sharing perspectives and insight—is a key component of our communication/leadership-driven culture.

A great example of what I'm talking about is taking place in downtown Las Vegas in the exciting revitalization project initiated by Tony Hsieh of Zappos. Tony is creating a vibrant community where employees can live, work, and play together, all within walking distance, to encourage the kind of creativity and innovation Zappos is known for. "We want to accelerate the kind of serendipitous collisions that can happen between people in close-knit communities because that's how new ideas happen," Tony told me. Those are precisely the kinds of daily interactions we like to see at The Container Store, so that our employees can constantly develop new approaches to solving customer problems while helping one another stay focused on the core values of our company.

Unlike some companies, we don't work on a "need to know" basis. Rather, we ask ourselves, "Who will benefit from having this information? Who needs this information to help them do their job better and to help them be the best employee, the best leader, the best person they can be?" This type of "whole-brained" approach to business, this 360-degree thinking and execution, is one of our many key differentiators. It makes every employee truly a vital part of our company's cognitive process.

I've heard top-level people at other companies tell me they'd be afraid to communicate that much—they would be very concerned and mortified if key information went outside the company. It's a fair point. We know that some of the information we share could quite possibly fall into the wrong hands. But we also believe that the advantages of our honest, transparent, and thorough approach to communication far outweigh the possible disadvantages. And it's really consistent with our belief in valuing our employees, valuing one another, making sure we all feel appreciated, included, and empowered, and have the training necessary to be successful in our jobs.

In this respect, a business is like a football team. If all the players don't know the score in the game, how can they contribute when it's their turn to play? How will they know what needs to be done? Imagine that the two-minute warning sounds: You're driving down the field, determined to pull out a last-minute, come-from-behind victory, and everything is intense and exciting. It's the ultimate team adventure, but suddenly you have two guys who've been sitting on the bench now running onto the field who don't even know the score. It's going to be almost impossible for them to have a big impact.

That's why we give all store employees sales results from their market area for the previous day, along with our new goals for today, and gather everyone together for a short huddle before the store opens every morning and as shifts change—so they can fully participate in achieving our goals. When everyone has a complete understanding of what we're doing, how we're doing it, and why we're doing it, we all become more productive and happier members of the team.

Everyone at The Container Store is encouraged, and really expected, as members of this great team, to seek out information. The resources in our company are so abundant, we encourage everyone to ask questions, to seek out tenured coworkers for their perspective, and then to share that perspective with others.

That's an example of what we mean by thoughtful and courteous communication and leadership.

As Melissa likes to say, leadership is not something you do *to* people, but rather something you do *with* people. And, of course, to lead effectively, we must breathlessly communicate. Yes, we breathlessly communicate. It's hard, but it does result in higher productivity, happier and more motivated employees, and a superior level of customer service.

As I've mentioned before, I believe that if you're lucky enough to be somebody's employer, you have a moral obligation to make sure your employees wake up and look forward to coming to work in the morning. And the best way to do that is first by surrounding them with amazing 1=3 colleagues with whom they can accomplish great things, and then by communicating with them so thoroughly that they really feel they're part of the team.

Communication, of course, is a two-way street. That's why we give employees many ways to communicate, both with management and with one another. All voice mail numbers are published so you can easily leave a message with a comment, question, suggestion, or celebration; cell phone numbers of managers are also published. Employees are encouraged to speak with their manager (or anyone else in the company) about any decision that affects their jobs. If they feel they haven't been "heard" by their immediate manager, they're encouraged to contact that manager's manager. Yes, we give them the permission to talk to anyone in the company and not feel they're bound by any rigid hierarchical rules.

Heck, we don't even have a human resources department at The Container Store. That's because our communication is so constant and thorough we don't need a separate department to address employee concerns—it's already part of our culture. As Melissa observes, "If you can surround yourself with secure people who understand constructive criticism, transparency, and being candid and caring about others, then you don't need the kind of traditional HR department where employees go to share their grievances and complaints. If an employee has a problem or issue, or anything they want to share and be candid about, they should feel confident in talking about it to whomever they want without retribution."

Hearing regularly from our employees also helps us advance their careers, because we're so tuned in to their goals and ambitions. And they learn about new company initiatives or store openings they may want to be a part of. One of my favorite questions for the staff when I go into a store is "If you were chairman and CEO and you owned one hundred percent of the business, what are the two or three things you would do? What's the first thing you would focus on?" I have spent thirty-six years hearing what we've been doing great, so I really want to know what we can do better. How can we innovate? There are always areas of opportunity. We want to liberate the spirit of communication in everyone so they can talk as much as they want about how we can make something better. Our Communication IS Leadership principle really pushes for that.

———— ◁◦▷ ————

Ensuring that our large group of part-time employees stays in the loop is a great example of that. Imagine how daunting it might be to keep up with our brand of constant communication if you're a single mom whose second job is here at The Container Store. A single mom doesn't have time for anything! Well, we try to make time for her. There's scheduled time to read, watch, or listen to whatever information is currently available. The most pertinent, timely written information is compiled in what we call our "Prime Time In the Know On the Go" notebook. During their scheduled time, they might find themselves studying the following:

• A Communication Board in each store's break room that includes current product information, training materials, sales goals, and a chart with titles and photos of everyone in the Dallas headquarters and distribution center so every employee knows who's who;

• "Melissa's Weekly Message," with her perspective on various developments in the company, written in Melissa's inimitable, energetic, and always inspiring style;

• "The Gumby Gazette," which discusses community events, employee promotions, and new initiatives;

• "News from the Oasis," a biweekly publication from our training and development department;

• A video of a town hall–style presentation that Danny Meyer and Walter Robb gave at our offices about Conscious Capitalism and hospitality.

Our transparent communication means our employees know virtually everything about our business. We find that these details build real trust as employees see the proof in the numbers and that we truly do make employees our number one priority.

For example, during the Great Recession, this constant flow of communication meant that all our employees knew exactly how far sales had fallen and that freezing salary, 401(k) matches, and hiring was done out of absolute necessity and for one reason only—to preserve everyone's jobs. It was a thing of beauty, amazing and touching, to watch the whole company support that difficult decision—and all because they had exactly the same information management had. It's human nature to want to feel warm, safe, and secure—and constant communication helps that happen.

I could go on about the hundreds of channels of communication that flow through our organization. But the best way to get to the heart of our Communication IS Leadership principle is to talk about Melissa Reiff, since she embodies the concept better than anyone I've ever met. I thought I was good at communicating, but Melissa made me—and everyone else—realize we could be so much better. When we hired her, I knew Melissa was a phenomenal talent, one of the sharpest business minds I've ever encountered. But none of us had any idea what a profound effect she would have on us, bringing The Container Store to a whole new level of excellence and helping us meet the enormous challenge of evolving from a small regional chain into a beloved national brand.

———◦———

Melissa was national sales manager at Crabtree & Evelyn in Boston in the mid-'90s when she came up with an idea to develop products for us. Sharon and I had been good friends with Melissa and her husband, Ron, ever since she began representing some of our vendors as a manufacturing rep in Dallas some fifteen years earlier. After moving to Crabtree & Evelyn, Melissa worked with Sharon, and with Peggy Doughty (now our fabulous vice-president of visual merchandising), to create a proprietary line of scented shelf paper and other fragrance line accessories that we liked so much we launched them in all our stores.

One night, after a long day of training our sales staff in the new product at our store in Rockville, Maryland, Sharon and I took Melissa out to dinner. Sharon and I started talking about how we were both spending at least half of our time on marketing and advertising, making it hard to find time to get everything else done. "Wow, marketing for The Container Store—that sounds like something I would love to do," Melissa said. As the wine flowed, Sharon and I found ourselves confessing that we'd always wanted to work with her (in fact, I had been quietly kicking myself for years for not hiring her before Crabtree & Evelyn did). Melissa said that was amazing, because she'd always wanted to work for us, too. She loved her current job, but missed Dallas, where she had gone to college at SMU.

As the night went on, we told Melissa how special she was and how much we loved her, and it was humbling when she said she adored us, too. Even after all those years, it was the first time we'd really had this type of open conversation with her. And we decided to make her an offer.

A few weeks later, we were thrilled when Melissa accepted our offer to become vice-president of sales and marketing. It was a big step for us because until then we had always promoted vice-presidents from within—she was the first to come from the outside. But everyone quickly saw what Melissa could accomplish with the sheer force of her talent, integrity, energy, and loving personality. Her greatest strength was clearly her ability to communicate and to rally the troops as she created the most detailed, comprehensive marketing plans we'd ever seen. "I promise you there will be no surprises," she told me. "I will put myself in your shoes and communicate with you exactly the way I would want to be communicated with."

Melissa can't tell you exactly how the phrase "Communication IS Leadership" developed, and in her usual, self-effacing style, she says it's entirely possible someone else coined it first. Other thought leaders have expressed similar ideas, including James Humes, a speechwriter for several presidents, who

once said, "The art of communication is the language of leadership." But I do know this: The formulation "Communication IS
Leadership" did not exist at The Container Store before Melissa
arrived, and it perfectly articulated a principle we had always
valued highly but performed instinctively, without thinking too
much about it. We began using the phrase more and more, thanks
to Melissa, and during our Staff Meeting in 2008, when we celebrated our thirtieth anniversary, we surprised her by formally
establishing it as a Foundation Principle. You should have seen
Melissa's face—you could have knocked her over with a feather.
"It's a moment I'll never forget," she says.

———◁◦▷———

But ever since that pivotal Houston Staff Meeting back in 1989,
we knew that the most important thing we needed to communicate to our employees was not reams of data, but the philosophical
principles our company was based upon—and whatever technology we adopted during the dawning digital age, from e-mail to
the Web, had to serve that purpose. During this period of fast
growth, we knew it was critically important that our employees
become even more deeply trained in the Foundation Principles
that made us successful in the first place.

I'm convinced that our ability to successfully communicate
those principles to our employees is what allowed us to make
the transition from a small regional chain to a thriving national
brand. As we grew, we also began communicating more with the
outside world about our unique workplace and culture. In 1999,
we decided to enter *Fortune* magazine's 100 Best Companies to
Work For competition, and were blown away when we placed
number one! That was the first year we entered (it was the third
year of the list—we just didn't know about it the first two years!).
Here we were going up against the best companies in America,

nobody really knew who we were, and we were flabbergasted to come out on top. Then we were even more astounded the following year when we placed number one again!

We've been on quite a roll ever since then, making the *Fortune* list fifteen years in a row, placing second twice, and making the top five six times! I think if you take an average of our place on the list over the years, you'll find we're among the highest-ranking companies in the country. And a retailer, for that matter! I should point out that this is not just a bunch of magazine editors throwing darts at a list of companies. *Fortune* partners with the Great Place to Work Institute, a highly respected global research and consulting firm, to crunch reams of data from anonymous employee surveys, called the Trust Index, and detailed company submissions. It's really quite an elaborate process, and two-thirds of the score comes from those anonymous employee surveys. To be chosen for this honor year after year—well, it's hard to express how overjoyed and proud that makes us feel. And it only makes us work that much harder to live up to our reputation as one of the best companies in America to work for.

Our Communication IS Leadership principle has also played a crucial role in our hiring process. As I've mentioned, today fourteen of our top nineteen executives—and almost 70 percent of all our employees—are women. After all, guess who tends to communicate better? If you believe that a company thrives better in an atmosphere of love rather than fear, who's more comfortable with showing affection? If you believe that collaboration and teamwork are crucial to a company's success, who's better at leaving their egos at the door and working together as a team?

In recent years, I've been glad to see research that supports this view of women executives. In 2012, the *Harvard Business Review* published a comprehensive survey of over 7,000 leaders of some of the most successful and progressive organizations in the world. While the majority of leaders in the study (64 percent) were men, women scored higher than men in a remarkable twelve of the sixteen competencies considered critical for outstanding leadership. It's not surprising that women ranked higher in what are typically considered "nurturing" qualities—the ability to develop talent, build relationships, and so on. But women actually outscored men to the highest degree in two other traits—taking initiative and driving for results—that are usually considered male strengths (in the study, some women attributed that result to the fact that they have to work harder to prove themselves). At higher executive levels, the gap between the higher women's scores and lower men's scores grew even wider.

Those conclusions certainly match my own experience as we hired and promoted so many amazing women, including Melissa, who became executive vice-president of stores and marketing in 2003 and then president of the company in 2005, later adding chief operating officer to her title. I like to say she's the best president in the United States, and that I'm incredibly lucky to have two such close and trusted confidantes in Sharon and Melissa. They complement each other perfectly, like two hemispheres that make a complete world. Sharon handles the merchandising sphere, which includes product development and buying, vendor relationships, visual sales, supply chain, store branding and design, and anything related to our products. Melissa's domain is the other hemisphere, which focuses on day-to-day operations and our sales performance, and also includes finance and accounting, information technology, real estate, logistics distribution, loss prevention and legal matters, marketing, store leadership, training and development, and recruiting. Melissa really drives the organization to perform with excellence. Any retailer needs strong leaders in both hemispheres to succeed, and we're fortunate to have the very best in the country at both positions.

Of course, we do keep a few men around, just to keep things interesting. Garrett and I both got into retail because we loved helping customers, training employees, and organizing displays in the store. But as the company grew, I found myself gravitating toward other areas where I was needed, like our store expansion strategy and finance. Being a liberal arts student, I stayed away from math courses during my long and colorful career in college, but I did work hard to develop my finance skills while at The Container Store and was surprised to find I was pretty good at it. Then I remembered something my mom said when I was little: "He thinks he's not very good at math, but if you just put a dollar sign in front of it, he's the best you've ever seen." (My golf buddies will agree, and swear that I don't start playing really well until we start betting!)

My mom was someone who understood that Communication IS Leadership—though, of course, she wouldn't have expressed it that way. Jackie Tindell was so smart and loving and such a strong leader in our family and community of friends. In fact, my mom communicated so well that my dad usually couldn't get a word in edgewise—which is pretty much how some of us guys sometimes feel at The Container Store, surrounded by all these world-class women. It's hard to keep up, you know? But I could talk to my mom about anything. She was my go-to person whenever I was wrestling with any problem at all. She listened deeply and attentively, but it was more than that. I was really interested in hearing what she had to say. I respected her insight into things. And I always felt unconditionally loved and supported by her—and my dad as well. That was such an incredible gift they gave me.

Since I'm talking about my mom, I should probably mention something that's pretty hard for me to talk about. In 1997, I was living my busy life—we opened our seventeenth and eighteenth stores in Denver and Atlanta that year—when my mom was diagnosed with cancer. I was devastated. She went through chemotherapy, but I had trouble accepting how serious it was. One day when I was over at my parents' during that difficult time, I got into the car with my nephews, Ty and Kip, and went out to pick up some lunch. I played some of my favorite music for them (I think it was Tony! Toni! Toné!), and we were driving around leisurely, just talking, enjoying the music. When we got back, the hospice workers were in the driveway. "Kip, come on, hurry up, hurry up," they said, and took me into the house.

My mom was in her final moments, just waiting for me to get home. "She was just holding on until you got here," somebody said. And then I hugged her. And then she died.

Mom wouldn't let go until I got back—I was so struck by that. And what an idiot I was to leave in the first place, driving around, wasting precious time! But I never really expected her to die. I actually believed she had a decent chance of overcoming it. The doctors later said, "Well, of course, what she had was incurable. There was really never any chance." Well, why didn't the doctors tell us that at the beginning? Mom and Dad could have traveled all over France; she would have lived her last six months totally differently. Instead, she stayed home and went through painful chemo treatments when there actually was no hope of beating the cancer. Clearly, those doctors were not being brave or transparent in their communication, and that made me very angry—though, in their defense, I'm sure part of it was that we simply believed what we wanted to believe.

My mom's funeral was at a big Catholic church in Dallas called St. Rita's. The number of people who showed up absolutely flabbergasted me. Some were associated with The Container Store, but my mom and dad also had so many friends. They were very social people. They never met a stranger, as the saying goes.

They would go on a trip and make two or three lifelong friends. They would go out to dinner and start a conversation with someone in the restaurant and end up exchanging Christmas gifts and then traveling the world together. All those friends showed up, and it was so good to be around so many wonderful people who loved her.

Fortunately, my dad is still around and I remain very close to him. Now in his eighties, he still shoots his age in golf whenever we go out together. But of course nobody can replace your mom. She really understood me. She was so very bright and wise, and I always took her advice, ever since kindergarten. And she usually turned out to be right! I miss her so much. But in so many ways, I know she is with me still.

————◄○►————

As I learned from both my mom and my dad—and as Melissa and Sharon always remind me—great communication creates tremendous trust. That's why Communication IS Leadership. There can be no leadership without trust, and there can be no trust without open, transparent communication. It was that sense of trust that helped us persevere just before the turn of the millennium, when we faced one of most serious challenges in our history.

In early 1999, we received word that our beloved vendor Elfa was for sale. This came as a complete shock. Elfa had been by far our best-selling product, accounting for almost 25 percent of our sales. But now, suddenly, giant retail chains and housewares manufacturers were trying to acquire elfa, a small company of 300 employees based in Sweden. If any of them succeeded in taking the company over, it would be ruinous to elfa, and ruinous to us at The Container Store, too.

By then, The Container Store was responsible for 40 percent of elfa's sales. That's pretty remarkable, since elfa is a complex, metric-based component system that is very hard to sell for most retailers. But we had spent the previous two decades perfecting our sales methodology with our highly trained staff. We had also become the sole elfa wholesale distributor for all of North America three years earlier, so we devoted considerable resources to showing other retailers how to sell it.

We had spent a great deal of time and focus building the value of the brand—not just for us, but for everyone who sold it. In short, The Container Store and elfa were deeply intertwined and highly dependent upon each other. Separate us and we would both die. Worse, we had hardly any time to make an offer. Anyone interested in buying elfa would have to submit a bid within a week. There seemed no way we could make a plausible bid. Our revenues were $170 million, and elfa's were $50 million. It would be like a snake trying to eat a chicken. We didn't have the cash on hand to make such a big acquisition, we had never gone into debt in our history, and there was no way a bank would lend us that kind of money. Trying to win elfa over those corporate giants would be like David taking on Goliath.

On the other hand, losing elfa was unimaginable. Any of those big corporations would certainly try to sell elfa products through mass merchants, which would be like trying to sell Armani in Kmart. Elfa would have to change from an upper-end specialty-store product to a discount item sold at low prices and in huge volumes. The other bidders simply wanted elfa because they knew our sky-high sales numbers. What they didn't know was how to sell elfa, and that elfa would not thrive in a typical low-service retail environment. The end result would be that elfa would surely go out of business—and I firmly believed it would be devastating to us, too.

Our only hope lay in the great relationship we had established with elfa, thanks to our Foundation Principles. We had spent two decades filling the other guy's basket to the brim by creatively crafting a mutually beneficial relationship and doing everything we could to help elfa prosper. We developed some truly outstanding products together, such as the ventilated shelf and closet rod, which was revolutionary in the industry for its extremely light but exceptionally strong construction. Our trust level with elfa was so high that its employees knew they could always count on us, and that we would not abandon them for a competitor. That trust allowed them to plan and invest and to grow their business. We taught them how to market and sell elfa to other retail customers, allowing them to use our beautiful photography and marketing materials.

As a result, astonishingly enough, just one of our stores sold more elfa than another entire national retail chain.

It's funny, but I had an intuitive feeling from day one that the retail industry would fail to recognize the true value of elfa. Some people believe in the efficient-market theory that good products will somehow find their market eventually. But I can think of many instances when the market isn't efficient at all, and doesn't recognize the value of a product until an entrepreneur comes along and creates a market. "One of The Container Store's secrets," our vendor Andy Van Meter once told me, "is that your company recognizes the value in products that the market doesn't. You can make a big success out of a product that no one else in the industry even understands."

Several of our Foundation Principles played a big role in our success at selling elfa products, including "Intuition does not come to an unprepared mind. You must train before it happens" and "1 great person = 3 good people." That's because our highly trained staff of great employees have the skills of interior architects to design an elfa solution to any storage and organization problem a customer might have. And by using Man in the Desert Selling, our employees constantly go beyond offering customers that proverbial glass of water to devise complete solutions using elfa.

But none of those Foundation Principles would have helped us in the chase to buy elfa without the trust we had established with its employees. And that was due to the faithful execution of our powerful Communication IS Leadership principle. By then, elfa knew everything about our business—how we price the products, our margins, and endless details about our customers—the kind of information other retailers don't share with vendors, fearing it might leak out to competitors. We became very close friends with elfa's management team, taking business trips and vacations together and sharing our lives with them. The owner of elfa at the time initially leaned toward maximizing his profit by selling to one of the large bidders, but CEO Stefan Ferm and most of the employees were enthusiastic about wanting The Container Store to win the bid. They loved our company culture so much, they wanted to be part of it. And they agreed with our view that their company probably had no future if elfa was to be sold through mass merchants.

At some point, it became clear to elfa's owners that selling to anyone beside The Container Store would not only mean losing their best customer, but also that the hearts and souls of most of elfa's management team and employees were with us. It became an extremely risky proposition to sell to another bidder for a simple reason: There might not be anybody left there to run the company.

In the final round of bidding, facing off against two house-wares giants, we submitted a bid that was not as high as the others, but close enough for elfa to say yes! And yet the deal threatened to fall through: We still could not come up with the financing because the banks were balking at loaning us so much money. My closest confidants were very caring and supportive during the whole ordeal. But with the future of both companies hanging in the balance, there were moments when I felt as lonely as little David must have felt battling Goliath. If I failed, hundreds of great employees in both companies would most likely lose their jobs.

Then, out of the blue, a dramatic breakthrough: Stefan, elfa's CEO, made a brave decision not to sell his stake to the highest bidder—passing up millions in profit—and instead agreed to exchange those shares for a stake in The Container Store. That lowered the amount we had to borrow, and the bank gave us the green light—just barely. Amazing! The owners of elfa quickly accepted our offer, and soon thereafter, the deal was done. Cheers broke out at elfa headquarters in Västervik, Sweden, and at The Container Store in Dallas. Somehow, miraculously, David and his slingshot had knocked out the giant.

What Stefan did took real courage. As a poker player, I know how hard it is to sit on your chips when everyone around you is cashing in. But by holding fast, Stefan showed how deeply he believed in us, gambling that his stake would ultimately be worth more as a part owner of The Container Store. And that's exactly what happened. Stefan moved his family to Dallas, enrolled his kids in school here, and served as our vice-president of international operations and later as chief financial officer.

Dallas is night-and-day different from the sleepy, idyllic fishing village of Västervik. But Stefan made the adjustment, and it proved beneficial to both companies. When Leonard Green & Partners bought The Container Store in 2007 (about which I'll tell you more later), Stefan sold his shares for far more than what he would have received in 1999. Then he retired from the company. And it was all due to the great trust we had established with him through our long and wonderfully open, transparent, highly communicative relationship.

Anytime a company makes an acquisition, it's a challenge to blend two distinct corporate cultures—and that challenge is even greater when those companies are based in different countries. But we were very fortunate that both companies shared so many

core convictions: that life and business are about much more
than just making money, that producing a quality product matters, and that specialty retailers have an important mission in our
era of mass merchandising. The management of elfa shared our
view that employees must be treated as multidimensional human
beings rather than cogs in a machine. The employees of elfa also
found our Foundation Principles completely in sync with their
existing beliefs.

But soon after, we found ourselves in a quandary: Should we
continue to wholesale elfa to other American retailers? On one
hand, it was clearly in our best interest to make elfa an exclusive product found only at The Container Store; after all, why
should we supply competitors with our top-selling product? On
the other hand, many of those "competitors" were actually small,
family-owned furniture and hardware chains and single stores
that relied on elfa for a significant portion of their sales. Cutting
them off cold turkey could be disastrous for them.

This was not the first time we had faced a dilemma like this.
In 1980, just two years after opening our first store, we beat out
several larger competitors to become the wholesale distributor
for elfa across a five-state territory in the Southwest. We had
no money or track record, but elfa could see that we knew how
to sell its products better than anyone else. In 1992, we took
on the Western US district, too. We had no great desire to be
wholesalers—our main motivation was simply to be assured of
getting enough supply to satisfy the huge demand for elfa. Then
in 1996, elfa told us it had decided to use just one distributor for
all of North America and asked if we were interested.

It was a flattering offer, since we were the only existing distributor elfa trusted to offer the North American market to. But
it put us in a deeply uncomfortable position. If we said yes, we
would be taking over the business of other regional elfa distributors, some of whom had become dear friends. If we said no, elfa

said it would simply hire an outside firm and we would lose not only our distributorship, but also access to the large volume of products our customers were demanding.

The business world is full of such predicaments, of course—and how you react to them is a big test not only of your business skills, but also of your character. In the end, we said yes to elfa, but we didn't abandon our former colleagues. We quickly created a plan to help the other distributors make up for the business they lost. Rich Klein, who sold elfa in parts of the United States, remains one of my closest friends today partly because we both worked so hard to find a way to navigate this difficult situation. The Container Store ended up buying other products from Rich's company, replacing the business it lost and then some, and everything worked out extremely well for both of us.

Then, as noted, after buying elfa three years later, we faced a similar situation. Refusing to sell elfa to competing retailers could mean watching good, honest folks go out of business, people who could easily go to their graves cursing us and telling their grandchildren about how The Container Store had destroyed them. So we continued to wholesale elfa across America, even ramping up the volume for a while. But elfa is so difficult to sell that the other retailers just weren't moving much of the product (which means that either we're great retailers or we're lousy wholesalers!). So in 2007, we started the process of making elfa exclusive to The Container Store. But rather than severing ties with those smaller retailers immediately, we've spent the intervening years helping them make a gradual transition to similar products that serve the same market but are much easier to sell, creating more win-win situations.

Both of those stories are great examples of how to fill the other guy's basket to the brim, even sometimes with competitors, and how any businessperson can do the same. You're limited only by your imagination and determination. It also shows the importance of constant, open communication—especially when the situation gives you a bit of heartache, as it was with Rich Klein. Sharon and I both love Rich and his wife, Lynn, dearly, and we've spent many wonderful vacations together over the years. Fortunately, our relationship—as it was with other elfa distributors and retailers—was already so strong and trusting because it had so much transparency. Not only did we weather that particular storm, but our relationships grew deeper and stronger because of it.

Relationships—isn't that what business is really all about? Our experience with elfa, from the miraculous way we acquired the company to managing our complex role as wholesale distributor, shows how crucial human relationships are—and why the quality of those relationships is often the difference between failure and success. How can you have strong relationships without honest, open communication? In my view, you can't. That's why Communication IS Leadership has been such a powerful Foundation Principle for us.

Without great communication, everything falls apart. With it, anything is possible.

8

The Best Selection, Service & Price

As I mentioned, Stanley Marcus was an early fan of The Container Store and a special mentor to us very early on. I loved him so much. He was so generous with his time and his praise. Imagine. Stanley Marcus thought what we were doing was not just worthwhile but extraordinary. His time with us inspired me to spend time with young entrepreneurs, which I delight in doing.

I loved to talk to Stanley about selection, service, and price, which later became one of our Foundation Principles. Stanley Marcus always said that if you do one of these things really well, you'll be very successful. He said if you do any two of them well, you'll have the number one business in your niche. Then he said you can't do all three because price is absolutely mutually exclusive to both selection and service.

Neiman Marcus, which Stanley and his family ran for most of the twentieth century, would seem to prove his point. It's one of those rare stores with fantastic selection and service, but no one has ever attributed great prices to Neiman Marcus.

That's because excelling in all three areas is pretty unheard-of in retail. One of the few companies that actually manages this extraordinary feat is Total Wine & More. Owner David Trone and his team transform 30,000 square feet of selling space from what could be an average warehouse wine store into a beautifully specialized experience with a friendly, knowledge-able staff that makes wine very accessible through its breadth of selection and price point. You can't drive by the store without seeing the parking lot full, and the company's double-digit sales growth is astounding to watch.

Without a doubt, offering the best selection, service, and price is retail Heaven. What could be better than shopping at a store with great prices and fabulous service that's universally acknowledged as having the most celebrated collection of products in retail? Well, that's why we want to do it. Never in the past thirty-six years have we been satisfied with merely dominating our niche. Our goal is to be the best retailer in America. To achieve that, we made our merchandising strategy—selection, service, and price—one of our seven Foundation Principles.

———◦———

The Container Store gets a lot of credit for having the best customer service around. Nobody ever debates that. I talked about our approach to service in Chapter 5 when discussing Man in the Desert Selling—because, to us, service and selling are the same thing. And people tell us that customer service is our core competency.

Our people really do want to help you. Since we're a solutions-based form of retail, not an items-based form of retail, we want our customer to come in saying, "My closet is driving me nuts. Is there anything you can do to help me with that?"

But we don't just give the customer that one shoe rack she might have thought was the answer to her prayers. Because then she would get home and still be frustrated with her closet and, worse, mad at us. Instead, after an engaged conversation with one of our staff, she leaves the store ecstatic, with creative solutions, and hopefully does a little dance in her closet every time she opens the door in the morning. It's an inspirational, creative process between the salesperson and the customer.

———◄○►———

As for selection, I've already described how Sharon and her amazing team of buyers curate the world's most celebrated collection of storage and organization products by creatively crafting mutually beneficial relationships with our beloved vendors. A short stroll through any of our stores reveals the variety of items we offer, from 120 types of food-storage containers to 40 kinds of laundry hampers. I find it so exciting that we offer the world's most extensive collection of…just fill in the blank… shoe storage, hooks, hangers, decorative packaging…on and on throughout the sixteen lifestyle sections of our store. The store is built on wondrous selection. Nothing excites me more.

Even with such a wide selection, we're also zealous about quality. Some retailers divide their wares into three categories: good, better, and best. We found that standard too low, so our merchandising strategy is "Better, Best, Exceptional." Isn't that better? I just think the world is better off devoted to Better, Best, Exceptional rather than Good, Better, Best. We won't carry anything that's merely good. Insisting on durable items that meet our customers' expectation of quality, we start with Better: our least-expensive products, which are similar to higher-quality items at big-box retailers. Then we have Best: products that have added features or benefits and may cost a bit more. Finally, there is Exceptional: the finest on the market, which you likely can't find anywhere else and which will basically last forever. So, for example, in the garment-rack section at The Container Store, you'll find products with varying price points placed right next to one another so customers can touch and feel them and know exactly what kind of value they're getting for their money.

And yet, even with all these choices, we doggedly try to keep our customer from feeling overwhelmed by the myriad options throughout the store. Unlike many stores, which are set up like an obstacle course, with narrow aisles jammed full of products stacked high in a messy jumble, we work hard to set up our displays so it's easy to cruise through our aisles to find what you want and bypass what you don't. Our displays are clear, simple, and direct, all to help customers make meaningful choices. The result is that you feel as relaxed, organized, and energized in our stores as you'll feel back at home when you're living with your solutions. Whenever anyone asks Sharon which of our 10,000 products she likes best, she always says she doesn't have just one favorite—they're all special to her. That's probably because she knows each one so well.

My favorite is probably the Eagle Creek Pack-It Folder, which keeps your shirts, pants, and suits folded and wrinkle free and fits compactly in your suitcase (a thin plastic board helps you fold your shirts perfectly, making it a breeze to pack and unpack). And for home, my favorite is the FlipFold, which folds clothes to a uniform nine-by-twelve-inch size and makes it easy to neatly organize your drawers and shelves. There's nothing that makes me happier.

So yes, we're proud that we're universally applauded when it comes to service and selection, but we don't get nearly enough credit for our prices. That's because people just assume that a thriving specialty retailer—especially one offering such amazing customer service for free, including sophisticated custom elfa design—must have high prices to pay for all that. But let me give you a little quiz: What do you think is the average price for products in our stores? Keep in mind that our best-selling product is elfa, and an elfa solution can cost hundreds, even thousands of dollars because it's a component system (an entire solution versus just one product).

If you said $20 or $30, you'd be way off. The average price is just around $8. Another amazing statistic: Fully 80 percent of our products at The Container Store cost under $20. And we're stunningly competitive even with the mass merchants.

———<o>———

We're not the only retailer that gets an unfair reputation when it comes to price. But it's the retailers that focus solely on price that get the credit for great pricing. And it's surprising to me how overcredited discounters are for pricing and how unfairly retailers who focus on service and quality are marked as overpriced.

That's because price is mostly an issue of perception rather than reality (and it's also why some stores get an undeserved reputation for being inexpensive). Let's face it, no customer has time to compare all your prices to a competitor's. Customers can't even do much "showrooming" with us—checking out a product at the physical store and then buying it more cheaply online from somebody else. You can't showroom solutions. You can't showroom proprietary products. You just can't find those items anywhere else, online or offline (many products that look the same really aren't, because ours are of higher quality and will last longer). That makes us largely immune to competition from the giant online retailers that threaten many other brick-and-mortar retailers.

As for those products not exclusive to The Container Store, sometimes ours are less expensive than the mass merchants' and sometimes the big chains are cheaper—it depends on which store is having a sale. No store has the best price all the time. The days of being able to guarantee the lowest price are gone, because today most store managers have the power to change the price on any product at any time to stay competitive. Since customers never know exactly how much something is selling for at any given store, retailers just have to battle it out. Online retailers scramble the equation even more by offering free shipping and even occasionally avoiding their states' sales tax.

The perception that a store has high prices, whether true or not, is hard to change. A customer only has to see one product offered at a lower price elsewhere to think your whole store is overpriced. For example, my dad is not a very sophisticated housewares consumer. He's probably spent less than a hundred dollars in housewares his entire life. But to this day, he thinks we buy things for $1 and sell them for $9. I always give him a hard time about this. I say, "Dad, we don't do that. It's more like we buy something for a dollar and sell it for around two dollars, and that's pretty great for this business." He says, "No you don't, you buy it for one dollar and you sell it for nine dollars." And this is my own dad! But it's interesting that the more sophisticated a housewares consumer is, the better they think our pricing is. My mom was a very sophisticated housewares consumer and always understood that we were surprisingly price competitive for a specialty store with great service and selection. "You know, your prices are lower than all the department stores and other specialty stores you compete with," she used to tell me. "And you are even less expensive than the mass merchants half the time."

I've always said, "Don't worry about what people think. If we focus on that, and put signs on our counter that say 'We will meet or beat the best price in town,' we will lose our hard-won reputation for selection and service. Because people think there's no way we can be the best in all three areas. But the sophisticated consumer, like my mom, will know the truth—and she is our target customer."

But after all this, I must confess that the Great Recession a few years ago made me rethink my position. Price perception is more important than I thought—especially during an economic downturn. During the financial crisis of 2008, that terribly difficult time when consumers were tightening their belts, we permanently lowered thousands of retail price points. And we let people know about our great prices. In retrospect, I wish we had done this much earlier, because it turned out that our reputation for great selection and service didn't suffer in the least. We learned a valuable lesson: that many of our customers and all of our best customers are like my mom, sophisticated enough to know how well we execute this particular Foundation Principle—that we really do offer the best selection, service, and price.

How do we achieve this amazing feat? We do it by buying low from our vendors, thanks to our creatively crafted, mutually beneficial relationships. Most people think whatever retailer buys in the biggest volume always gets the lowest price. And yes, while volume certainly helps, other factors can be more important. The big discount chains buy more of the commodity storage and organization than we do. But for the few items we carry, we actually buy them more cheaply than the mass merchants do. How do we do that? We do that by having a better relationship with the vendor than the big chains do. And let me tell you, nobody is going to beat mass merchants on volume. But they're easy to beat on relationship. That's how the little Container Store can compete with those huge discount retailers.

Understand that these relationships don't happen overnight. They take years to develop. And because of that, it's hard for other stores to come close to the tight bonds we've spent decades developing with our vendors. We help them succeed in so many ways—displaying their wares beautifully, helping them develop new products we know our customers will love, finding efficiencies to keep their costs down. The vendor, meanwhile, does great things for us, like delivering quickly and giving us exclusive products, a better price, or a bigger supply of hot items. Creatively crafting these mutually beneficial relationships is one of my favorite parts of the business, and it's identical to building ideal relationships with your employees.

On the other hand, if you achieve high margins by selling high, rather than buying low, you'll be nothing more than a sweet little specialty store with no volume.

Having low prices and high margins creates a tremendous economic incentive to turn those high-margin products into your biggest sellers. It's another thing the world thinks is impossible. I'm mystified that so many retailers put so much effort into building up the volume of their low-margin, commodity-type products—mostly because that's the way things have always been done. But why not perfect the selling methodology of your highest-margin products? Why not give those products the best shelf space, train employees in those products more, advertise them more, and work harder with vendors to create high margins for both of you? In other words, why not spend more time in the gold mine rather than the copper mine? It's the best way for any business to succeed.

That's exactly what we did with elfa from day one, when it became our highest-margin item and our biggest seller. When new employees join us, it doesn't take long for them to figure out how important elfa is to this company. They understand that it's a good idea to get very good at selling elfa and to learn everything there is to know about it (we like to say, in our internal training and communication initiatives, "All Eyes on elfa"). Owning elfa gives us the huge benefits of vertical integration, of course—since we're the manufacturer, importer, distributor, marketer, and retailer. If we didn't own elfa and have this vertical integration, the product would easily sell for more than twice what we sell it for. And in spite of the gross margin and great pricing, elfa is the greatest value in the store. You can get an unattractive particleboard chest of drawers that costs the same or more. And it's particleboard! But elfa lasts a lifetime and it looks much better the whole time it's lasting.

The final price tag, however, is less important than offering products that "transcend value" and evoke a powerful emotion in the customer. What I mean by that is that the value of any product you buy should transcend the actual price you pay at the register. When Stanley Marcus befriended us in those early days, he taught us that if you buy something that costs maybe 20 percent more but functions maybe 150 percent better, is, say, 200 percent more beautiful, and, on top of that, might last 600 percent longer, then that item has real value. Isn't that a great definition of value? Then Sharon came along and said, "Transcending value is when you do everything Stanley Marcus says and, on top of that, you create an emotional response by the customers. Because that's what people want—an emotional connection."

Think about some of your favorite things: your favorite pair of shoes, your very favorite tie, your absolutely favorite car among all the cars you've ever owned. I mean, those are not just worth what you paid for them. The merchant has succeeded in transcending value for you. I think it's the highest art form of the merchant.

I have a certain necktie, and when I wear it, I don't hear three or four people tell me, "Nice tie." I hear something like fifteen people tell me, "Hey, Kip, that's really a cool tie!" And I bought that tie in New York at Bergdorf Goodman. I probably paid $200 for it. But every time I wear it, by the end of the day, I start to think, "I must be looking pretty damn good today." So you think that tie was worth what I paid for it? Transcending value and evoking an emotional connection. That's what we look for in every product we include as part of The Container Store. That's what we're trying to create with our vendor partners when we develop products together. We want to create the customer dance. We want our customer to do a little dance every morning when she opens her closet door. That's a key reason why people don't just say they like The Container Store, they love The Container Store. People want emotion. That's what they really want from a product, retailer, or brand.

Or take a trash can. I like to say that even a trash can really can make you smile. If it has high quality and innovative design, fits in that space in your kitchen perfectly, looks great, and functions beautifully, you're not only happy with your trash can, you love it. Let's be honest—you're actually proud of your trash can! You might even show it to your sister-in-law or your next-door neighbor. No, that's not aberrant behavior—you're just passionate about something and want to share your enthusiasm.

Here's a true story that gets to the heart of what I'm talking about. One day, a gentleman came into one of our Atlanta stores straight from his divorce proceedings. The papers had just been signed, and the first place he stopped on his way home was The Container Store. Why? Because his ex-wife had gotten everything in the settlement—including one particular trash can. That trash can was so special to him that he needed to replace it immediately. Yes, it was only a trash can, but to him it mattered. The man was ready for a fresh start, a new beginning—and fortunately, we were able to help him.

Over the years, as we developed our approach to offering the Best Selection, Service & Price, we knew there was one final frontier where we had yet to prove ourselves. You can't really call yourself a national retailer without a presence in Manhattan, where the competition is fiercest and customers are notoriously hard to please. In early 2003, after many years of looking, we finally found the perfect spot on Sixth Avenue in the Ladies' Mile district of Chelsea, where America's most famous department stores once stood. Could The Container Store and its unconventional style of doing business thrive in the toughest retail environment in America? We were about to find out.

———◦———

I was sitting in my office in March of 2003 when Val Richardson, our vice-president of real estate, came in. "So, Kip…" she said. "Are we ready to finalize this deal?"

I smiled and welcomed Val into my office. We all feel fantastically fortunate to have Val on our team; she is truly the best retail real estate executive in the country. Val can do it all—find the most promising markets for our customer base, locate excellent spaces, negotiate with landlords, and close the deal in a way that works for everybody. Previously, John Mullen was responsible for new store locations (he joined our management team as vice-president of real estate in 1991). John found and negotiated many of the wonderful locations we still have today, including one of our finest locations, in the affluent New York suburb of White Plains. We're also forever grateful to him for finding Val to replace him when he retired in 2000. Val's arrival was another case of the universe conspiring to assist us. After earning a sterling reputation at Barnes & Noble and Ann Taylor in Manhattan, she had already decided to move back to Dallas, her hometown, when John approached her about the job.

One of Val's first assignments was to find a great spot in Manhattan. Once we decide to go into a certain market, we're extremely thorough and meticulous about finding the absolute perfect location, as we did with recent store openings in Palo Alto and in King of Prussia, Pennsylvania. When we searched Las Vegas, we held out for a long while before settling on a truly A+ location—a former Borders bookstore in Town Square with a great mix of local and tourist traffic.

We used to think we had to confine ourselves to the very largest metropolitan markets, like Los Angeles, Chicago, Dallas,

Boston, and Atlanta. And we will continue to add stores to those great markets. But we discovered something very important shortly after the Great Recession. We were delighted to find that smaller markets, with maybe 2 million in population—places like Indianapolis, Raleigh, Charlotte, and Nashville—love us just as much as the LAs and the Chicagos. In fact, the grand-opening hoopla and buildup are arguably even greater as the whole town goes nuts about finally getting their own The Container Store.

Much of what I jokingly call the Indianapolis-ing of TCS has to do with pent-up demand. The best location in Indy costs far less than the best location in, say, Atlanta, and the sales are about the same. So these stores immediately become extremely profitable. We get invested capital back in just about two years and achieve what we call a first-year, four-wall EBITDA of almost 25 percent. And while our new Farmers Market store in Los Angeles will do great, there are so many Indys out there.

That's one reason we're so optimistic about our future—literally hundreds of such new markets exist around the country, giving us a tremendously long runway for continued growth.

When it comes to growth, I often hear, "You have so few stores. Why have you grown so slowly?" And I always say we don't measure our growth by our store count, we measure it by our sales. In fact, over the last thirty-six years I haven't seen anyone grow faster for longer. Clearly, our historical average compounded annual growth rate of 21 percent has come not from opening hundreds of new stores but from maximizing the potential of each one, even relocating to a bigger, better spot in the same city or renovating the existing space. This has been a hugely successful strategy for us, generating the kind of stunning growth rate that is extremely rare in retail while still leaving us hundreds of potential new markets. It's good to be immature in retail. I feel like we're a racehorse ready to get out of the barn and run. Imagine having 68 or so stores and feeling extremely confident that we can expand to at least 300 stores in the United States alone—almost five times more than our current store count.

And today, after thirty-six years of successful expansion, we're a "first call" for landlords and developers. We feel like the belle of the ball. It's taken us thirty-six years to achieve this, and it's the greatest achievement for a high-growth retailer. The best locations, the best pricing—it's retail Heaven. Again, it's that superabundance of opportunities thing I talked about earlier.

Val did a great job finding and negotiating for the Sixth Avenue space in Manhattan, a historic building previously occupied by a Today's Man clothing store. It was an incredibly complicated deal. Today's Man was going out of business, there was a long procession of bankruptcy court filings and lawyers, and we had to deal with two landlords to get the space—20,000 square feet on the street level and another 20,000 feet in the basement to handle the huge volume of products the store would need. Somehow, Val managed to pull the deal together in a matter of weeks.

Still, I hesitated. First, the rent was astronomical. For that kind of money, we could open six stores elsewhere in the country.

Just as worrisome, this was a quick turnaround. By the time the paperwork was completed, we would have only six months to get the store up and running—a process that usually takes a year. In this case, we would have to completely renovate the historic building while preserving and showcasing some of its wonderful architecture. None of our stores had more than 60 employees, but suddenly we would have to hire and train more than 200 top-notch 1=3 employees to serve the tens of thousands of customers we hoped would flow through our doors each week. Those were huge numbers for us. I remembered what happened in Houston in 1988 and 1989, when we couldn't handle the high volume or hire and train enough good workers fast enough.

Many other factors gave me pause. Most Manhattan shoppers don't use cars, so we would need a delivery service, something we had never attempted before (and we told ourselves back in the beginning that we'd never need or start one). Other retailers in New York told me horror stories about employee theft. And there was a high-volume Bed Bath & Beyond right across the street—not to mention scores of other stores only a short walk, cab ride, or subway ride away that would test our commitment to Best Selection, Service & Price as never before.

I have been called a percolator. That is, I like to take my time making decisions, to really think things through from all angles. But this time there was no time. Val was being patient, but I knew everybody was waiting—the bankruptcy court, the lawyers, the landlords...

So I did what I like to do in situations like this: I called Gordon Segal.

Gordon, of course, is a true retail legend. He started Crate & Barrel in Chicago with his wife, Carole, in 1962, shortly after they got married and couldn't find the kind of elegant and inexpensive housewares with Scandinavian design they found during their honeymoon in the Caribbean. "There's got to be other young couples with good taste and no money like us," they thought. Talk about predicting the future! As baby boomers came of age, Gordon turned his little shop in Chicago into a famous nationwide brand that in recent years has gone international, an incredible accomplishment.

I was thrilled to meet Gordon in the 1980s at various trade shows in Chicago, Europe, and dinners and such, and we soon became dear friends. Every chance we got, we hung out to talk shop, and we agree that those were some of the best conversations we'd ever had. Gordon has been such an important mentor to me, along with Stanley Marcus—in fact, we went to Stanley's memorial service together in 2002. To be influenced by those two men, two of the greatest merchant princes of our time—well, that made the memorial service a very powerful moment for me.

Gordon knew the Manhattan market well, having brought Crate & Barrel there eight years earlier. After hearing my concerns, he said simply, "Do it." What about the trucks parked on Sixth Avenue that obstruct the view of the store? And the street vendors and guys hanging out on the sidewalk? What about the rent? The sales volume? I had a thousand questions, but to every question, Gordon said, "Don't worry—you'll do great. You won't regret it."

That was the final push I needed. After some last consultations with Sharon and Melissa, we took the plunge. It's funny, but despite all the challenges ahead of us, I immediately felt a certain calming confidence. And why not? I was surrounded by the best retail team in America. I just knew that together we would find a way to get the job done and have a ball doing it.

—◁◇▷—

We completed the renovations during the summer of 2003 and prepared for a late-November opening. For us, that was a very short time, because every new store opening is quite an elaborate process—and an incredibly fun and exciting one, like adding a new member to the family.

We "Grand Open" unlike any other retailer. It is, without doubt, one of the most successful aspects of our business. Our goal is for each store to immediately—from day one—perform like a mature store, as opposed to opening slowly with a strategy to ramp up sales over several years. To accomplish that, we must do a tremendous amount of work on the front end. Understanding the local community we're becoming a part of—and ingratiating ourselves—takes time, money, energy, and focus.

Our process begins, of course, with assembling a great 1=3 store team, starting with managers, whom we hire months before an opening. And once the team is on board, as you know by now, we provide weeks of formal training before a single customer ever sets foot in the store. Of course, we spend a lot of time teaching the new employees about Conscious Capitalism and our seven Foundation Principles. Top executives from our Dallas head-quarters, managers of other stores, and area and regional directors who oversee stores in various geographical regions fly in to offer support, training, advice, and encouragement to the new team.

During the week of the grand opening, our product buyers personally deliver hours of training directly to the team, explaining each product, how it works, and how to sell it. This is unique in the retail industry. Employees love it because often our buyers know more about the products than the manufacturers themselves. You might even say that our buyers are the rock stars of the housewares industry. Melissa and Sharon also do presentations about our unusual company culture, company goals, and merchandising strategy, and other executives explain our extensive marketing campaign—from ads in newspapers and magazines and on radio and billboards to deft uses of direct mail and social media and tons of free publicity from bloggers and the local media. We invite all the local movers and shakers to our grand-opening party, knowing they'll be so impressed they'll quickly spread the word among their friends and colleagues.

It means so much to our new employees to have the company support them in every way possible, and it really seems to touch them to hear directly from us—being trained by the folks who were there when the doors of our very first store opened. They understand they're a select bunch—since only 3 percent of all applicants are hired—and when they gather for that first huddle before the store opens, they have a deep, visceral understanding that they're not working for some anonymous retail chain. Now they're part of a close-knit community based on ethical values that performs a crucial service for customers who adore us. It's a very powerful experience to feel so much love and respect from their coworkers and management, to be part of such an amazing team. On the last day of training, tears of joy, gratitude, and camaraderie are overflowing.

About six months before opening, we create a marketing partnership with a nonprofit that helps us stoke excitement and build the buzz in that market—The Container Store is coming to their city! We look for an organization with supporters in our target demographic: busy women who need organization in their lives, who like to shop and are passionate about the charity's work. Before the Vegas opening, for example, we partnered with the Junior League of Las Vegas. For months before our opening, we appeared at that group's fund-raising events and provided product giveaways for their swag bags, auction items, and elfa closet makeovers.

The Thursday night before the store opens, we host a private preview party in the store for the nonprofit members and our customers in the market. It's a real party, with a dance floor, a band, great food and drink. We then give 10 percent of our weekend sales to the nonprofit. Not 5 percent of the after-tax profit, but 10 percent of total grand-opening-weekend sales. And long after the grand opening, we continue to enjoy a relationship and partnership with those nonprofits in our communities.

Now, about that party—oh, what a bash! Melissa always works from an "everything matters" standpoint, and her team takes that to heart, lavishing attention on every little nuance as if it's the most important thing in the world—which for us (the organization experts) it is. That party—like the entire store-opening process—is a masterful display of organization and execution, like putting on a flawless wedding for 2,000 people. Guests can't actually buy the products on the shelves until opening day, which only whets their appetites even more. Vendors attend because they know it will be a great time and they feel like an integral part of the team. There's lots of dancing and excitement. One thing this company really knows how to do is throw a party, something I know my family back in New Orleans is proud of—in fact, they come to a lot of our parties.

A certain amount of bravery goes into opening stores so aggressively—and we have had times when investors, and even some in our management team, have questioned it: "Can't we open a store without doing all that?" The answer is no. We actually tried cutting back once or twice, and those stores ended up being far less successful than they should have been. In every other instance, we stuck to our approach, and our grand openings have always been ridiculously successful.

Here's the bottom line: In thirty-six years, we have never closed a store because of underperformance. We've only moved undersized, older stores to better, larger locations. In short, this is pretty remarkable.

On Saturday morning, just before the doors open, some of our top executives and other great employees treat the new staff to a choreographed song-and-dance routine. Wearing hats that symbolize the community we're entering—showgirl headpieces in Vegas, Mickey Mouse ears in Orlando, Stanford caps in Palo Alto—our talented troupe breaks into song to the tune of "Another Op'nin', Another Show," from the Broadway show *Kiss Me, Kate*:

> *Your first big day is about to start*
> *With Man in the Desert, you'll fill the cart*
> *At nine o'clock they'll be through the door*
> *Another opening of another store*
> *Another opening, just the greatest opening of the Las Veeeegaaaas*
> *   store!!!*

Before every opening, we conduct a search and pick one Super Fan of The Container Store, who wears a crown and a sash that says SUPER FAN. She gets to be the store's very first customer, pushing around a special gold shopping cart (she also gets a gift card and free products). In Las Vegas, we picked Lisa Wolfrum, who did an inventory of her home and calculated that she had purchased over 150 Container Store products—and there wasn't even a store in her city yet! She'd bought most of it during trips to San Diego, where her husband's family lived, and often made up excuses to drive there just so she could shop at The Container Store. That's the kind of passion and loyalty we hear about from our customers constantly. So we like to return the favor: When our Super Fan enters the store wearing the sash, a long line of employees cheers like crazy.

When the doors finally open to the general public, we're ready to go! A line of hundreds of customers is snaking around the building. As customers charge into the store, it feels like floodgates opening. Employees are cheering and giving them high fives. Within minutes, the place is jammed. Talk about an Air of Excitement! This is what I love so much about retail—all that unbridled joy and energy as our new employees eagerly help customers solve their problems. Great music plays from our sound system and sunlight streams through our floor-to-ceiling windows. We all hit the sales floor just like in the good ol' days—chatting up customers and showing new employees what Man in the Desert Selling is really all about.

I've been known to get teary-eyed on occasion. And those Saturday mornings, from the song-and-dance number to the cheering employees to the crowds of customers packing the store, well, those can be some of those occasions. I walk around, deliriously happy, watching it all like a proud papa.

———<◊>———

As we prepared to open our Sixth Avenue store, we thought Manhattan would be a great market for us. After all, New Yorkers have less space than just about anybody and they have less time than just about anybody.

But how would we handle the huge volume we expected—or more precisely, the volume we needed to make the store profitable? And to get the whole thing up and running in just a few months? All of our Foundation Principles would be tested as never before.

Knowing this would be our highest-volume store, we of course had to keep our shelves well stocked, even on the busiest days, when thousands of customers would flood the aisles. Many retailers use multiple warehouses around the country—or have their vendors ship products directly to the stores—but from the very beginning we've used a single centralized distribution center in Dallas to receive shipments, exercise quality control, and then ship products out to each store. This creates many efficiencies and frees up our store staff to focus on customer service rather than replenishment. It's also great for our company culture to be so close to the products and allows our buyers to simply walk out to the dock whenever they need to check out a product.

But our Sixth Avenue store would have to be different. To ensure enough supply, we would have to set up a mini distribution center in the basement that would also be responsible for taking the large number of orders coming in by phone and online, as well as handling delivery and customer pickup orders. We had never done anything like that before. We also had to hire people to work around the clock to keep this distribution system humming, another first.

We couldn't uphold the reputation for good customer service that we'd worked so hard to achieve for decades unless we found lots of 1=3 employees—quickly—in a city not always known for great customer service. Would New Yorkers interviewing for jobs find our approach to business hopelessly naïve and corny? We know from experience that our unique company culture simply will not work unless all our employees truly understand it and embrace it.

———◦———

I'm inspired by other business leaders who are constantly thinking about how to maximize the positive impact their companies have on society. By cofounding Whole Foods Market, for example, John Mackey has probably done more to increase the health and life-spans of American consumers than just about anybody I can think of. Whole Foods has changed our way of thinking about nutrition, health, animal husbandry, and sustainability, and that has changed every other grocery chain's approach, too. That's why *Esquire* magazine named him one of the Seventy-Five Most Influential People of the Twenty-First Century. There is no doubt that John has enhanced the quality of life of millions of people by being deeply conscious of his wake and always considering the impact his business decisions can have on the world.

We didn't call it Conscious Capitalism at the time, but leaders like John gave us inspiration when we faced huge challenges like opening that first New York store. Fortunately, we had a phenomenal team led by store manager Don Leary, who had previously managed our highest-volume location until that point, in White Plains, and is now a regional director in California. Don started working part-time in Tysons Corner in 1994 because he felt burned out by his other job, a stressful executive position at a nonprofit health group in Washington, DC, and wanted a change of pace.

"I thought, 'This is crazy!'" he recalls. "Here I am, running million-dollar nonprofits, and now I'm selling plastic containers?" But Don found the job so challenging and rewarding that he decided to make his career at The Container Store, moving up the ranks at stores in Maryland, in Chicago, and on the East Coast. "Going from a nonprofit to a for-profit company, I didn't feel like I was changing my real desire," he says. "If you really do care for people, it's a logical progression. We create a great experience for customers, and all the employees are happy. So the idea of giving to other people in a different way really resonated with me."

Don and his team went into overdrive, assisted by our Dallas headquarters, hiring and training 200 employees quickly, setting up the Manhattan logistics operation down-stairs, and moving into the renovated space—which, despite the huge volume we expected, was actually the same size as every other location, about 25,000 square feet. We loaded Don's team up with all the support it needed so it had every conceivable resource at its disposal. "We were so energized by the opportu-nity and excitement, and felt so supported by the home office, that nobody ever said, 'What? How are we going to do this?'" Don recalls.

Meanwhile, our marketing team pulled out all the stops to let people know we were coming to town—securing billboard space in Times Square and making our grand-opening party one of the hottest events in the city, with 4,000 guests dancing to the reggae, rock, and soul tunes of the rollicking Cafe Wha? house band. We were honored that New York City mayor Mike Bloom-berg cut the ribbon on Saturday morning—especially since he rarely found time for such events. (When our doors finally opened, we were confident, but, of course, you don't really know whether you have a hit or a flop until the crowds start to arrive—or don't.)

In the store's first minutes, only a few people trickled in. In fact, the first few hours were nerve-wracking: "Where is every-body?" Later, we realized what was happening: New Yorkers don't get up early on Saturday morning (particularly not in Chelsea)! The city that never sleeps was actually sleeping in, then enjoying a leisurely brunch. By late morning, the crowds finally started to arrive, and amazingly enough, it turned out to be our biggest grand-opening weekend to date. Now, more than a decade later, they still haven't stopped coming. Sixth Avenue remains by far our highest-grossing store and has become almost an institution in the famous Ladies' Mile corridor.

How did we make it in New York? Mostly by knocking the ball out of the park when it came to offering the country's most discerning shoppers the Best Selection, Service & Price.

New Yorkers were thrilled and delighted with our selection. The city had very few big-box retailers back then—and even today, most stores in Manhattan tend to be quite small—so I think customers were shocked to see our astonishing varieties of hangers, food-storage containers, and trash cans, thanks to our replenishment system working at a fever pitch downstairs in the basement as products flew off the shelves. And the funky, hip feel of many of our products—the reason so many celebrities from Taylor Swift to Kim Kardashian swoon about us in their Twitter feeds, and Brooke Shields raves on *Today* about The Container Store as her go-to place when she's stressed—seems tailor-made for style-conscious New Yorkers. As for our service, it became legendary in Manhattan almost immediately. People were amazed when we carried their bags out to their cabs for them. They just couldn't get over that.

Three years later, after we opened our second Manhattan store, at Lexington Avenue and East Fifty-Eighth Street, a group of customers got into the elevator with Robin Soumas, who was then the store manager. "Where did you get these people?" they asked. "They can't be New Yorkers. They're too nice—they must be from Texas, right?" Robin laughed and assured them everyone on the staff was from New York. We hired such amazing people, in fact, that the feared employee theft problem other retailers had warned us about failed to materialize in our New York stores.

It's funny, but every time we've expanded—first beyond Dallas, then beyond Texas, then around the country—people have worried about whether we could find enough 1=3 employees to continue our tradition of offering superior customer service and Man in the Desert Selling. But every time, without fail, we've found great employees, proving that people who believe in the universal truths of the Foundation Principles really are everywhere.

As for price, New Yorkers immediately began raving about that, too. Holding firm to our policy of keeping the same prices in Manhattan as elsewhere really helped us. Sophisticated shoppers understood how extraordinary our prices are. I believe that our New York stores ended up being far more successful than they would have if we had taken the short-term approach of simply raising prices.

As we were preparing to open the Sixth Avenue store—and even after it was up and running—we found ourselves constantly saying, "Well, New York is different." And there are some things we do differently there. Because folks in Manhattan tend to be in a rush and don't have cars, we created our own proprietary technology called GoShop! Scan & Deliver. It's a handheld device that allows you to scan products, pick a delivery date, and let us gather the items and deliver them to your door—for just $25 in Manhattan. No shopping cart, no checkout, no dragging bags home—just zap the products you want and go. (Right now, it's only available in New York, but we're looking into whether it might work in other areas of the country.)

GoShop! was a huge hit from day one. A group from IBM came to tour the store to learn how our state-of-the-art technology worked. The *New York Times* wrote a glowing article that read, "There is no need for a shopping cart, no tension when you try to hail a taxi with seven bags on your arm, no pinched look from the doorman, no neck strain as you haul the goods upstairs. They are delivered to your door...by the end of the day."

Now, we didn't do everything perfectly in our Sixth Avenue store. We failed to anticipate the huge demand for delivery, forcing us to scramble to catch up. We had to figure out how to bundle and bag products for customers heading home by subway or bus. And our distribution and logistics system needed plenty of tweaks to keep up with the huge volume. At such moments, it was tempting to make exceptions to our usual way of doing business because, "Well, New York is different."

But when it came to our core values, in the end, we didn't change a thing. I'm convinced that our success in New York City came because we chose to embrace our Foundation Principles with renewed vigor and allowed those principles to guide us toward solutions to whatever problems we faced. GoShop!, after all, is really just a high-tech way of making sure we live up to our promise to offer the Best Service. As Don Leary reflects: "I think once we all held hands and said, 'Why should New York be so different? It's a Container Store, it just has more volume,' that made a big difference. Instead of trying to overdo everything, we learned how to keep it simple."

9

Intuition Does Not Come to an Unprepared Mind. You Need to Train Before It Happens.

I've always believed in the power of intuition, going back to my boyhood days fishing and my college years playing poker. After all, when it comes to predicting the habits of trout and gamblers, your rational mind can only take you so far. Much later, as a businessman, I noticed that many of my best decisions also happened when I trusted my intuition.

In the summer of 2007, I faced a critical decision that would affect the future course of our beloved company. We had to choose among top bidders who were all hoping to buy a majority share of The Container Store. If our intuition was right, our company would continue its phenomenal upward trajectory; our shareholders, management team, and employees would all prosper; and we could continue to help our loyal customers improve their lives. But if we chose the wrong financial partner, our life's work could be ruined by new owners who didn't understand our quirky culture, thus bringing our fairy-tale run to an inglorious end.

I'll get to that story in just a bit, but now I'd like to explain why we think intuition is so important. A few years after we started The Container Store, I read an interview with the writer Roy Rowan about his book *The Intuitive Manager*, in which he told a story about Albert Einstein.

Like most of us, Einstein had the experience of sitting on a stationary train and looking over at a train on a parallel track that was pulling forward. It gave Einstein the sensation of moving backward. However, unlike the rest of us, used the experience, in a flash of intuition, to help him conceive the theory of relativity. Have you ever seen those wheels spinning backward? Probably. Did you think "E=MC^2" when that happened? Me neither. The difference is that Albert Einstein had a lifetime of studying physics and mathematics. Intuition doesn't come to an unprepared mind. You need to train before it happens.

"A new idea comes suddenly and in a rather intuitive way," Einstein once said. "But intuition is nothing but the outcome of earlier intellectual experience."

I placed the Rowan interview in my Philosophy Epistle File and kept thinking about it until one day I realized that Rowan had perfectly articulated our training philosophy when he summarized Einstein's experience: "Intuition does not come to an unprepared mind. You need to train before it happens."

That statement was so profound that I made it one of our seven Foundation Principles. For us, it means that we want our employees to use their intuition—their wonderful life experience—to anticipate the needs of our customers and to recommend the appropriate solutions. We know that to help our employees do this, we must first provide all the necessary information—the training—so they know how best to apply their intuition. This is why we have a tremendous, never-ending commitment to training.

All full-time employees of The Container Store, as I've said, receive nearly 300 hours of training in their first year (compared to the national retail average of only 8 hours); part-time employees at The Container Store get nearly 200 hours in their first year. In short, when you're hired by us, you receive about 40 hours of training before you ever reach the sales floor. And that's just the beginning. Training continues—day in, day out, year after year. This ongoing process is a critical part of our employee-first culture.

We live in a society where people are brought up to believe that only logic and not intuition should be used in business. But someone very wise once said that "intuition is the sum total of one's life experience." If that's the case, why would you leave it at home when you go to work in the morning? Sure, we all need to use logic and analysis in our lives, but you'll be so much smarter if you use both logic and intuition—your left brain and right brain. Einstein certainly had the necessary background in mathematics and physics, but it took a daring moment of intuition to contradict Newton's laws of physics and to come up with his theory of relativity.

I've only met one person who disagreed with me about the importance of employees' using their intuition. It happened when Garrett and I were giving a presentation about our Foundation Principles to *Fortune* magazine's Most Admired Companies in America. We shared the stage with a woman who said, "Kip, I don't think I want my employees using their intuition." And I said, "That's so weird, because we really never hear anybody disagreeing with our Foundation Principles, just like nobody disagrees with the Golden Rule." And she said, "Well, I want my employees to strictly use logic and to follow procedure and use no intuition whatsoever." I said, "Really, that's so interesting—please tell me more about your business." And she said, "We manage and operate nuclear power plants." I said, "Okay! I agree with you! You definitely don't want any intuition there!"

So I guess there are a few exceptions. But in nearly every other situation, you don't want to straitjacket employees with a manual about how to do their jobs. Instead, we unshackle our employees to follow their own individual creative genius. That's when you get achievement and excellence and wild amounts of creativity and productivity plus great happiness from your employees. And that's very exciting.

The truth is, many employees are afraid of using their intuition because they don't want to make a mistake and be humiliated, reprimanded, or fired. That's why it's so important to create an environment that's safe and secure and warm—so people feel brave enough to take chances and make mistakes. They must know that their managers and coworkers have their backs in an atmosphere of great mutual respect. When managers create a climate of fear, rather than love, this approach won't work. You get nothing close to full productivity, innovation, or individual creative genius.

Before we open a new store, I tell our new employees, "We know you may be a little nervous anticipating waiting on that first customer. But guess what? We know you're great because we only hire great, 1=3 employees. And you have more training than any retail salesperson in a new store in America. So go ahead and be vulnerable. Say, 'I don't know.' Go ahead and screw up. That's how you learn, by making mistakes, by taking chances. It won't matter—we'll still think you're fabulous. In fact, we'll probably give you a hug."

———◄○►———

It all sounds wonderful, but intuition requires proper training. The better you are at something—whether it's dancing, playing the violin, or Man in the Desert Selling—the more reliable, brilliant, and touched by genius your intuition will be. I've been fly-fishing all my life. So if I'm teaching you to fly-fish, and I intuitively think there's a trout under that rock, there probably is. If you've never fished before and you think there's a trout under that rock, there probably isn't.

Of course, training is more than just receiving information from management. We want our employees to have an obsession with learning and to seek out new information to further their development and career. If they forget some bit of training, that's okay. All they have to do is ask somebody, because everyone at our company wants to help.

One reason training is more important at The Container Store than at other retailers is because our motto is "We sell the hard stuff." We actually tell our buyers to look for products that are hard to sell. Why? Because we know other retailers won't touch those products, giving us an exclusive and yet another reason for customers to shop with us. It may seem crazy to base a store around things that are hard to sell, like our elfa shelving system. But we make it work, selling tons of products like elfa that make people come back for more—a new shelving system for every closet in the house (like potato chips they can't stop eating). And we make it work because our deep commitment to employee training creates unparalleled customer service.

Our Gift Wrap Wonderland during Christmastime is an excellent example of how superior training pays off. Being helped in our gift wrap section is like visiting an art museum with a friend who is a connoisseur of fine art. You walk away from the museum with a greater understanding of and love for the paintings. You become so eager to own some of it, to show it off to other people, that you begin to feel like a connoisseur yourself.

When we train our employees, we emphasize that they are the peers of the customer. Since many of our employees *were* customers, they're in a perfect position to tell our shoppers the story of a product and to explain how it will solve whatever organizational problem they have.

———◄◌►———

In none of our stores will you ever hear an employee say, "That's not my department." That's because all employees are trained in every product in the store, including our elfa system. This is no simple task, since we carry thousands of multifunctional products and designing an elfa space is a mix of art and science. But it shows how seriously we take our commitment to customer service and to making every employee a storage and organization expert.

Each of our stores has its own manager of training and a full-time sales trainer, which is virtually unheard-of in retail. They give first-year, full-time employees more than ninety hours of development training—all designed to help them reach their full potential, using skills assessments, performance reviews, training videos, and coaching. More than forty hours are devoted to company communication, including conference calls and events training; another thirty hours to learn the cash register, order processing, and various sales campaigns; and twenty-five hours to training in selling elfa. And everyone hired at our home office in Dallas works at one of our nearby stores for a period to help them truly understand our company culture, store operations, and the customer experience.

We also devote more than thirty hours of training to our Foundation Principles and Conscious Capitalism (which are really one and the same thing). As I mentioned earlier, most people can't even remember the Ten Commandments—that universal set of values we all think we know by heart—so we believe it's critical to constantly reinforce our company's core values. We want our employees not just to remember the words of our Foundation Principles but to truly absorb them and apply them to their jobs every day.

One employee described our training this way: "Training is more of a burden or an afterthought at most other companies. The level of excitement and intent in training is so strong at The Container Store, not like anywhere else I have ever been." Another employee came up with a perfect definition of training as we practice it: "Training is the time to let the culture wash over you."

Our most ambitious and spectacular training event is something we call Staff Meeting, which we hold intermittently at our Dallas headquarters—sometimes every eighteen months, sometimes every few years. At our last Staff Meeting, 330 employees from our stores, home office, and distribution center gathered for three days of inspiration, celebration, reflection, and company updates. It's quite a production but well worth it because we keep each Staff Meeting alive long after it's over by emphasizing its themes and then distributing its content often through our many channels of constant communication. (I'll discuss Staff Meeting more in the next chapter.)

People always ask me, "How can you possibly recoup your investment in all this training?" My answer is "Let me count the ways."

The most obvious is that our employees stay with the company practically forever. They can tell we really mean it when we say we want this to be the last place they ever work—why else would we spend so much money training them? With a turnover rate of less than 10 percent—compared to the industry average of about 100 percent—we save millions of dollars by not having to go through the long process of searching, interviewing, hiring, and training employees who meet our high 1=3 standards. People join our company and they never leave.

After all, doesn't it make more sense to hang on to your employees and let all their training and experience accrue so they perform their jobs brilliantly? Man in the Desert Selling doesn't just happen—it requires lots of teaching and practice. When a customer who came in for a shoe box leaves with the elfa closet makeover that's really the solution she needs, it suddenly becomes clear that all that training has paid for itself, and then some. In fact, I often tell employees that the only way we're ever going to get our training investment back is by convincing them that using their intuition is a wonderful thing.

Our commitment to training also pays off in our relationships with vendors, who know that our employees really know how to sell their products, and to tell the story behind each one. That's a big reason vendors give us such terrific pricing—and that, in turn, means we can afford to pay and train our employees so well in an inspiring, never-ending virtuous cycle.

There's another, subtler payoff. As every educator knows, teaching makes you better at whatever subject you're teaching. Talking about intuition so much has made our top leadership team more adept at using our own intuition, especially when it comes time to make a critical decision. For example, in the fall of 2006, we decided we needed to pursue a financial partner. As we began to navigate the unfamiliar world of Wall Street bankers, lawyers, and private equity firms, we had a feeling that our final decision—one that would determine the fate of our company— would have to come straight from the gut.

———◦———

Like a lot of entrepreneurs, we started our company with whatever funds we could rustle up at the time. We've always funded our expansion through proceeds of the business—we still do today. And in truth, we were so focused on running the business that we had no real long-term ownership strategy. In the fall of 2006, when some of our existing shareholders wanted liquidity, and still holding on to my longtime dream of putting more stock into the hands of the employees, I didn't think we could go any longer without a different ownership strategy. I had become increasingly insistent that our executive team and other key employees be granted stock in the company. This is vitally important to me, and has been from the very beginning, because it's clear that only through their tremendous effort and loyalty has our brand become so successful. By the end of 2006, we had thirty-eight stores and nearly $500 million in sales. I also knew that even our most selfless and dedicated employees would be crazy not to consider the great job offers they were getting regularly from *Fortune* 500 companies, especially publicly traded firms that could offer lucrative stock options. Word was spreading about The Container Store, and other companies definitely wanted a piece of our magic.

I knew, too, that continuing to sell shares here and there, as we had been doing, could eventually result in our losing control of the company. We needed a plan. I sought advice from the Container Store's banker, my great friend Norman Bagwell, then Dallas president of JPMorgan Chase, and he suggested I speak with Rob Holmes, head of JPMorgan's global retail investment banking—his group was renowned for its banking practices as the best on the Street. Rob was very excited about the chance to work with us and introduced me to Jim Woolery, then a senior partner at one of the best mergers and acquisitions (M&A) law firms in the country, Cravath, Swaine & Moore, with whom he had worked on several major deals. "The Container Store is a real darling of the retail space," Jim told me. "You have never done an IPO or been sold and you are still operated by the founders, so the company is almost in a pristine state from an ownership standpoint, which is rare for firms with your life-span and success."

I showed Rob and Jim around our home office in Dallas and explained our Foundation Principles, our yummy culture, how we try to stay flexible like Gumby, and the power of our ripple-effect wakes. They were polite but confided later that they had been rolling their eyes. "Here we are, a couple of grizzled, typical New York banker-lawyer types," says Jim, "and we come into your Dallas headquarters, where everybody's very energetic and enthusiastic and happy and smiling. That was very odd for us to deal with. We were kind of looking at each other funny out of the corners of our eyes. But, of course, you got to us. You broke us down."

We're used to that kind of reaction. We know the secret of our success—that it's the culture that drives the value of the business; our company's performance metrics prove that to even the most cynical folks. As I told Jimmy Elliott, then head of global M&A at JPMorgan, when we began the process, "This may not be the biggest deal you ever worked on, but I promise you, it will end up being the most joyful thing you have ever done."

We concluded that we would immediately stop selling small pieces of the company and create a clean ownership slate by selling a majority stake. The timing was perfect, Jimmy Elliott said: The M&A market was red hot, the likes of which the financial markets had rarely seen.

Over the next few weeks, I had a series of long, soul-searching discussions with Garrett and his family, and with Sharon and Melissa. Finally, we came back to Rob with our thoughts. We would consider selling, but only if three conditions were met: (1) Our existing leadership team would retain complete operational and strategic control; (2) Our management team and 200 or so employees would receive robust equity in the company to keep them with us for a long time, which we believed was a pre-requisite for serving our unique culture; (3) Our beloved exiting shareholders would receive maximum value for their shares. If any of those three terms was not met, the deal was off.

Even as we ticked off those conditions, I knew how outland-ish they must sound. We would be asking bidders for what bank-ers call a control premium—a higher share price paid in exchange for gaining control of the enterprise—but in this case, they would not get control. Which, of course, would seem to defeat the whole purpose of paying a control premium. Normally, the majority owner expects to have the power to pick the board of directors, to hire and fire the CEO and other key employees, and to set strategic direction. Giving that up would be like buying a house and then letting the seller decide what color to paint it and how to decorate it. "That's never been done, as far as I know," Jim Wollery said, "and I've been around for a while."

As I've mentioned before, we like to paraphrase Goethe and say that at the moment of commitment, the universe con-spires to assist you. In our case, I often joke that even our bank-ers and lawyers conspire to assist us! Because after listening to our conditions, Rob Holmes and Jim Woolery didn't say we were crazy. They actually thought we might pull it off. Several once-in-a-lifetime factors were converging at that moment: The M&A market was incredibly hot and so was The Container Store, which dominated a storage and organization market that was taking off, giving us lots of room to grow.

Perhaps most important, Rob and Jim could see that we were no ordinary company. They understood—and would help potential buyers understand—that many competitors had tried to crack this huge market and failed, that we knew this busi-ness better than anybody else, and that putting somebody else in charge would surely kill the goose that laid the golden egg. "There is a zeal at your company and all of your employees have it," Jim said. "It's in the cafeteria, it's in the warehouse, it's in the marketing. It's in the stores, it's everywhere—and we understand you have to protect that."

The key to achieving our goals, they said, was to announce to the world that The Container Store was conducting an equity auction, then notify all interested parties that if they wanted to compete, here were the rules, and let the market decide whether our conditions were reasonable. For a deal like this, Rob said, we could expect about ten bids, maybe fifteen at the most. We announced the auction in February of 2007 and the bids started coming in. And coming. And coming, and coming, and coming…When our deadline finally arrived, we were all astonished—119 bidders!

Most of the bidders were private equity firms, some were major retailers, and all were excited to be in the running. Rob was excited but later confessed, "We don't even know how to run a process with a hundred and nineteen bidders—what do we do?" The investment banking world had never seen anything like it, he said, before or since.

One candidate was Warren Buffett. The Oracle of Omaha called while we were opening our St. Louis store, so I had to apologize and told Warren we would call him back on Monday. We had a good chuckle over that when we finally spoke—I said, "I'm sure not too many people do that to you!" It was my first encounter with Warren, who was warm and friendly, casual and funny, and relaxed in a folksy, paternal way. I just adored him. He's one of those people you feel comfortable with immediately, as if you've known each other for a long, long time. He doesn't try to put on airs or show you how smart and powerful he is. The comfort level was profound—after all, he was talking to entre- preneurs who had built a business he admired and wanted to buy. Those are exactly his kind of people. Warren would have been a perfect fit for our culture. He holds on forever to the companies he acquires and has a great reputation for giving the existing management team tremendous autonomy.

But it soon became clear that Warren would not pay the highest price. After all, that's how he became the greatest investor of our time—mostly, he buys low. So we would not get the best possible deal for our exiting shareholders. Also, it would probably have been tough to convince him to put substantial stock into the hands of employees. As much as I would have loved to have Warren Buffett as my business partner and guide, he was clearly not the best choice at the time for the existing shareholders or for our employees.

Another candidate was a large retail chain—a famous brand name. When Rob asked its CEO why he wanted to do this deal, he said, "The kind of interaction they have with customers in their stores is something we try to create every day, in every one of our stores. They do it better than anyone." He was searching for the answer to a single question: "How do they create that magic?"

To separate the great bidders from the not-so-great, Rob suggested putting everyone through three rounds of bidding. In April, as the first bids were coming in, Sharon and I had a personal crisis. A seventy-nine-cent fixture in the upstairs bathroom sink of our Dallas home broke and flooded the entire house. We had to bring in professional cleaners, who looked like astronauts walking around in their hazmat suits, but black mold spores still spread like crazy throughout the house. It was so bad we had to dry-clean, bleach, or throw away just about everything we owned. We moved into a condo at the W Hotel Residential Tower that was being sublet for a few months by a professional hockey player heading out of town for the off-season. The hotel's Whatever/Whenever service definitely made it hard to move back to the suburbs.

So there we were, in the middle of the intense process of

selling our company, working ridiculously long hours every day and coming home at night to the hippest hotel in Dallas, surrounded by all these beautiful folks forever dashing off to the latest art gallery opening or concert at the House of Blues next door. "Kip, we're so worried about you," they said. "All you ever do is work!"

Over the next few weeks, we reviewed the bids and eliminated contenders one by one, eventually ruling out 110 bidders and settling on nine semifinalists to invite to management presentations at our home office. It would be their first in-depth look at our company. In most auctions, these sessions last about ninety minutes, Rob explained, maybe two hours. Instead, we created a presentation that would start at 9 AM and last until 5 PM, with a forty-five-minute lunch break. We would place a heavy emphasis on our Foundation Principles and quirky culture.

"You have got to be out of your frickin' mind!" Rob said when he read our outline. "All this Gumby, Foundation Principle crap, it's not gonna work. There is no way in Hell we can do that."

Your audience will be hard-core, bottom-line Wall Street bankers and lawyers, Rob said—and they would have the same attitude he did when he first met us. "I didn't care about the magic in the store or yummy culture or creating a climate of love," he said. "I only cared that you have X revenue today and you will have X plus Y revenue tomorrow, and here is your return on your money. Here are the future growth opportunities, here's how many stores you can build. I didn't care about that touchy-feely stuff."

So Rob put together his own management presentation. That's how the process usually works—the banker writes it and the management team presents it. "No way," I told him. His version had great numbers and charts, but the company's soul was missing. Finally I told him, "Let us do our presentation for you once, and you can tell me what you think."

Rob sat there, bracing for the worst. "Most of the time, these practice runs are awful," he says. "The CEO is too dry, or comes across as arrogant, or disassociated from the business. So you have to coach them and really practice." But when he saw ours, he was blown away. "I have to admit, it really works, because the Foundation Principles are the main points that add value and drive the earnings," he told us. "It's not abstract nonsense that you can't prove. And the way you're presenting it shows off the culture you're trying to protect."

We set up the meetings and started off each presentation with a short company video and what I call our magical mystery tour of our home office and distribution center in the Dallas suburb of Coppell. The place is so huge—1.1 million square feet—that the Empire State Building would fit inside it were you to lay it down on its side. When we started the project in 2002 (having outgrown our previous 350,000-square-foot space), we made a list of words to describe what we stand for—"love," "communication," "synergy," "organization," "partnership," "collaboration," "inclusive," "team"—and designed the building to be a physical representation of those values.

In 2004, when we moved in, the result was spectacular. We honored our vendors by displaying their products throughout the building like masterpieces in a museum. We named each conference room after a Foundation Principle (we'll say, "Meet you in the Fill the Other Guy's Basket conference room"), and we created a strong sense of connection in the design so all employees feel linked to one another, regardless of what department they're in.

Our atrium, designed like a town hall, is where our staff often comes together to celebrate, share announcements, and hold impromptu meetings. It's a blast to host our vendors—often hundreds at a time—to celebrate events like our *Fortune* magazine 100 Best Companies to Work For honor or our annual holiday party. We also have community events there, like creating Easter baskets for needy children or hosting a school-supply fund-raiser, both benefiting Community Partners of Dallas.

As you might imagine, every part of the building is neat and organized, from the offices to the distribution center, where our products come in from vendors and are shipped out to the stores. Employees zip around in motorized forklifts, guided by voice-activated headsets that tell them which boxes to snatch from the towering shelves of products and bring to the waiting trucks. Inspired by the Dutch painter Piet Mondrian, we painted sections of the distribution center walls in large blocks of primary colors. Employees walk around smiling, happy to be there, loving their jobs, and greet every visitor with a big, warm hello. I never get tired of hearing the ooohs and aaahs from visitors who are amazed by the place. Heck, *I'm* still amazed every time I see it.

Our guests were stunned to see, near the atrium, our wall of photos of hundreds of employees who have been with the company for ten, fifteen, twenty, twenty-five, thirty, thirty-five years—something rarely seen in the retail industry. And they were knocked out by the comments when they stopped to ask employees about working here. The giddy, effusive praise was so natural, not canned or rehearsed, that they kept whispering to one another, "Holy cow, I've never seen anything like this!"

Being so awestruck by the tour made our guests listen raptly to everything our executive and top leadership team covered during the formal presentation—from business strategy to merchandising to financials. They especially loved the Foundation Principles. And why not? How can you disagree with the Golden Rule, especially when it generates the kind of financial performance we've produced for thirty-six years? They could see that our philosophical principles were not just "touchy-feely stuff," as Rob called them, but actually the engine that drives the profitability that brought them all here in the first place.

We also took each group out to dinner, which for me is

200

UNCONTAINABLE

always a great test of character. How do they treat the waiters? Are they pleasant or difficult to be around in a relaxed social setting? Those dinner sessions were very revealing. We eliminated one private equity firm that had made the highest bid up to that point because one member of its team was a total jerk during dinner (we agree with Stanford professor Robert I. Sutton's best-selling book *The No Asshole Rule*, if you'll pardon my—or rather Sutton's—French). Worst of all, the bidder completely ignored Melissa and Sharon and spoke only to the men at the table, which, for us, is a cardinal sin.

During the process, some of the bidders tried to figure out how serious we were about retaining control. "You're not really going to make us do this, are you?" one asked Rob. Another said, "Is everyone else agreeing to this?" Rob politely replied that it was not negotiable. We've seen so many successful mom-and-pop businesses lose their heart and soul—the passion and love the company was founded upon—as soon as they bring in outside investors who start calling the shots. That wasn't going to happen to us. "If you're not comfortable with that, fine," Rob told them. "You can pull out anytime, we have plenty of bidders." We also had great leverage because as a private company, we didn't have to sell. If we didn't get what we wanted, we would simply stop the process.

After our management presentations, eight of the nine candidates made bids, all for a majority stake. We were astounded at how high the bids were, ranging from thirteen times to sixteen times the standard measure of profitability, EBITDA. Even that lowest bid ranked among the highest ever offered for a retail company (a healthy company, excluding distressed firms), according to most observers. Companies in our position often just accept the highest offer, but it was more important for us to dig deeper and find just the right owner, one who truly understood our culture and mission.

From the beginning, one candidate stood out. Early in the process, Rob had suggested that we meet with Jon Sokoloff, managing partner of Leonard Green & Partners, a private equity firm based in Los Angeles. Private equity guys don't have the greatest reputation in the media, but when Jon came by our Dallas home office for a visit, he seemed like just the opposite of the caricature you hear so much about—you know, the cynical plunderer pursuing short-term profits at the expense of all else. Leonard Green actually tried the conventional distressed-asset-turnaround strategy when Jon joined the company in 1990, back when it was a small $200-million fund—"We bought a lot of crappy companies and tried to fix them up" is how he put it—but that strategy proved to be hit-or-miss. The world was changing, and the controversial "leveraged buyout" mania of the '80s was fading.

So Leonard Green's strategy evolved into its current, far more sustainable mode of investing in best-in-sector, growing companies like J.Crew, Neiman Marcus, and Petco and then leaving them alone to run their business. "We don't come in with an army of efficiency experts to tell our companies how to do things better," Jon explained. His firm's small staff of twenty-five will sometimes make suggestions, of course, and will step in when absolutely necessary to protect its investors, mostly sophisticated institutional players like pension funds and insurance companies. But that is only as a last resort.

I was impressed by how well Jon listened—"God gave us two ears and one mouth for a reason," he often says—and he was fascinated by our Foundation Principles. "The most meaningful asset a company has is its culture, its work force, and the value of the brand name," Jon told me. "Those are all things that don't show up on the balance sheet. It's very important that we don't come in and mess up those very intangible but critical assets that companies have spent decades creating."

All of this was pure music to my ears. But could we trust Jon and Leonard Green? What about the other candidates, some of whom expressed similar sentiments? To me, that's where intuition comes in.

Finding an investor is a lot like finding a spouse. There's a courtship period when you're trying to impress each other and to say all the right things, hoping you've found a great match. But you can't really know how it will work out until you take the plunge and say "I do." We did our due diligence on Leonard Green and the other candidates, of course, but ultimately we had to rely on the intuition we'd spent our lives developing. If you believe, as we do, that "Intuition Does Not Come to An Unprepared Mind. You Need to Train Before It Happens," then you could say we'd been "training" for this moment for nearly thirty years—forming partnerships, negotiating vendor deals, and hiring employees, all the while assessing people's character and trustworthiness before reaching a decision.

A very wise person once said that in selecting business partners, employees, or friends, everything is a commodity except for judgment and integrity. That is so true. Those two qualities are not easy to discern, of course, but that's exactly what I look for in people I choose to hang out with. Would Jon and Leonard Green—or any of the other candidates—really let us keep the keys to our car and let us drive, so to speak, and not search for loopholes in our contracts that would allow them to take over our company? Thousands of employees at The Container Store and their families were counting on us to make the right decision.

As I've mentioned, I like to take my time making decisions—really let things percolate—especially ones as important as this one. I would have loved to do management presentations for dozens of candidates, leaving no stone unturned, even if the process took a year. But in June, Rob called and said time was running out. There were unmistakable signs that the booming M&A market had started to cool. Some banks were attaching restrictive clauses to loans to protect themselves in case certain performance benchmarks were not reached. "We should move now," he said.

By then, we had narrowed the bidders down to three finalists: Leonard Green and two famous blue-chip investment firms. Since we no longer had the luxury of time, our intuition was more important than ever. As we'd predicted from the start, this crucial decision would have to come from the heart.

Our management team determined that the right choice was Leonard Green & Partners. Why? The resounding answer when we asked our team: Jon Sokoloff. My intuition, and Sharon's and Melissa's intuition, told us the very same thing. We were so impressed by Jon's intelligence, compassion, and humility, and we trusted him completely—everything we wanted to feel about the people our beloved company partnered with.

You should know that Leonard Green did not make the highest bid, but its offer was high enough that we knew our exiting shareholders would be ecstatic. Leonard Green offered the best terms on governance provisions, allowing us to retain control, which was a huge factor. "I think some private equity firms would think we were nuts to agree to what we did," Jon said. But to protect itself and its investors, Leonard Green insisted on "triggers" that would allow it to take control only if certain financial performance targets were not met. That seemed fair to us, and we felt confident those triggers would never be set off. Our new six-member board of directors, evenly apportioned with three members from each firm, would consist of Sharon, Melissa, and me from The Container Store and Jon and his colleagues Tim Flynn and Kris Galashan, whom we also trusted completely.

Leonard Green also offered the highest equity distribution

deal for our employees—"one of the highest I've ever seen," Rob said. They understood, better than anyone else, that owning 50 percent of a dollar is better than owning 100 percent of a nickel. In this case, it meant that owning a smaller percentage of the company by giving equity to key employees will eventually pay for itself many times over when those employees drive the company's growth and profitability to new heights.

Keeping our hugely talented management team feeling appreciated and rewarded—and safe from firms trying to lure them away with lucrative stock options—is critical to keeping our unique culture thriving. After all, they're the ones who built and are building this company, and we hope they'll spend the rest of their careers with us as we expand across the country and internationally. The biggest drawback to Leonard Green's offer was the same one we faced with all the private equity firms: Their business model requires them to hold on to an acquisition for only three to five years before selling. "Our business model is simple," says Jon. "We turn one dollar into three dollars." That short time frame was hard to swallow—would we have to go through this agonizing process all over again in a few years? As I've mentioned, I'm a long-term-relationship guy. That's why Warren Buffett's offer was so appealing—he hangs on to companies forever. But to get the maximum value for our shareholders, we had little choice but to sell to a private equity firm, and they all operate basically the same way.

Leonard Green & Partners, however, had an advantage over the other bidders: With certain highly successful acquisitions, it will hold the asset much longer.

We gave Rob the green light to call Jon. "We want to move things along," Rob told him, "and we want to move things along with you." Jon was delighted. He booked a flight to Dallas immediately and notified Leonard Green's lawyer, Howard Sobel of Latham & Watkins. Turned out Howard was on vacation, listening to monks chanting in a fourteenth-century chapel in a remote valley in Provence, when his BlackBerry buzzed. He and his wife, Ileene, grabbed a train to Paris, then flew to New York, a twenty-hour trip. It was the weekend before the Fourth of July. Howard lived in his Manhattan office for a few days, showering in the gym downstairs, while in Dallas Jon worked long hours with Rob, Jim, and The Container Store team until the deal was done.

Exhausted but elated, we announced the acquisition to our employees on Monday, July 2, 2007. We reminded them that when we began our search in February, we had promised not to do the deal unless we accomplished three goals—getting maximum value for shareholders, retaining control of the company, and putting equity into the hands of employees. Now we were ecstatic to announce that all conditions had been met and Leonard Green was our new partner. "The Container Store will remain every bit as yummy, quirky, and exciting and every bit as true to its values, philosophy, and core concepts as we are right now," I told the media the next day. And that's exactly what has happened.

——◦——

Immediately after the deal was done, I became ill. I had always thought I was immune to stress, the kind of guy who says, no matter what the problem is, "Don't worry, I'll fix it—just put it on my shoulders, I'll carry it." But I seem to have developed what I call the Finish Line Syndrome: I'll go and go and go and keep on going until I cross the finish line, and then I just collapse. This process was by far the most stressful, difficult, and lonely ordeal of my life, and for the first time, stress manifested itself in a physical way—a stomach ailment that made it extremely difficult for me to eat. That was especially hard for me because I love good food and wine—so for about a year, it was pretty miserable.

Adding to the stress of the equity deal was our home

renovation, moving to a temporary home, and having our life turned upside down. In late August, a few days after the last details of the Leonard Green deal were finalized, we were happy to leave the W Hotel—the hockey player had come back for the new season—and to move into a new home we'd bought in Dallas, an extremely contemporary house where we live today. We ended up selling the old place—a magnificent house we had spent years building—and that made us sad, but we love our new place. It has a pond full of bass and a small garden where I grow herbs for the wonderful meals Sharon cooks.

Fortunately, I recovered fully from my illness. I haven't become a vegan, but I now consume vastly less animal fat and very little dairy. I have also eliminated as much stress as possible, to the point that Melissa doesn't like to fly with me because I insist on leaving for the airport so early!

The Leonard Green deal turned out to be fantastic for everyone—it was truly beyond our wildest dreams. The whole process was one of the greatest examples of the stakeholder model that you'll ever see. Conventional business thinking would see the stakeholders affected by this deal—Leonard Green, its investors, our shareholders, management, and employees—as competing with one another. But it was truly a win for all parties because one stakeholder didn't have to take from the other's pocket to succeed. We couldn't have the exiting shareholders feel as if the employees were getting too much, or vice versa. This was the most beautiful win-win-win I've ever seen—for the exiting partners, the new partners, the employees, the culture, the customers. It was the ultimate manifestation of Conscious Capitalism.

"Kip, you were right—this was the most joyful thing I've ever done in my whole career," said Jimmy Elliott of JPMorgan. When the process got difficult, he and Rob were great sources of inspiration, with Rob often reminding me, "Kip, you are on the side of the angels."

There was definitely magic in this deal. It allowed us to give stock to over 200 employees—not options, mind you, but actual stock that finally rewarded these deserving folks with a real piece of the company. The exiting shareholders, meanwhile, were able to sell all their shares at the top of the sizzling M&A market, and each got a stunning return on their investment.

After the deal was done, The Container Store was owned entirely by Leonard Green and employees, creating a more unified ownership structure and one that would lend itself readily to putting more stock into the hands of employees. Many of our minority partners resisted exiting at first—they loved being associated with The Container Store and were excited about our growth potential—but we assured them they would end up being ecstatic with the final result. Everyone was thrilled, proud, and joyful.

The deal was also great for Leonard Green—though it hardly looked that way at first. No sooner was the ink dry on our contracts than the M&A market cooled and the credit markets shut down. "People think of the recession happening in 2008, but the capital markets actually collapsed on July Fourth 2007," Rob says. "Most people just didn't know it yet." When the full brunt of the Great Recession hit in 2008, our sales declined for the first time ever, and everybody was rattled. "For a company to lose that much in revenue was shocking and frightening," Jon Sokoloff says. "That is not what anybody bargained for."

But that was exactly the moment when everybody realized what a great partnership we had. Our sales didn't fall nearly as much as those of most housewares retailers, but things were bad enough that according to the triggers spelled out in our contract, Leonard Green was legally entitled to take full control of the company. Jon and his team could have appointed another board member to give it a 4-to-3 majority, basically allowing it to do whatever it wanted—fire me, fire Sharon and Melissa, install their own team, and create whatever kind of culture they wanted. But Leonard Green never exercised a single governance right that they were entitled to. They simply kept the faith and believed we were the best captains of this ship, even during those terrible storms. That singular moment told us everything we needed to know about Jon and the folks at Leonard Green.

There is no doubt in my mind that just about any other private equity firm would have taken control. Most would have demanded layoffs and huge cuts in the high cost of our employee-first culture, especially for pay, benefits, and training. And that surely would have ruined the company and ended the magic. Soon after the deal was completed, Leonard Green got lots of calls from consultants who had worked with other bidders. "You know, The Container Store's expense structure is way too high," they said. "That place could be run much more efficiently." Jon listened politely, as always, and occasionally forwarded individual suggestions to us. But ultimately he left us alone to do our jobs, exactly as promised.

It got to the point where I finally had to call Rob and say, "Hey, those Leonard Green guys never call—what's the matter? Are they mad at me? Don't they like us?" Later, Jon explained: "You guys were doing great, considering everything. We had much bigger things to worry about."

Jon went on, "The Container Store is a truly special business with an amazing management team and very special culture, and, most of all, incredible growth prospects. Some retailers provide a great return on capital, but they already have three hundred stores. So what happens after they open the next twenty-five or thirty stores? You run out of runway. But The Container Store could eventually have three hundred more stores in the United States alone, and then there's the international market. So we have an endless runway for the future."

The Leonard Green deal was also good for Sharon and me. We were required to sell and did sell about half of our position in the company, and that was both daunting and disturbing. It was the first time we'd ever sold significant company stock—and the first time, after nearly thirty years, that we derived any real wealth from the company's success. Over the years, we'd found it funny that people assumed we were wealthy because The Container Store was so successful. But until the Leonard Green deal, our wealth was just on paper. "Kip, you need to monetize this," friends would whisper. "You've got the world by the tail—you need to cash in your chips."

In fact, I think we needed to learn the lesson of carpe diem a little bit and enjoy a more comfortable lifestyle. And this liquidity event, combined with the fact that Sharon and I had saved half of our income for decades, allowed us to enjoy it and not worry about money. But what the Leonard Green deal really gave us was the chance to continuously get more equity into the hands of our beloved employees.

—◦—

In August of 2012, to celebrate the fifth anniversary of the acquisition, we were thrilled to announce that stock options would be awarded to 283 deserving employees. This included our 15 vice-presidents at the time, plus 268 other exceptional employees throughout the company—not based on title, duties, or tenure, but solely on contribution. To arrive at the final list of recipients, we did some deep soul-searching and called up all the wisdom (and intuition) we could muster, hoping it would provide inspiration to all employees as we continued our effort to give more folks a share of the company.

Sharon and I were always willing to dilute ourselves in favor of the employees. And this was the consummation of our selection of Leonard Green as our financial partner. They were bullishly willing to dilute themselves as well, and together we were able to make a hugely significant equity contribution to our employees.

Leonard Green understands all this. Its investors will now earn a far greater return than if Jon and his team had taken the narrow, zero-sum approach and refused to dilute its ownership stake. That's why I'm proud to say that Leonard Green has become truly a Conscious Capitalist private equity firm. I know what an oxymoron it is. It makes us all smile. But we're very proud of our partnership and exactly that.

It's not altruism. We are capitalists, albeit conscious ones. And even we find it astonishing that giving up equity today can make our stake worth far more tomorrow. At this point, our main motivation is that we just think it's right and just to share the wealth, to watch our employees' dreams come true, to see them buy new homes (or whatever their version of a ranch in Colorado is) and send their sons and daughters to college, and to see our company continue to grow and thrive.

Why don't more companies and investors operate this way? It takes a lot of faith, even bravery, and a genuine spirit of generosity. You have to leave behind old business habits of short-term, zero-sum thinking. You have to talk about things like vulnerability, intuition, and love. And, of course, you have to work hard—though when your work feels like play, that part is easy. Sharon and Melissa have all those qualities and abilities in abundance, and that's why I feel so blessed to be their partner. And why I'm so grateful that in 2007 our well-trained intuition told us to choose Jon Sokoloff and Leonard Green, who intuitively behave this way, too.

These principles are so powerful, in fact, that I'm convinced that all business will be conducted this way in the future. It has to, for the simple reason that doing business this way works better than any other methodology. And that will be a huge boon to humankind. That's why I'm so eager to talk about the next stage in our company's development, when we teamed with John Mackey and helped forward a movement I'm proud to be a part of—Conscious Capitalism.

10

Air of Excitement!

Three steps in the door, and you can tell whether a retail store has it—that "Air of Excitement," which also happens to be our seventh and final Foundation Principle. It's what I've always loved about retail, even as a kid, that magical world of possibility stretching out before you when you walk through the door.

Air of Excitement is really the inevitable result of faithfully following all the other Foundation Principles. When you do everything else right, all the principles we explored in previous chapters—1=3; Fill the Other Guy's Basket; Man in the Desert Selling; Communication IS Leadership; Best Selection, Service & Price; and Intuition Does Not Come to An Unprepared Mind—lead to this very happy outcome.

In retail, customers can always sense when employees are having fun, when they love their jobs and are excited about helping. Folks are always telling me, "Your people are so happy! How do you do it? What do you put in the drinking water?"

Well, the simple answer is that they all have that Air of

Excitement and are eager to spread it. My neighbor in Colorado, Jim Oates, used to be president of Leo Burnett—the acclaimed ad agency in Chicago that created Tony the Tiger and the Pillsbury Doughboy. The agency came up with a TV ad for Schlitz beer that captured the essence of what I'm talking about: A cabful of people is out for a night on the town, looking for a good nightclub. They poke their heads into one spot that's dark and has no music playing and say, "No, that's not it," and another where there's no people and it's not very clean—"Nope, not right," until they finally find the right spot and say, "Yeah, come on, this is it!" Then the voice-over says, "When it's right, you know it."

That nightclub had an Air of Excitement. Everybody really wanted to be there, customers and employees alike. Parties are the same—either they have that magic or they don't. Perry's, that dime store in Lake Charles, Louisiana, where I used to hang out as a kid, definitely had an Air of Excitement. It was the highlight of my day—that's why I went there all the time. The Container Store has had it from day one, probably because we were so excited to be doing what we loved best—helping customers with cool products they'd never seen before. Zabar's, the specialty food store in Manhattan, is legendary for its exciting atmosphere, especially around lunchtime. Whole Foods has it—you can just feel the passion every time you walk into those stores. So does Southwest Airlines. The mood and the vibe are night and day compared to most other airlines. That's why these brands are so beloved. They strive to achieve that feeling every single day.

I think of retail as theater. So why not put on a show? Everything you think should be done in the back room really should be done on the sales floor. If you have to disassemble a display and you get up on a ladder, that's when customers come up to you and really want you to help them—because they can feel the energy of an exciting store. Retail is hard, but you don't have to be serious all the time—make it fun! I like people with big booming theatrical voices and I love hearing laughter. When someone is out on maternity leave and brings the baby into the store for the first time, everybody goes crazy, cooing over the new baby, and sometimes the mother will apologize and say, "Sorry to interrupt." But I always say, "No, this is great. This is Air of Excitement at its finest! Look how excited everybody is!"

Herb Kelleher, of Southwest Airlines, taught us that it's okay to have fun at work. And he's one of the most fun people in the whole world. Once I was flying on Southwest from Austin to Dallas and Herb was on the same flight. He said, "Kip, come over here and sit with me." So we take off and he gets up and says, "Let's you and me be the flight attendants!" and we both start handing out pretzels. He introduced me to everybody on the plane, and people kept saying how much they love The Container Store and Southwest Airlines. It was a blast, the most fun I've ever had on a flight.

We make sure all our employees understand that they have a responsibility to sustain that Air of Excitement, to nurture it, to enhance it. So if an employee has an argument with her significant other that morning, she needs to leave it at the door—and her coworkers shouldn't hesitate to talk to her, draw her out, and help her move on. For me, maintaining an Air of Excitement is an almost magical, cosmic thing.

In the Catholic Church, they light a candle to represent God's presence, and as a boy I wondered how the priests kept that candle lit twenty-four hours a day, seven days a week. But I understood they had a responsibility to keep the flame going all the time. When the candle burned down, they carefully transferred the flame to the next candle. That's how I think about our responsibility to sustain that Air of Excitement—we must be vigilant in keeping that flame alive.

Maintaining an Air of Excitement can be a challenge during times of crisis—like after 9/11 or during the Great Recession.

But we never let our energy lag during these trying moments, because that's when people really come together, go out of their way to help one another, and become true neighbors. During both of those national emergencies, we got reports from all over the country about people coming into our stores just for comfort—sometimes not to buy anything, but just to be around warm, caring people in a happy, orderly place. This also happens on the most ordinary days. One customer told us recently, "I was so frazzled after a bad experience at a department store—the saleswoman was so rude and unhelpful—that afterward I went over to The Container Store for no reason other than that I just wanted somebody to be nice to me. I needed a hit of whatever they give those employees."

You can't force that feeling of warmth and caring—it has to be authentic and come from the heart. That's why it's so important that the hugely talented people we hire also be genuinely kind, loving people. We want our employees to relax and to just be themselves.

Since retail is theater, it's crucial that our stage be set up perfectly. That's why we take such great care with our interior design and the presentation of products—to make sure the look and feel of our stores reflect The Container Store's mission. After all, if you're the storage and organization experts, you can't have a messy, disorganized store. Our stores are bright, spacious, and clean, with a minimalist, modernist look. Like our company culture, the atmosphere is casual, sophisticated, and fun.

—◇—

When you enter The Container Store, you immediately feel at ease because the store is so easy to navigate—wide aisles, clear signage for various areas of your home (Closet, Kitchen, Office, etc.)—and you can see nearly all the merchandise without feeling overwhelmed. You'll notice that most of our products are out of their packages. That idea goes back to my childhood, when I developed a fondness for the way grocery stores display colorful baskets of fruits and vegetables and neat rows of canned goods on shelves. When we opened that first store back in 1978, most of our products came in bulk from commercial vendors and weren't even available in retail packaging. And the products were so unusual that we decided to let customers play around with them—it became a fun discovery to brainstorm different uses for the products. Sure, it would be easier to sell our garment bags in a package, but that wouldn't serve the customer, who needs to touch and feel that garment bag to see how high-quality it is.

Most retailers call this part of the business visual merchandising, but we call it visual sales because we consider it a critical part of our Man in the Desert Selling philosophy. We call it visual sales because "visual sells." Brian Morrison, our senior merchandise director, coined the phrase and really led a rallying cry that now everyone has adopted. He has a wonderful Texas accent—so his special emphasis when articulating "SALES" and "SELLS" makes the point terrifically well when we're training our staffs. Again, Air of Excitement! Brian and Peggy Doughty, our vice-president of visual merchandising, do a tremendous job with this. Our goal is "perfect product presentation," which means that the customer can clearly understand everything about the product immediately, even if our sales staff is busy helping other customers.

All sales-floor employees are constantly pulling products to the front edge of the shelf and making sure they're straight, even when helping a customer. That's why you'll often hear our employees talking about "fronting and straightening while selling." They're like great party hosts, carrying on sparkling conversations while guests don't even notice they've been simultaneously refilling glasses, replenishing food trays, and picking up empty plates.

Our stores aren't the only place in our company where you can feel an Air of Excitement. Our home office and distribution center in Dallas are bursting with it, too. I've never understood why people think an office should be quiet. Let's make it vibrant, alive! Our distribution center has an amazing Air of Excitement because of all the fabulous folks who work there. That's pretty unusual in our industry, given the hard physical work and often sweltering conditions (we use giant fans to keep the place cool during those scorching Dallas summers). We have a great video of one of our distribution center employees, Cale Meeks, keeping spirits high, shouting to coworkers. "All right—let's do this!" "Woo-hoo, Janet!" "Duane, come here so I can give you a high five!" It's a relaxed, happy environment, and because of that, it's also incredibly productive.

To keep an Air of Excitement flourishing throughout the company, we do lots of celebrating throughout the year with fun, silly events. Here's a sampling:

• We Love Our Employees Day, held every Valentine's Day. A couple of years ago, we distributed to employees a fun *Mission Impossible*–inspired video of Sharon, Melissa, Garrett, and me wearing white painter's coveralls and red Converse Chuck Taylor sneakers and climbing a ladder to the roof of our distribution center, getting down on our hands and knees to paint, then high-fiving one another and shouting as the aerial camera panned back to show our creation—a 58,800-square-foot valentine with a heart and the words "We Love Our Employees." Our rooftop love note is still clearly visible to thousands of passengers every day on flights coming in and out of the Dallas/Fort Worth airport. We promoted the valentine with a full-page ad in the *New York Times* and sent employees free boxes of products donated by vendors and Valentine's Day munchies. Every year we try to outdo ourselves in showing employees how much we love them and congratulate them on a job well done!

On We Love Our Employees Day in 2014, we launched our Employee First Fund, which provides financial assistance to employees experiencing an unforeseen emergency, a major medical situation, a catastrophic event, or some other challenge they're not financially prepared to deal with. The fund is supported by contributions from The Container Store, employees, and other company stakeholders. You can imagine the Air of Excitement felt throughout the company when we made that announcement.

• Our Annual Chili Cook-Off. Each department in the home office/distribution center picks a theme and competes for the Best Chili, Hottest Chili, Best Cornbread, Best Dessert, Best Booth, and Best Individual and Team Costume. Our vendors donate prizes and volunteer to be judges. We've been holding this event for over twenty years, and it's such a crazy, riotously good time that I look forward to it every year.

• Our Annual Distribution Center Derby. Each department makes a toy soap box derby car to race, and everybody gathers in our distribution center, cheering like crazy, to watch the cars zoom down the tracks. The cars are highly creative and silly—one might be made of LEGO, another adorned with a tiny statue of Betty Boop. To add realism, we park a real NASCAR race car outside the building.

And as you might imagine, we celebrate moms on Mother's Day and dads on Father's Day; eat hot dogs together on the Fourth of July; go to baseball games; have an ice cream social at the end of the summer; celebrate Halloween with candy, costumes, and a Haunted House Parade; have Family Movie Night under the stars with food, balloons, and free face painting for the kids; and of course throw fabulous holiday parties in December.

Sometimes it's the little touches that matter most, like

finding your desk decorated with balloons and signs on your birthday, receiving a heartfelt card on the anniversary of the day you joined the company or an engraved silver spoon when you have a baby. These days, people often spend more time with their coworkers than with their own family, so we encourage our employees to bond in ways very much like a close-knit family.

You might wonder how we get any work done with all this celebrating. Sure, all these events cost money and temporarily take employees away from their jobs. Most management consultants would probably come into our headquarters and say, "Look at all these silly events—cut them out! Put these people back to work!" But the idea that the time and money spent on a toy-car derby can simply be subtracted from more "productive" work is classic zero-sum thinking.

What conventional business minds don't understand is that all the positive feeling this activity generates is really the fuel that drives our company. Without it, we'd be just another retailer with no spark, no Air of Excitement—and, I'm quite certain, no profits. When I visit a store, I often ask the managers, "Is that all you got? Can't you be more fun than that? Can't you come up with more creative, cool ways to make this place more fun for people who work and shop here? And can't I do a better job in encouraging you that it's okay to do that?"

People in management can easily get into the habit of being too regimented, too militaristic. I realize that especially when I look at a company like Patagonia, whose founder, Yvon Chouinard, wrote a book called *Let My People Go Surfing*. When surf's up, he tells his employees to go surfing—right in the middle of the business day! When I read that, I thought, "Gosh, we could do so much more!" Sure, we have great sales and earnings, but I'm convinced they'd be even higher if we had more toy-car derbies, more Chili Cook-Offs, more fun and games. Most of the time, I really don't think we're doing enough.

I've talked before about the power of our rippling wake—the inevitable consequences of our actions—and there's no doubt that our company's Air of Excitement flows out far beyond the store walls and boomerangs back to help us. Communities like Raleigh, North Carolina, go crazy over us when we open stores there, but that enthusiasm also happens in big markets like Manhattan, Chicago, and Los Angeles. The local and national media notice it, for sure. Our Air of Excitement has generated huge amounts of positive publicity everywhere from *USA Today* and the *New York Times* to top magazines like *Real Simple*, as well as on HGTV and *Today*, *Good Morning America*, and *Oprah*. In fact, during Oprah's last "Favorite Things" show before she moved to her OWN network, members of her studio audience went berserk when she told them they were all getting a free closet makeover, courtesy of The Container Store. Remember those images of teenage girls screaming when the Beatles landed in America? Well, that was nothing compared to how these women reacted as the curtains parted and they caught a glimpse of their dream closet: "*Yaaaaaaaaaaaaaaaay!*"

One way to tell whether your company has an Air of Excitement is to ask, "If we went out of business, would anybody care?" For a lot of companies out there, the honest answer would probably be no. But I can say with all humility that I'm sure lots of people would miss The Container Store. The kind of customer feedback we get is astonishing—personal, heartfelt, emotional, probably because we're helping to solve some of their most maddening problems and giving them back precious time.

———◦———

Air of Excitement—that's a great way to describe how folks at our company were feeling when the Great Recession finally began to ebb in 2009 and our sales resumed their upward trajectory. Amazingly enough, we continued to open new stores even during those difficult years, albeit at a slower pace, and have posted wonderful sales and profits every year since 2010, despite the economy's painfully slow pace of recovery. It was such a testament to the spirit, hard work, and ingenuity of our entire team that we avoided layoffs during that frightening 2008–09 period. Yes, it was painful to institute a freeze on salaries, 401(k) matches, and hiring, not to mention cutbacks on training and Air of Excitement events—all extreme measures we had never taken before. But because we communicated so well, our 1=3 employees not only understood that all these steps were necessary to preserve every job, but they enthusiastically supported one another. We truly held hands and weathered the storm together.

As the economy stabilized, we went right back to business as usual, eventually restoring full funding to everything from pay raises to 401(k) matches. We also began opening stores at a faster pace than ever before. A lot of people said, "Why are you doing that? You're throwing caution to the wind!" Our answer was that with the economy improving and hundreds of untapped markets nationwide, we felt we were just hitting our stride.

We were also fortified by our appointment of Jodi Taylor as chief financial officer just after the Leonard Green deal was finalized in August of 2007. During our nationwide search, everybody kept saying, "Jodi is the best in the country," and wow, were they right! She had been in retail for twenty-two years and helped a small firm in South Carolina grow into a big, publicly traded chain called Baby Superstores that was eventually acquired by Babies "R" Us. Not all financial executives get the Container Store culture, but Jodi certainly does. She has become as valued and trusted an adviser to me as Sharon and Melissa and was crucial in helping us emerge from the recession financially stronger than ever before.

By 2011, we were in a celebratory mood, so we decided to hold a Staff Meeting, our first since 2008. Talk about an Air of Excitement! Earlier, I described Staff Meeting as a training event, especially for its emphasis on our Foundation Principles. But it's also a huge celebration—of our beloved employees, our culture, our mission, our customers and business partners, and the affection we have for one another—and it's a great illustration of our Air of Excitement Foundation Principle in action. Staff Meeting feels to me like an old-fashioned revival. I don't want to sound overly religious, but I can't think of a better simile for the feeling that emerges from Staff Meeting, when hundreds of our 1=3 employees gather to celebrate our accomplishments and to gear up for the challenges ahead.

We met in our Gumby Cafe for three days in late June of 2011, the cafeteria jammed with employees and special guests while another large group upstairs participated via video conference. Our motto for the event was "It's a New Day!" and our theme, displayed on banners and logos everywhere, was "Connection, Communication, and Community." Staff Meeting is a hugely ambitious undertaking—pulling key managers and employees from their jobs for most of the week and flying folks to Dallas from around the country—but well worth the time and expense. There's so much material to absorb at each Staff Meeting that it often takes years before the company has fully digested the last one and is ready to do it again.

The 2011 event was certainly a far cry from our first Staff Meetings, when we would fit around a small table in our first office/distribution center on Dairy Milk Lane. But now here we were, more than 300 employees in attendance, celebrating our growth into a beloved national brand. The employees got updates about everything from financials to real estate to operations, and our management team presented inspiring hourlong seminars on each of the seven Foundation Principles. There were also candid, talk show–style conversations with our investors (Jon Sokoloff of Leonard Green), vendors (Les Mandelbaum and Paul Rowan of Umbra), elfa management (new CEO Per von Mentzer), long-time employees (Barbara Anderson, retired), community friends (Dr. Sandi Chapman of the Center for BrainHealth at the University of Texas at Dallas), and our top leadership team (Sharon, Melissa, and me).

We were also treated to mind-blowing talks by some of the most provocative thought leaders of our time, and were highly honored when these luminaries accepted our invitation to speak. Chip Conley, CEO of Joie de Vivre Hotels and author of *Peak: How Great Companies Get Their Mojo from Maslow*, explained what business leaders can learn from Abraham Maslow, best known for his "hierarchy of needs." My good buddy Roy Spence, the advertising wizard and author of *It's Not What You Sell, It's What You Stand For*, discussed why every company must articulate a clear purpose to succeed today. Bert Jacobs, cofounder of the Life is good apparel company, threw Frisbees into the crowd and challenged us to embrace our life and work with open hearts. The scientist and entrepreneur Paul Zak, author of *The Moral Molecule*, held us spellbound with his tales of traveling the world to discover the biological basis for virtuous behavior. David Cottrell, an authority on leadership and author of *Tuesday Morning Coaching*, enthralled us with his wisdom about management and business. Marti Barletta, author of *PrimeTime Women*, offered stunning insights into the economic and social power of the women's market.

And, of course, there was plenty of time for partying and fun. We booked a three-piece blues band, and some surprise special guests sat in. As I mentioned before, Paul Rowan and Les Mandelbaum of our vendor Umbra are both accomplished musicians, so Paul dazzled on the harmonica and whipped up the crowd with his vocals while Les laid down a funky beat on the bass. I even got into the act, singing a version of the old Jimmy Reed song "You Got Me Dizzy" that brought me back to my college days in Austin, when we played and listened to music all night long. At the end of one day's events, Sharon, Melissa, and I were onstage delivering our closing remarks when the whole crowd broke into a flash-mob dance to the Black Eyed Peas tune "I Got a Feeling," which they had been rehearsing for days in secret; we were so caught off guard that it didn't really sink in until we left the stage and said, "Hey, wait a minute—did that really just happen?"

So it was an incredible week—intellectually stimulating, emotionally powerful, information packed, cathartic, wildly fun, and so inspiring that we all returned to our jobs as if walking on air. Of excitement.

———◦———

One of my favorite events of Staff Meeting was sitting onstage for a freewheeling conversation with my old college roommate, John Mackey. Sharon introduced us to the audience, telling the story about how John moved out of the apartment I shared with him and two other guys in 1976, shortly before Sharon moved into the adjacent apartment. "And it's kind of funny," she said, "because neither one of them remembers ever discussing retail." That's true. As I mentioned earlier, we talked about philosophy, poker, and what most college boys talk about—girls.

For more than three decades, John and I got together occasionally; we followed each other's careers and read media reports about the big success of these two little Texas start-ups, Whole Foods in Austin and The Container Store in Dallas. In June of 2008, a writer for *Time* magazine, Justin Fox, invited us to sit for a joint interview to talk about our approach to business.

Those thirty-two years melted away in a flash. The first thing I noticed was that we were both dressed the same way we'd been dressed back in school—John in khaki cargo shorts and a T-shirt and I in my usual jeans, polo shirt, and sneakers. As we started talking, we were astonished at the parallel tracks our lives had taken. We had both dropped out of UT Austin to cofound a specialty retail store in the same year (1978), and both stores had been very successful from day one. Most incredibly, we ran our companies with nearly identical core values—treating employees well and harmonizing the needs of all stakeholders, from vendors to customers to investors—and had created company cultures infused with love and compassion. As the interview progressed, we agreed that business does not have to be a zero-sum game, that every action can be a win-win for all parties involved, that happy employees make for happy customers and ultimately happy investors, that Milton Friedman was wrong in saying that a company's main obligation is to maximize shareholder value, and on and on...

"I remember the reporter would ask us a question and when you gave your answer, I was sitting there shaking my head saying, 'Man, that's exactly what I would have said!'" John recalls. "It was eerie." Soon we were finishing each other's sentences and practically rolling on the floor laughing at the craziness of the whole situation. You know those stories you hear about twins being separated at birth and creating lives that are nearly mirror images of each other? That's what it felt like as John and I talked about our companies.

After that meeting, neither of us could wait for the next time we could get together to compare notes. John told me he had been influenced by two business school professors, both of whom I've been very pleased to get to know since: Ed Freeman, the father of stakeholder theory, whom I discussed earlier, and Raj Sisodia, John's *Conscious Capitalism* coauthor, now a marketing professor at Babson College, who also cowrote a 2007 book called *Firms of Endearment* (with David B. Wolfe and Jagdish N. Sheth). Raj and his colleagues showed that enlightened companies such as Google, JetBlue, Whole Foods, Costco, and Patagonia that follow the stakeholder model and bring qualities like love, joy, authenticity, and empathy into their business actually far outperform the S&P 500 over a ten-year period. As John put it, "That research was catalytic in getting us to realize, 'Oh my God, we think we have a better way of doing business here!'"

John settled on the term "Conscious Capitalism" to describe this approach, an adaptation of the phrase "socially conscious capitalist enterprise" that Nobel laureate Muhammad Yunus used to describe his Grameen Bank in the mid-'90s. John also started a nonprofit organization called Conscious Capitalism, Inc., devoted to developing and spreading this message. As we talked, John became convinced that The Container Store was among the best practitioners of Conscious Capitalism he had ever seen—and I began to realize that Conscious Capitalism and the Foundation Principles were really one and the same thing! What a remarkable convergence—over the last three decades, John and I had been using different words to develop and describe the very same business philosophy. That's when I told John I would do everything I could to help promote Conscious Capitalism and help business leaders understand that this approach is not just the right thing to do, and doesn't just feel great—it actually works!

The best way to learn about Conscious Capitalism is to read John and Raj's brilliant book of the same name, which lays out their inspiring vision of how business can transform society in a way that transcends the products or services it offers. Unfortunately, capitalism has a bad reputation today—people see it as heartless, rapacious, damaging to society—but when it's practiced in a conscious way, I'm convinced that it can be the most powerful tool for positive change the world has ever seen.

In defining Conscious Capitalism, John and Raj have identified four key tenets: (1) having a higher purpose beyond generating profits; (2) harmonizing the needs of all stakeholders to create win-win outcomes for all; (3) having leaders who are motivated primarily by serving the firm's higher purpose and creating value for all stakeholders; (4) creating a conscious culture based on qualities like trust, accountability, transparency, integrity, loyalty, egalitarianism, fairness, personal growth, love, and care.

In a truly conscious company, these values permeate the entire firm, starting with the CEO and board of directors. This makes Conscious Capitalism fundamentally different than "corporate social responsibility" and "cause marketing," which tend to push a company's "good works" off to the side into separate departments that deal with areas like community outreach, charitable contributions, or marketing. The Container Store does a tremendous amount of charitable work of all kinds, in our home base of Dallas and in the communities where our stores are located—and we're extremely proud of those partnerships, which are a critical part of our mission. But Conscious Capitalism requires much more than that. Its principles must be felt from the building maintenance staff to the chairman of the board, with a total commitment to creating win-win outcomes at every level of the company.

Corny as it may sound, much of Conscious Capitalism comes down to having leaders who are inspired to spread values like generosity, humility, teamwork, and caring throughout the whole organization. But the hardest thing is to get people to understand that this is not about altruism. We are fervent capitalists who believe that this method, in addition to doing good for the world, is actually the best path to higher sales and profitability. This creates a paradox—not making profit your number one priority actually makes you more profitable. I like John Mackey's idea that this dynamic operates much like happiness. "People who make personal happiness their primary goal in life probably aren't very happy," he told our employees at Staff Meeting. "Happiness is better found by following a higher purpose through love, family, caring, sharing, through your own development. If you do those things passionately, you will discover, 'Wow, my life has been so amazing. I am so happy.'"

To shed some light on this paradox, while we shared the stage at Staff Meeting, I asked John, what place does love have in the workplace? His answer: "The more interesting question is 'Why is there not more love in the workplace?' My working theory is that it's because men have dominated most corporations, and most business. And historically men have often believed that love is weakness and that competitors are going to run over you. But one of the great trends in America is that women are taking over, and women in general are much better communicators. You know, gender stereotypes are difficult, and always dangerous, because you end up being misquoted, but in general women bring with them their full selves to the workplace. And why should the workplace be anything less than full human communities where we have heart, and love, and great relationships? And that has been missing in too much of corporate America for too long."

I couldn't have said it better! At this point, I should probably add that there are some things that John and I disagree about. Politics, for example. John is an outspoken libertarian who sometimes gets people riled up with his public statements about health care reform and other topics, while I'm more of a fiscally conservative moderate Democrat (making me vastly outnumbered in the Texas business world!). But John's political views have nothing whatsoever to do with Conscious Capitalism—indeed, at any gathering of Conscious Capitalists, you'll probably find more people whose politics are closer to mine. And whether you're on the left or the right, or believe in big government or small government, it's hard to argue with a philosophy that says business can have a big impact on the world by being more conscious, more ethical, more empathetic. John loves a good debate and feels strongly about the power of free speech, and I admire him and love him for being so committed to his beliefs.

Even before he founded Conscious Capitalism, John already had an incredibly positive impact on the world. As I said earlier, through his devotion to healthy eating and wellness, he has—in my opinion—single-handedly done more to extend our life-spans than just about anybody in America. Thanks to John and his co-CEO, Walter Robb—and Walter is one of the best chief executives and best retailers in the country, bar none—Whole Foods has revolutionized the nation's eating habits and influenced the biggest retailers and grocers in the country to carry healthier food. Whole Foods is opening locations in food deserts—underserved areas that supermarket chains tend to avoid—spurring others to do so as well. Thanks to the company's emphasis on sustainable agriculture and seafood, animals are being treated more humanely, shrimp are living better lives, and fewer pesticides are being used on our food. That's why John is often mentioned in the same breath as folks like Bill Gates and Steve Jobs—he is a truly revolutionary, transformative figure.

I was honored to be asked to serve on the Whole Foods board of directors shortly after John and I renewed our friendship. I was really blown away by that, because I've always been stunned at what great works of art Whole Foods stores are. And when Whole Foods was struggling through the Great Recession (like everyone else), I was happy to be in a position to introduce John and Walter to Jon Sokoloff of Leonard Green & Partners, which invested heavily in Whole Foods in 2008. It was a huge decision for Whole Foods to choose Leonard Green, but basically it boiled down to the fact that John Mackey knew we'd been through the process and Leonard Green & Partners were the only one right for us. So it was John Mackey trusting me and me having trust in Jon Sokoloff, which resulted in a partnership that has been just superb. Just perfect. Once again proving how well Conscious Capitalism works—especially when times are bad—Whole Foods came roaring back so strongly when the economy improved that when Leonard Green finally sold its shares in late 2012, it had more than quintupled its initial investment. By investing in The Container Store, Whole Foods, and later Danny Meyer's Union Square Hospitality Group—and appearing on Conscious Capitalism panels at events like the National Retail Federation's annual convention—Leonard Green seems to be becoming the nation's leading Conscious Capitalist private equity firm. We were ecstatic to be able to play a role in that.

Shortly after John and I gave the *Time* magazine interview, I began attending Conscious Capitalism events—typically meetings of entrepreneurs, executives, academics, and various thought leaders—and every time I talk about our Foundation Principles, the audience goes crazy. If John Mackey is the founder of this movement, I seem to have become one of his apostles—a role I cherish because I believe in the Foundation Principles and Conscious Capitalism with all my heart and soul. I don't need notes for these speeches—for me, it's as easy as falling off a log. Sometimes when I'm talking about Conscious Capitalism, my eyes well up. It happens all the time—but people like that part, too.

At the first formal Conscious Capitalism gathering retreat outside Austin, one of the original guys from Blue Man Group, the theater troupe, came up to me to rave about the speech, then said, "I am your best customer in New York and I had no idea that you and The Container Store stood for all these things. Why are you keeping this a secret?" Well, out of modesty, I guess. But that's one thing I love about the Conscious Capitalism movement—it gives us a great platform to tell folks about our quirky, yummy culture. And the phrase "Conscious Capitalism" is probably a better term than "Foundation Principles" to tell people outside our company how they can apply our approach to their own lives and business.

Talking about what we stand for has been great for business, too. We train our sales staff to talk to customers not just about our products, but also about the Foundation Principles and Conscious Capitalism. Customers love it! We often get reports from the sales floor about how much customers enjoy hearing about our values and culture, and our blog at whatwestandfor.com, gets tremendous traffic. People are glad to know their dollars are going to a company they can truly believe in and feel a part of, which in turn deepens our emotional connection to our customers.

Through the Conscious Capitalism movement, I have also met and befriended many people I admire, like Zappos' Tony Hsieh, whose best-selling book, *Delivering Happiness*, describes his realization that his company's true purpose had less to do with selling shoes and other apparel online than with making people happy; and Vineeta Salvi, founder and chief empowerment officer of Vidya Solutions, who uses the wisdom of various spiritual traditions to enhance business practices and performance. Inevitably, people start asking which companies qualify as being "Conscious Capitalist." I've discussed this at length with John and my great friend Doug Rauch, CEO of Conscious Capitalism, Inc., and former president of the Trader Joe's grocery chain. We all agree that our group will not attempt to rank companies on how consciously they run their business or issue any sort of *Good Housekeeping* Seal of Approval. We're pitching a big tent, which means we're committed to being nonjudgmental, even if that means letting sinners in. We'll just learn from one another and work to improve the way we do business. If we're only going to welcome saints, it will be a very small tent indeed.

In the long run, such questions won't matter anyway because the principles of Conscious Capitalism are so powerful that, as I mentioned earlier, I'm convinced everyone will do business this way in the future. For one thing, the digital and social media revolution will make it impossible not to behave this way. If you mistreat your employees, produce inferior products, despoil the environment, or cheat your business partners, the world will surely—and instantly—find out about it. That's why I've always loved and believed in transparency. It's the best way to choose friends and employees. Life is too short to deal with people who are opaque. But more than that, I believe Conscious Capitalism will prevail because most people are fundamentally good and truly want to do the right thing.

Sure, there are always exceptions—some people with deep-seated insecurities will bully, cheat, and steal to get ahead—but I've noticed that the success of The Container Store, Whole Foods, and other such companies seems to give people permission to behave the way they really feel, deep in their hearts, is right. The truth is, as companies that embrace Conscious Capitalism are showing, the best way to succeed beyond your wildest dreams is by following the Golden Rule. Now that's a revolution.

"The principles of Conscious Capitalism will spread because they're going to win the competition" is how John explains it during Staff Meeting. "It's just very hard for traditional business to compete against a conscious business and win."

Even companies that behave well realize they can do better. For example, our Japanese vendor Kentaro Ohyama of IRIS Ohyama, seeing that fourteen of our top nineteen company leadership positions are held by women, went back to Japan and completely changed the composition of his male-dominated work force, giving women greater responsibility and advancement. Our vendor Steve Catechi of AMAC says he now strives to creatively craft the same kind of mutually beneficial relationships with his vendors overseas that we do with his company. He also gives his employees great latitude to use their intuition to make decisions, rather than demanding they do things a certain way. "I wouldn't do any of those things if I hadn't seen them in action at The Container Store," he says.

I'm also very encouraged by today's millennial generation, which seems to love the message of Conscious Capitalism.

They're far more enlightened and morally grounded than the baby boomers and are starting scores of inspiring companies with a social mission—firms like Tom's Shoes, which gives away a pair of shoes to someone in need every time a customer buys a pair, or Warby Parker, which does the same with eyeglasses. Young people are excited to learn about The Container Store and Conscious Capitalism in business schools. I'm often asked to speak at prestigious business schools—which I always find ironic and fabulous, since I dropped out of college myself.

As John Mackey points out in his book, capitalism is one of the greatest gifts to humankind. Along with science, capitalism has lifted people to a higher standard of living than ever before in history, allowing art to flourish and people to rise up the pyramid of Maslow's hierarchy of needs to achieve their highest aspirations. That's true cause for celebration, and capitalism can play an even greater role in addressing the problems of the twenty-first century. Conscious Capitalism is actually part of a much larger movement of business leaders who are all heading in the same general direction. Some have spoken compellingly about Natural Capitalism (Paul Hawken and Amory Lovins); the Triple Bottom Line of People, Planet, and Profits (John Elkington); benefit corporations, which exist to benefit society, not just shareholders; Shared Value Capitalism (Michael Porter of Harvard Business School); Creative Capitalism (Bill Gates); and Enlightened Capitalism (Sir Richard Branson). I have vast respect for Howard Schultz of Starbucks and his calls for greater corporate citizenship. "Charity alone will not solve the world's problems," former president Bill Clinton says. "Capitalism can help and at the same time put people back to work."

What I find so exciting about companies becoming an ever more powerful force for good is that it's also great for business. It's truly a win-win proposition all around. The more The Container Store finds ways to improve the lives of everyone we touch, the more our sales and profits grow. Our customers love us more, and our employees earn more and enjoy their jobs more. Every company that does the same boosts the economy, creating greater prosperity for all. That's the power of our wake, the awesome power of the universe conspiring to assist us, which is the most delightful aspect of all.

That was a huge part of the Air of Excitement that everyone felt when Staff Meeting 2011 concluded. And we still feel it today, every day. For many of us, my old college friend John Mackey's voice still resonates as we go through our days: "If anything is more important than love, I don't know what the heck it is," he told us. "And I have a feeling, when I am on my deathbed, I am going to be thinking about all of the relationships and all of the people I have loved in my lifetime. Love is the most important value, and if we are going to transform America's corporations, then love is going to have to be front and center of it."

So much to be done, so much joy to spread...let's go!

11

The Best Is Yet to Come!

It's a gorgeous summer day in Colorado. I'm standing in a stream, drawing swirling shapes in the air with my fishing line, watching the fly glide onto the water. A gentle breeze rustles the trees and a single cloud drifts across the blue sky. The Rocky Mountains rise in the distance like sentinels keeping watch over this sacred place. Everything is sun splashed, like a dream.

At moments like this, my mind sometimes wanders back to the summer of 2008, when Sharon and I came up here to wrestle with the tough decisions that helped The Container Store emerge from the Great Recession stronger than ever—and did so without layoffs.

But the truth is that I'm usually too wrapped up with fishing to think about much of anything else. That's what I love so much about this place—it takes me back to my childhood, when there was nothing more important than enjoying the moment, fishing rod in hand, feeling the sun and the breeze, happy just to be soaking it all in.

As I said early in this book, I like to joke that the only two things I'm really good at are fly-fishing and organizing closets. That's only a slight exaggeration, but it does get at a certain truth—that for all the wonderful blessings Sharon and I have received, what makes us happiest are simple pleasures, like taking a walk in the woods or standing in a stream reeling in a big trout. I turned sixty in 2013, and such milestones can't help but make you think about the future. And every vision Sharon and I have about our future includes lots of happy time up here at our Colorado ranch, just hanging out with our dog and dear friends and family who can join us for hikes, fishing, golf, great conversation, and delicious food and wine.

But I'm certainly in no hurry to retire! I love this life so much—guiding the company's strategic direction, planning new initiatives, dreaming up ways to entrench our Foundation Principles deeper into the fabric of our company culture, getting to work with amazing 1=3 people every day, extolling the virtues of Conscious Capitalism every chance I get, and watching our company grow bigger and bigger by expanding into new markets and improving the lives of more and more customers every day. And yet I'm also aware of how critical succession planning is. I have seen entrepreneurs create fabulous companies but then fail to plan for a successor and end up watching their beloved creation—the sum of their life's work—morph into a soulless bottom-line company they don't even recognize.

That will never happen to The Container Store. We've done a fantastic job of developing people who can replace me, Sharon, or Melissa at any time. Our executive management team has an average of seventeen years' tenure. Many of them grew up in The Container Store's culture and still have twenty-plus years of leadership ahead of them, giving us strong and deep leadership bench strength heading into the future.

In fact, I'm quite sure that five or six of our top executives would actually be better CEOs than I am. That doesn't make me the least bit paranoid—quite the opposite, it actually helps me sleep well at night. Because should something ever happen to me, God forbid, I know The Container Store would be in great hands.

That same supportive, collegial atmosphere permeates every level of our company, from management to the sales floor. We have depth charts in place for each leadership position and we have hugely talented people at every spot. What we don't have, fortunately, is power struggles. If any executive who really wants to be president or CEO is ever passed over in favor of a colleague, there will be lots of tears and hugs, of course, but no bitterness, and I'm confident that everyone will stay (at most companies, of course, the person passed over leaves). Truly, I know it's hard to believe—but when promotions happen around here, there's sincere mutual love and respect. It's not what you typically see in corporate America. Hang around with us for a while and you'll see this kind of humility and grace at every level of the company. One of our favorite sayings is "It's amazing what you can accomplish when you don't care who gets the credit." So I feel great that anytime any of our top leaders have to retire, our company will only get stronger and better.

———<○>———

It's been a good day of fishing, so I wade back to the shore. I pack up my gear, climb into the ATV, and head back to the ranch along a rutted dirt road. As the mountains come into view, I'm reminded that one thing I love about being up here is that feeling of timelessness. The Rockies began taking shape about eighty million years ago and will remain for many millions more. I think people have a natural desire to be around things that last a long time, that have that air of eternity about them. That's one reason people love to vacation up here. I think of business the same way. Our goal is to have The Container Store continue to thrive long after we're gone—not just for the next generation or two, but for hundreds of years to come. Sound crazy? I know lots of businesses in Europe that have been around for hundreds of years.

———<o>———

Leonard Berry was right on the mark when he wrote in his excellent book *Discovering the Soul of Service*: "Creating a successful service operation is unquestionably a difficult task. However, sustaining success can be even more difficult. Services are performances, and the challenge of sustaining the performers' energy, commitment, skills, and knowledge day after day, week after week, month after month, year after year—especially as the organization grows and becomes more complex—is daunting."

Daunting, perhaps, but hardly impossible. Berry's book cites a 1983 study on corporate longevity commissioned by Royal Dutch Shell that focused on twenty-seven companies in North America, Europe, and Japan that ranged in age from 100 to 700 years old. The author of that study, Arie de Geus, concluded that most companies don't come close to realizing their potential— but argues that it doesn't have to be that way. "The high corporate mortality rate seems unnatural," he writes. "No living species suffers from such a discrepancy between its maximum life expectancy and the average span it realizes. And few other types of institutions—churches, armies, or universities—have the abysmal record of the corporation.

"Why do so many companies die young? Mounting evidence suggests that corporations fail because their policies and practices are based too heavily on the thinking and the language of

economics. Put another way, companies die because their managers focus exclusively on producing goods and services and forget that the organization is a community of human beings that
is in business—any business—to stay alive. Managers concern
themselves with land, labor, and capital, and overlook the fact
that labor means real people."

Very well said. That's why Conscious Capitalism and the
people-oriented values of our Foundation Principles are the best
prescriptions for building a sustainable company. Since the beginning, our company has always been primarily about people, and I
feel a big responsibility to stay around long enough to make sure
that's the way things remain.

———◇———

I suppose when we venture abroad we'll find out how universal
our Foundation Principles really are. In the early days, people
told us that our quirky, yummy culture would only work in the
South, until we expanded everywhere from Southern California to Manhattan. Our products sell exactly the same no matter
the city. So I expect we'll hear the same thing about expanding
overseas. But I believe human beings are fundamentally the same
wherever you go. People everywhere respond well to kindness
and generosity, and employees truly enjoy helping customers,
working as a team alongside great coworkers, being trained to
become more intuitive, creating win-win situations with business partners, and striving to be the best.

Some cultures may be more comfortable than others with
the emotional openness of principles like Communication IS
Leadership and Air of Excitement. But I believe that all our values will ultimately be embraced when practiced with sensitivity
to local customs and traditions. A global reach is certainly nothing we ever even dreamed about when we opened our first little
shop in Dallas, but after more than three decades of phenomenal

growth, it has become impossible for me not to imagine that our message will someday resonate joyfully around the world.

————◇————

Heading up our driveway, I see that Sharon's car is gone. She must be in town. I carefully put away my fishing equipment on the elfa shelving unit in the garage and enter the house. For some reason, I'm reminded of the first executive retreat we held here, in 2006. Sharon and I had finished building the place two years earlier and decided to fly our vice-presidents in to do some bonding and to get closer as a team. On the last night, we had a party on the deck, and everybody was dancing and having a great time. It was very reminiscent of that giddy Air of Excitement you always feel at our grand-opening parties. Suddenly, Garrett collapsed on the floor. Later, we discovered he had suffered a stroke, but at that moment, nobody knew what had happened. Or what to do. Of course, everybody freaked out.

We immediately called an ambulance, and our ranch manager, Greg Zoellick, basically saved Garrett's life. Our house is in a very remote area, hard to find if you don't know where you're going, so Greg quickly organized the guests to fan out to several spots along the nearby dirt roads to flag down the ambulance and show the driver where to go.

The key to handling a stroke victim is fast action; any delays could be fatal. Amazingly, the ambulance arrived in just nineteen minutes, thanks to our team of guides. The paramedics examined Garrett and said they weren't sure he'd make it. But they put him on the gurney and wheeled him into the ambulance, and I hopped into the back with him.

At moments like that, you realize how precious life is, and how meaningless most of our day-to-day worries are. Like any longtime business partners, Garrett and I have had our share of disagreements, but suddenly all that seemed silly. I remembered how much I truly love him. I've known Garrett since I was in high school, and he's always been like a brother to me. Without Garrett, of course, The Container Store would not exist, so for that and many other reasons, my debt to him is immense.

When we arrived at the hospital, my job was to cut through the red tape to get him treated as fast as possible. The hospital called Garrett's wife, Cecilia, who was back home, to ask her approval to inject him with a drug that could save his life by dissolving the blood clot to resume blood flow to the brain—that is, if he had, in fact, had a stroke. If not, if it turned out that the cause of his collapse was something else, like an aneurysm, the drug could be fatal.

Knowing that Garrett would want to take the risk in order to avoid permanent paralysis, Cecilia gave the okay; they administered the drug, and we waited. A few minutes later, Garrett shocked everyone by sitting up in the gurney and starting to talk. He seemed fine, relatively speaking. We couldn't believe it! By that time, some of our guests had arrived at the hospital, and there were lots of hugs and tears. Of course, Garrett still needed more treatment, so he and I took another ambulance to the airport and flew to a bigger hospital. There, everyone from the nurses to the head of admissions moved quickly to give him the best possible care and the best room available. Garrett made a full recovery, thank goodness.

—◇—

I walk out onto the deck, into the sunshine, and take a deep breath of the purest air on earth. The view from here never ceases to astonish me, from the waves of graceful trees that surround our house—aspens, spruces, and firs—to the rolling valleys in the middle distance, to the majestic mountains far away, now turning shades of purple. The quiet stillness calms and stirs the soul.

No matter which direction you look, there's nothing but sheer beauty. It always makes me reflect on our purpose on this great earth.

———◅◦▻———

Among Conscious Capitalists, there's a lot of talk about defining a company's "purpose"—and, of course, that's a question that anybody can (and should) ask themselves: "What is my purpose on this planet?" When it comes to our Colorado property, our purpose is clear—enjoy it today while also preserving it for future generations.

Sharon and I know that we don't really "own" this land, that we're only passing through. So we're working to conserve as much of the surrounding area as possible. Excellent work has already been done to place thousands of acres of agricultural lands in conservation easements, and Sharon and I are happy to be able to help with that important mission.

Sharon and I also would love for part of the property to serve as a retreat for Conscious Capitalism events after we're gone. Being surrounded by such beautiful wilderness, where the forces of nature work together in exquisite harmony, could be tremendously inspiring for future generations of Conscious Capitalists as they seek to harmonize the interests of stakeholders. I'm hugely excited to think about their companies being as sustainable as the surrounding wilderness we're protecting.

———◅◦▻———

The Conscious Capitalism movement has given us an additional crucial purpose: to spread our approach and methodology far and wide to inspire more companies to operate consciously, with a noble intent, thus allowing more people around the world to benefit. I'm convinced that future historians will look back at our time as a turning point, when the popular narrative of the greedy, selfish businessman began to fade, replaced by a more humane vision of business as a powerful force for good.

The purpose of The Container Store, meanwhile, is just as clear: to improve the quality of our customers' lives through the gift of organization, fueled by our seven Foundation Principles. Those principles begin with our commitment to our employee-first culture, of course, but they also ensure that we ultimately create value for ALL of our stakeholders, including vendors, customers, community, and shareholders—so that everyone associated with our business thrives.

I like the comment a staff member of the nonprofit Children's Healthcare of Atlanta made after our party celebrating the relocation of our Buckhead, Atlanta, store in 2012 (when we contributed 10 percent of our first weekend sales to that group). She put it so succinctly: "The Container Store is the promise of a happier, better life."

And even after thirty-six years, it feels as if we're just getting started. In fact, I feel as if I'm glimpsing the future every time we have a new-store opening: watching the beaming faces of our new employees; watching our executives performing their choreographed dance routine, "Another Opening, Another Store!"; hearing the excited chatter of customers rushing in when our doors open for the first time. At those moments, well, I can get pretty teary eyed. It's hard to talk about because I get quite emotional, but I guess it comes down to the fact that people are just sweet. Deep down, they really are.

When I see those new employees working so hard, so happy to be on this amazing team and feeling free to just be themselves, doggone it, and working with great people they respect and admire so much, and then going home that night feeling so great about themselves, knowing that it makes them a better mother or father or sister, and that it even makes their kids turn out better—holy cow, watching all that, you'd have to be pretty hardhearted not to tear up. Sharon and I don't have children, so I guess when a new store opens, these are very much like the tears of joy a parent sheds when his or her child is born.

A new child, a new employee, a new store—they all reveal the power of our rippling wake, our unique and powerful legacy. In my favorite movie, *It's a Wonderful Life*, when Clarence the angel lets George Bailey see how miserable life would have been without him, you really feel the huge impact of one man's wake, and how George's approach to business affects so many people in his community. The reason that movie is a classic is because we all instinctively understand this. When each and every person in your organization understands the power of their wake, you have an unassailable advantage. Nobody else can compete with you because you're doing so much to help the universe conspire to assist you. It's really a lot easier to succeed if everybody is trying to help you win, and really hard if nobody can stand you and they're all lying awake at night trying to find ways to make you fail.

The sun has begun to set and the mountains are turning a bright orange. I hope Sharon and our dog Walter get back soon so they can see this incredible view from our deck before it fades. I also want to read Sharon an e-mail I received recently. It's from Mike Aplis, our project management director, who was recalling some remarks he made at our Service Awards dinner at the Ritz-Carlton in Dallas, when he celebrated his twentieth anniversary with our company. His wife, Maggie, is our logistics director, and they have two children, Katie and Eric. I pull out a hard copy of Mike's e-mail and read it again:

> Throughout my children's lifetime, they have only known our life as The Container Store. They see the passion we've had for this company and the people we

work with. We've raised our kids with the same philosophy that we run our company with—hard work, dedication, do what's right, and do it with intent and purpose, but, most importantly, love what you do and do it with passion.

As my children get older, they are getting ready for the real world. I have been reflecting a lot on their future and wondering, Will they have the same sense of purpose and love for what they do? Will they be treated as well as we have been? And that's when I get an uneasy feeling. The chance that they will have what we've had is pretty rare. Even I sometimes take for granted what we have, that it's like this everywhere. It's NOT! We have expressed this to both of our children, telling them that everything they see that we have as a result of working for this company is not "normal." I fear they've been sheltered from the real world because of this "Utopia" type place they have come to know...

I hear Sharon coming through the door and Walter barreling behind her. Great, we'll watch the sunset, make dinner, and get ready for tomorrow—a full workday, with a conference call scheduled with Melissa and lots of deadlines coming up. We wouldn't have it any other way. As with Monet painting the water lilies, it's awfully hard to tell the difference between work and play around here. And Sharon and I will both be excited to get out of bed in the morning to do whatever we can to help create a world where Katie and Eric can find great, well-paid jobs, full of challenge and achievement, joy and passion, just like their mom and dad. Now that's yummy!

Epilogue

As we put the finishing touches on this book, The Container Store embarked on yet another incredible journey, another defining moment when our Foundation Principles gave us tremendous strength and led the way.

On November 1, 2013, we rang the bell at the New York Stock Exchange, signaling our debut as a public company. The day was absolutely stunning, with more than 120 employees, family (my dad included!), and friends of the company joining us on the trading floor as we launched our ticker symbol, TCS. I asked Melissa to ring the bell, in honor of her late father, who was a stockbroker in Kansas City.

It was a surreal moment as I looked around me on that bell podium and down to the bustling trading floor. I was surrounded by my beloved management team. Folks like John Thrailkill, Melissa Collins, Audrey Robertson, Brooke Minteer, Joe Wilkinson, Matt Vonderahe, and Lucy Witte—people who started their careers with us so young like so many others and had tirelessly rolled up their sleeves to work so hard and are now vice-presidents of our company. And Joan Manson and Tom Birmingham, who formalized and created best-in-class loss prevention and IT practices, respectively, for the company. Eva, Val, Amy, Peggy, Casey, Natalie, Per, Jodi, Jeff. They were all there—every member of that special team—many enjoying the moment with a spouse or family member. And I could see my dad down on the trading floor looking up at me with pride. It was just electric and so very emotional. There was a palpable Air of Excitement as the big moment arrived—and lo and behold, the market welcomed us with open arms!

Our opening price of $18 per share more than doubled, to over $36, on that first day of trading, and the TV airwaves were full of stories about the amazing debut of The Container Store. For weeks afterward, media reports raved about the hugely successful offering of this quirky Dallas company, one of only a handful of instances all year when a stock doubled on its first day.

Our decision to go public, which we knew would affect so many people near and dear to us—well, as you can imagine, it wasn't made lightly. My seven years on the Whole Foods board helped tremendously as I watched and learned how a public company could operate under the tenets of Conscious Capitalism.

I talked to lots of like-minded leaders I admired at public companies—Herb Kelleher at Southwest Airlines and Jim Sinegal at Costco. And I looked at all the other alternatives. Go with another private equity partner? Could we find love again like we had with Leonard Green? Well, with half of all marriages ending in divorce, I wasn't willing to risk it. The IPO was the route to go. So to feel, hear, read, and see the resounding, unequivocal support for our IPO on that day touched my heart deeply and had me smiling from ear to ear, nonstop.

Why did we make this dramatic move after thirty-five years? In short, to get more stock into the hands of our beloved employees and to maximize the autonomy of our culture and management team. As I've said over and over again, it's been a longtime dream of our leadership to find a way for more employees to own a part of the company—and the IPO allowed us to make that a reality! This path also gives us a more visible stage on which to continue creating a company that we hope others will choose to emulate—and that's so inspiring to think about.

Jon Sokoloff and Leonard Green were absolutely ecstatic about the outcome. Leonard Green held on to a significant portion of its shares and remains a long-term partner and investor. Heck, those guys were beaming right along with the rest of us all day. And I'm happy to report that going through this challenging process made my relationship with Jon and Leonard Green stronger than ever.

As part of our IPO journey, we were also thrilled to add to our board a dream-come-true group of business leaders who all embody the principles of Conscious Capitalism.

Our two-week road show with Melissa and Jodi, traveling across the country meeting with potential investors, was a grueling and gratifying process. But as with Jon and Leonard Green, it also brought us even closer together. Much as in our 2007 private equity deal, we packed our presentations with examples of our quirky culture, talked about our Foundation Principles and Conscious Capitalism, and dispensed lots of hugs and love.

In fact, in our S-1 SEC filing to shareholders, I wrote a letter that made sure that all the important non-spreadsheet, non-banker/lawyer stuff was strongly underlined and accentuated: "How to define The Container Store culture?" it read. "I would have to say that first and foremost we're an employee-first, yummy company....We have built a culture that champions a collective focus on our wake, team, mutual support and respect, grace of authority and servant leadership, and leadership based on love rather than fear. We believe The Container Store's magic will continue to flourish in our next step as a public company."

"A 'yummy' IPO?" the media asked (and the public tweeted) with more than a hint of incredulity. Well, of course! We started the road show selling our beloved story, and after talking a lot about the fact that we wanted long-term investors, we were pleased to see that by the end of the process, the investors were selling to us. They turned over the formal presentation materials with all the financial charts and graphs and said things like "Tell me more about your Foundation Principles." That was joyful.

And just as we had in 2007, we communicated as much as we could to our employees (within the guardrails of the SEC quiet period, of course) to ensure that they felt safe and secure and informed. "Like we've done with so many things, we will pursue this IPO in our very own TCS way," read my memo to employees. "More details coming on that soon too. I just want to reiterate how proud I am of each and every one of you...We will continue to lead and make decisions about our beloved company based on our love for each other."

From the moment the opening bell rang at the New York Stock Exchange that morning, we were beside ourselves with excitement for a simple reason: We had just created tremendous, widespread value for so many of our employees, vendors, friends, and family. We're very proud of the directed share program we offered to ALL of our employees (full-time, part-time, seasonal—EVERYONE!), which allowed them to purchase shares of stock at the strike price of $18 per share.

These were not options, mind you, but actual shares of stock. So when the stock soared on that first day of trading, employees who sold automatically doubled their investment. And by all accounts—including our bankers, lawyers, and others involved with the process—our directed share program was the most robust that anyone can remember, at 14 percent of the total shares issued. As this book went to press, almost 25 percent of our employees owned stock in our company. Wow!

We were also proud and excited to announce a separate stock options program that allowed us to set aside part of the company's future value for a group of more than 1,100 employees who have been instrumental in the company's growth and success.

In fact, any full-time employee who had been with the company for more than two years received stock options. That was a life-changing event for many folks.

After our IPO, the outpouring of responses I received from our employees was overwhelming, and so touching:

"The thought of how many folks were able to actually participate in the IPO is astounding!!!!" wrote area director Christina Wilt.

Mary Burke, general manager of our Rockville, Maryland, store, wrote, "I know that we were all on a high throughout the day, watching the numbers, celebrating with each other. We had customers celebrating, too! The icing on the cake for me was getting in my car to go home, turning on NPR like I do every night, and having *Marketplace* be all about us. I was bursting at that point!"

Debra Heberling, store manager in Oak Brook, Illinois, was struck by the photographs of our meetings with investors that we sent to employees. "The pictures of the presentation room with the flags displaying our Foundation Principles made me want to stand up, put my hand over my heart, and pledge to continue working each day to fulfill the promise inherent in each one."

After our first day as a public company, we partied TCS style that evening at Danny Meyer's fabulous North End Grill in lower Manhattan with all our family, friends, employees, and partners. It was truly a grand, euphoric time, with lots of dancing and hugging.

But, of course, just beneath the surface were simmering questions that we knew we would soon have to answer. As we toasted and danced, we knew that tomorrow would bring a whole new set of surprises and challenges and that we were facing a future we could only begin to imagine.

As we grow into a much bigger company, as we open dozens and possibly hundreds of new stores, as we listen to stockholders and analysts, as we begin to surf the waves of powerful market forces beyond our control, we know that many twists and turns await us that will test our skills, resolve, and Foundation Principles as never before. But I just loved what someone said about our IPO not being an exit strategy for leadership or the company, but rather an entrance strategy into doing even more for all of our stakeholders with even greater commitment and enthusiasm.

But that will have to be the subject of another book. So for now I'll just quote another part of Debra Heberling's excited message after our IPO, which perfectly sums up our present situation: "It really does feel like we are at the start of the next part of our journey as a company—and the best IS yet to come!"

Index

Note: The abbreviation KT refers to Kip Tindell